Communication and Imperial Control in China

Harvard East Asian Series 51

The East Asian Research Center at Harvard University administers research projects designed to further scholarly understanding of China, Japan, Korea, Vietnam, and adjacent areas.

Communication
and Imperial Control
in China

Evolution of the
Palace Memorial System
1693–1735

Silas H. L. Wu

Harvard University Press
Cambridge, Massachusetts 1970

Distributed in Great Britain by Oxford University Press, London

Preparation of this volume has been aided by a grant from the Ford Foundation

Library of Congress Catalog Card Number 73–119078
SBN 674–14801–0

Printed in the United States of America

To my mother

Foreword

The governing of China is one of the modern world's great and future problems, if only because of the sheer size of the Chinese body politic. No precedent can be found in history to tell one how to arrange the government of seven hundred fifty million people within a single state, and the experience of modern China since 1912 suggests that it faces problems of government that are still unresolved.

Such problems must be understood in part genetically, by studying their historical origins, and any such study will reinforce the thought that the Chinese people today are in some degree victims of their past success. The unprecedentedly vast size of China today has been made possible and in fact unavoidable by the great achievements in the art of government that permitted the Chinese empire in its time to become the largest single human organization. These achievements included the early forms of bureaucratic administration developed under the Han in the second century B.C. as well as the examination system and the censorate set up under the T'ang in the seventh century A.D. But these well-known features of imperial administration are only some of the formal aspects of the Chinese polity. They had their ideological counterpart in the teachings of imperial Confucianism, their social counterpart in the local elite or "gentry" ruling class. All these elements of the old order gave it continuity, helped preserve it until recent times, and contributed to the vocabulary and repertoire of China's ongoing political life. Meticulously and copiously recorded, these achievements constitute a reservoir of experience on which the Chinese people are obliged to draw today even when most determined to strain out obvious evils from their inheritance.

It follows that the effort to understand China's problem of government must combine studies of the past and of the present, of historical as well as current behavior. The special merit of Silas Wu's monograph derives from two things: his textual mastery of the documents created by the institutional processes he is studying and his capacity to analyze these processes in the terms of present-day political science. Few can claim his level of competence in these two respects.

Dr. Wu attended school in Peking just after World War II and received his B.A. in history at National Taiwan University in 1954. He then studied at the University of California at Berkeley, at Yale, and at Columbia, where he took his doctorate in 1967. He is now associate professor of history at Boston College and an associate of the undersigned center at Harvard.

East Asian Research Center

Contents

Foreword from East Asian Research Center   vii
List of the Ch'ing Reigns   xiv
I. Concept, Method, Scope   1
II. The Early Ch'ing Deliberative Structure   9
III. Audience, Censors, Imperial Commissioners, and Tours   20
IV. The Traditional Memorial System   27
V. Origins of the Palace Memorial System in the K'ang-hsi Reign   34
VI. Factionalism and the Growth of the Palace Memorial System   52
VII. Changes in the Palace Memorial System in the Yung-cheng Reign   66
VIII. The Grand Council and the New Communication-Decision Structure   79
IX. Communication, Values, Control   107
Appendix: Sample Palace Memorials: Nature, Content, Uses   127
Abbreviations   151
Notes   153
Bibliography   181
Glossary   189
Index   197

Acknowledgments

In preparing this study I have benefited from the help of a number of scholars. I am particularly indebted to Professors C. Martin Wilbur and Chao-ying Fang of Columbia University for advice and criticism at the earliest stage. Among others at Columbia, I am grateful to Professors John Meskill and James Morley for valuable comments that helped me to avoid some of the pitfalls of oversimplification. During revision and expansion of the manuscript, I was honored with two consecutive summer grants from the East Asian Research Center of Harvard University. Professor John K. Fairbank, director of the Center, kindly read all the subsequent versions of the manuscript with great care and has made valuable suggestions. Further financial assistance was provided by the Faculty Research Committee at Boston College for expenses of securing archival material from Taiwan; and I owe much to Charles F. Donovan, S.J., senior vice-president and dean of faculties, and Thomas H. O'Connor, chairman of the History Department, for their cooperation.

For published sources, I have relied upon the rich holdings of the East Asian Library of Columbia University and those of the Harvard-Yenching Library at Harvard University. To Mr. Eugene Wu, librarian of the latter, and his many able staff members, my sincere thanks for courtesy and co-operation in facilitating research during the past three years. I am grateful to Mr. Chiang Fu-ts'ung, director of the National Palace Museum in Tai-wan, for permission to use the museum's early Ch'ing archives; Mr. Chia-chü Liu, archivist and expert on early Ch'ing history, helped enormously in the process of securing documents..

A number of friends have helped with the manuscript in various stages, among whom are Joseph Harrington, Charles Land, Harold Metzgar, James Millinger, and Jonathan Spence. Professor Spence kindly agreed to read the final draft of the manuscript.

January 1970   Silas H. L. Wu

Communication and Imperial Control in China

Evolution of the Palace Memorial System, 1693–1735

Shun-chih	1644–1661
K'ang-hsi	1662–1722
Yung-cheng	1723–1735
Ch'ien-lung	1736–1795
Chia-ch'ing	1796–1820
Tao-kuang	1821–1850
Hsien-feng	1851–1861
T'ung-chih	1862–1874
Kuang-hsü	1875–1908
Hsüan-t'ung	1909–1911

This book is concerned with the "communication-decision" structure that evolved during the early part of the Ch'ing dynasty. This structure, constantly modified in response to specific pressures and needs during the K'ang-hsi (1662–1722) and the Yung-cheng (1723–1735) reigns, became the accepted foundation for imperial government during the next century and a half of Ch'ing rule. The focus of the study is the key role played by the system of "palace memorials" (*tsou-che*), the new communication device informally introduced in the middle of the K'ang-hsi reign and firmly institutionalized during the Yung-cheng reign.

The term "communication-decision" has been selected as that which best indicates the general scope of this study. Though communication and decision are so interconnected in the governing process that, for example, political scientists can consider a "decisional system" as synonymous with a "communication network," [1] the term communication-decision gives a deliberate emphasis. In the Chinese example, communication can be seen as paramount.

Before launching into a detailed description and analysis of the K'ang-hsi and Yung-cheng periods, three basic questions should be considered: (1) What types of studies have been made in the field of Ch'ing imperial government? (2) What basic concept should be defined, and what method employed, in studying a historical bureaucracy? (3) On what general grounds can it be claimed that the K'ang-hsi/Yung-cheng period is a nodal point in the political and institutional history of modern China, and the specific subject under study a crucial issue in Chinese history?

Despite growing interest in the Chinese imperial bureaucracy — now generally regarded as the most elaborate, fascinating and, in Weber's sense, "modern" and efficient political machinery developed by any premodern society — it is unfortunately true that our knowledge of that bureaucracy is still at a rudimentary level. Lack of detailed Chinese evidence made Weber's generalizations on Chinese government largely hypothetical;[2] similarly, Karl Wittfogel's study of China as one of the subdivisions of an

"Oriental despotism," though supported by some historical examples, did not seem to have taken adequate note of contradictory evidence that might have led to very different conclusions.[3]

There are, of course, some studies by Chinese historians that have surveyed two millennia of Chinese political machinery in a general way;[4] and there are some excellent English-language studies of an institution or a level of government under a particular dynasty.[5] But the only detailed study of the central government of Imperial China is that by Hsieh Pao-chao: a pioneering work, which should have been long outdated, it is often the sole source of information on the Ch'ing imperial government used by Western historians and political scientists.[6]

These studies are significant contributions in that they have provided a clearer picture of imperial control techniques at the local and rural levels, of "gentry" functions, of the role of censors in bureaucratic control, and so forth. But the remarkable contribution made by the early Ch'ing emperors in the area that could be termed intra-governmental communication, which facilitated imperial control over the Chinese bureaucracy, has remained largely unexplored.[7] Surely an understanding of how the emperor operated must precede valid generalizations about the Chinese state.

A structure of communication and decision is a complicated political phenomenon. Necessary to define it are terms, or symbols, that are themselves clearly defined and an approach that is analytically consistent. Use of these terms reflects a concept of the content and dynamics of history, of the stream that runs within the banks; the confining banks in such a metaphor must consist of a broad approach to history and of specific views regarding the patterns of historical change.

As a first step, it is useful to adopt the Lasswellian definition of power, that it is "participation in the making of decisions." [8] The extent of power held by any political agent is measured by the extent of his participation in the decision-making process. Since communication is a crucial determinant in this process, its study is helpful toward understanding the extent of power held by a given agent in the decisional system.

The Ch'ing imperial power, taken in this sense of participation in decisions, may be seen as a function of other types of power. First, there is the hereditary power of the Manchu princes (*pei-le*). Second, there is representational power as held by the members of the various deliberative bodies within the Ch'ing central bureaucracy; this power was often insured through prescribed administrative procedures which were backed by a weighty accumulation of precedent and which rational rulers were cautious about violating. Third, there is advisory power as exercised by those brought into the system because of need for their special skills and information; this power was a potent factor, even if its wielders were outside the normal authority-responsibility relationships.[9] The differentiation of powers along these lines — imperial, hereditary, representational, and advisory — helps to analyze the power-concentration process in the early Ch'ing.

As a second step, it is necessary to realize something that should be a truism but is unfortunately nothing of the kind in many current studies of China: namely, that a discussion of communication involves the onerous task of deciphering a complex terminology. Precision of language is of great significance to the origins, development, and operation of the communication-decision system. To the problem of bureaucratic terminology, common throughout Chinese history, there is an additional problem in the early Ch'ing which is seen in other "dynasties of conquest," that of translation. The Manchu policy of using many Chinese methods and personnel so as to "rule the Chinese by Chinese" meant that a major duty of the *Nei-ko* (Grand Secretariat) was to translate Manchu documents into Chinese and vice versa. Despite the nominal continuity, therefore, this meant that there were important differences between the Ming and Ch'ing *Nei-ko*.

Like its counterparts in the past — and, indeed, in contemporary China — the Ch'ing communication system was a closed system, employing a special body of terminology for the use of the actors within the network.[10] Even some of the most eminent researchers into Ch'ing bureaucracy have been led into misconceptions through failure to grasp the significance of this terminology.[11] This gives some urgency to the task at hand.

Broadly speaking, two kinds of technical terminology can be found in the Ch'ing documentation. The first concerns operations and procedures of the communication system itself; the second is contained in information transmitted through the system, for example, the terms used in making civil appointments, in tax assessments and military planning, in judicial decisions, and so on. The volume of the second category is so huge that adequate deciphering and organization would demand the life's work of many scholars.[12] Because of the nature of the subject, this present study focuses mainly on the first category of operations and procedures.

As a third step, a typology of communications is essential. In the Ch'ing case, the major concern here will be with written, rather than nonwritten communication. The prescribed procedures, coupled with the geographical extent of the Chinese empire and the variety of problems to be handled, necessitated written communications that could be circulated and filed effectively. The basic form of the communication-decision process, inherited by the Ch'ing, was one in which the officials used "memorials" to submit information and the emperor responded with edicts.

But the Ch'ing system cannot be understood in terms of a simple memorial-edict process. Written communication has to be differentiated into subcategories, on the basis of the divergent means of transmission within the network. Commonly used modifiers such as "open" and "secret" are inadequate, since they allow too much ambiguity. Classification here will be made according to the following criterion: how many people were allowed to know about a given communication? A palace memorial (*tsou-che*) will be described as secret in nature if its contents were known only to the emperor and the original memorialist; this was a definition formulated by the K'ang-hsi Emperor himself.[13] Such a secret memorial would retain its secret character if the emperor returned it directly to the sender via its original incoming route. But if he made its contents known to a third party, the "inner grand secretaries," for example, and allowed their agents to return it, it clearly can only be classed as "semisecret." In other occasions, part of the contents of the secret memorial might be made known to the *Nei-ko,* a wide circle of officials, or even to the whole empire: it then became "semiopen." The modifier "open" is used here only for routine memorials transmitted to the emperor through open *Nei-ko* channels and later published through the mass-media *Peking Gazette.*

Such a "how many people were allowed to know?" approach, it is hoped, will be both accurate and fluid: accurate on the basis of available documentation as far as complex procedures are concerned, and fluid in that definition and description of the communication-decision process must follow every shift in practice. Here the historian simply follows the course of historical development in reverse. A historical bureaucracy involves the triune components of structure, process, and motives. Political structure reflects political process, in the Chinese case as in any other.[14] Process, in turn, reflects the changing relations between major historical agents — emperors, princes, officials — and these relations fluctuate through the interplay of human motives. Only such a wide-angled approach clarifies both *how* changes occurred in structure and *why*.

Consideration of motives leads to another methodological problem. In this study, that branch of current motivational theory will be followed which tends to de-emphasize the irrational aspects of human nature. As Allport puts it, "conscious values and intentions are important, far more important than Freudian and other irrationalist theories of motivation would allow." [15] To explain the differences between the K'ang-hsi and Yung-cheng Emperors' policies toward their bureaucrats, it is necessary to examine differences in their values.[16] Successful identification of these values leads back full circle to the differences in their control policies, and to those structural changes in the communications system which they made in order to implement their policies.

This study must be limited to those motivational factors of the leading actors which seem crucial to the particular system under observation. In other words, the K'ang-hsi Emperor's set of values here identified represents only one of the several sets of values that comprise his total motivation.[17] So, this volume focuses on structure and includes only the bare essentials on motive and political process; to deal at length with motive and process will require a separate study.

The core assertion here is that the K'ang-hsi/Yung-cheng period is a nodal point in the political-institutional history of modern China and that the palace memorial system is one of the keys to understanding that period. Before presenting detailed evidence and evaluating it, this period should be examined in the broader context of Ch'ing political history.

Looking forward in time, for a century after the suppression of the Three Feudatories (*san-fan*) in 1681 there were no major internal disturbances in China; not until the mid-nineteenth century did rebellions and Western pressures shatter the empire's political stability. Both Chinese and Western historians have seen this stability as rooted in the achievements of the K'ang-hsi and Yung-cheng Emperors. Some have stressed the "benevolent" role of the former, some the "despotic" role of the latter.

"Yung-cheng despotism" has received the most attention. Some historians have stressed the emperor's personality, some his control techniques. There is much emphasis on his secret police, or secret service, systems — terms with a fine contemporary overtone — which are assumed to have been cru-

cial to his attainment of political stability. Weight is also given to his ruthless "military control" and to his use of the Grand Council (*Chün-chi ch'u,*
literally office of military affairs). The historian Ch'ien Mu writes:

> Yung-cheng was a famous despot. His predecessor was K'ang-hsi,
> who can be considered as a good emperor in Chinese history; whereas
> Yung-cheng was indeed too despotic [*chuan-chih*]. If we just read his
> vermilion endorsements [written personally on palace memorials] we
> immediately discover how the Ch'ing emperors controlled China. At
> that time he was informed of all the activities in which the provincial
> authorities engaged. In probably every part of the Chinese Empire
> there were secret agents [*t'e-wu jen-yüan*] privately sent out by him.
> In many cases, therefore, even people's private lives, and trivial mat-
> ters concerning family members and their relatives, could not be kept
> from his notice. He also read all memorials carefully, and endorsed
> them in his own hand. Certainly he was intelligent and capable, but
> at the same time he was dictatorial [*tu-ts'ai*].[18]

In the same vein, Ch'ien Mu concludes from the Grand Council's literal
title (office of military affairs) that important imperial pronouncements
were classified as military affairs and hence that Ch'ing administration was
"under military control." He goes on to show how the "private decisions"
on administrative matters made by Yung-cheng were naturally more
despotic than those under the Ming dynasty, when the Six Boards checked
all memorials and edicts, investigated promotions and recommendations,
and supervised education.[19]

Such an interpretation is both pertinent and misleading. It is misleading
because of technical inaccuracies,[20] pertinent because it raises the whole
question of imperial control techniques: use of agents, lack of consultation,
special councillors, and the like. Keen Jesuit observers had come to similar
conclusions about the pervasive network of internal "espionage" in China;
they were inclined to take such a network for granted, coming as they did
from a Europe attuned to the spies of Hapsburg and Stuart courts and the
omnipresent agents of Richelieu.[21] But whether all these spy systems can
safely be lumped together is another matter. It is only after having studied
the K'ang-hsi and Yung-cheng systems that constructive parallels can be
drawn with Europe, Ming China, or the China of the twentieth century. And
only after careful examination of the nature of, and the reasons for, the
innovations made by the K'ang-hsi and Yung-cheng Emperors that their

importance as the founders of the great era of political stability can be assessed.

It is also necessary to look back in time if the full significance of this period is to be appreciated. This was the final phase of a process in the early history of the Manchu state, extending over a century, in which imperial power had been steadily expanding at the expense of other competing forms of power.

Before the period of Abahai's dominance (T'ai-tsung, reigned 1627–1643) the Manchu state was under the hereditary power of the Manchu princes (*pei-le*), who exercised collective leadership. Abahai subdued all rivals and made the *pei-le* part of the bureaucracy; imperial power grew at the expense of the bureaucracy during the Shun-chih reign (1644–1661). Yet, a Ch'ing "bureaucratic state" was not firmly established until the 1690's. Before that time, a government superficially patterned on the Ming model was in dangerous tension with the "state within a state" of Manchu nobility and bannermen.[22] Bureaucrats drawn from this privileged group could exercise hereditary power over both their own clans and their own followers and also over segments of the central bureaucracy. Manchus might well react against things Chinese. Thus, during the dictatorial regency of Oboi from 1661 to 1669, many of the Chinese bureaucratic forms that had been adopted during the Shun-chih reign were abolished. A restoration of Chinese patterns was begun by the young K'ang-hsi Emperor after he had eliminated Oboi in 1669; the restoration was completed in the 1690's, with the publication of the *Ch'ing Collected Statutes* (*Ta-Ch'ing hui-tien*).

Such a move from hereditary to representational power in the bureaucracy did not inevitably mean that imperial power would grow more autocratic. Bureaucrats, however active in the deliberative process, gained power through their access to information and their participation in decision-making as surely as a nobility had done through control of troops. Selfish and self-perpetuating factions were as great a threat to early Ch'ing rulers as they had been to Sung or Ming.

Counteracting such abuses of bureaucratic power was the crucial task for the K'ang-hsi Emperor. It was during the period from 1693 to 1735 that, first he, then the Yung-cheng Emperor, made an important contribution to the techniques for keeping bureaucrats under strict imperial control. The major innovation was in the field of communication. By introducing the palace memorial system — a direct and secret communication device — the emperor was able to check on the information supplied by his bureaucracy and concentrate almost all governmental power in his own hands. By the end of the Yung-cheng reign, the residual hereditary powers of the Manchu clansmen and the representational powers of Chinese and Manchu bureaucrats had alike been subdued.

Manchu acculturation was not a simple, one-way process. The Manchus did not humbly copy the whole Ming system; their technique of imperial control over the bureaucracy was a reciprocal contribution.

The power and position of the emperor in the early Ch'ing communication-decision structure was a function of the other components within the structure. Tracing changes in the latter automatically reveals changes in the former. In a strict sense, the emperor was the only one who made final decisions on all major state affairs; hence, only he could be referred to as the decision-maker, and all others are, in the Ch'ing documents, designated "deliberators." But because major imperial policy decisions were generally made on the basis of "deliberations" proposed by the various deliberative organs, the latter actually participated in the decision-making process; for the sake of simplicity we may therefore call them decision-makers as well, whereas the term "imperial decision-maker" may be an appropriate one to distinguish the emperor.

Generally speaking, the various agencies that were in charge of deliberations on governmental affairs fall into two categories. First, the Six Boards (*Liu-pu*) in the central administration were in charge of deliberating routine governmental business. (By routine is meant decisions governed by administrative precedents, regulations, and codes; the boards were guardians and interpreters of these regulations.) Normally the emperor would approve such deliberations, but in case of doubt he might refer the matter to a higher deliberative body for further consideration. In the area of weighty judicial matters involving, for example, capital punishment or serious offences committed by officials of high rank, there was an additional body called the Three Judiciary (*San-fa-ssu*) between the Board of Punishments and the next higher level.[1]

The conduct of the imperial clansmen was governed by a separate body of regulations. So it was with bannermen and Mongols. Decisions on matters pertaining to them were deliberated either by a separate organ — for example, imperial clansmen were tried by the Imperial Clan Court (*Tsung-jen fu*) — or in conjunction with the Board of Punishments, but never by the latter alone. More often, deliberations of this sort were referred to one of the higher bodies.

"High policy decisions" not governed by prescribed regulations under the guardians of the boards were referred by the emperor to one of the higher deliberative bodies for suggestions. Because the evolution of these various higher bodies reflected changes in the power structure in the early Ch'ing history, they will not only be typologized here, but their origins and developments will be traced briefly from the early days of the dynasty to the beginning of the new era under investigation.

By the middle of the K'ang-hsi reign, the accumulated structure of the deliberative apparatus was composed of three basic systems: (1) The Council of Deliberative Princes and Ministers (*I-cheng Wang ta-ch'en hui-i*); (2) The Assembly of Nine Ministries (or Ministers) and Censors (*Chiu-ch'ing k'o-tao hui-i*); and (3) various joint bodies of which the former two were the basic components. The first stemmed from an old Manchu tradition dating back to Nurhaci's time; the second was taken over from the Ming dynasty with slight modifications; the third represented a Manchu-Chinese amalgamation. The procedural relation between these systems, together with the system of memorials, will be analyzed in Chapter III; this section will trace only their establishment before the 1690's.

The Assembly of Deliberative Princes and Ministers. This body was composed of two subsystems, the Assembly of Deliberative Princes (*I-cheng wang*) and the Assembly of Deliberative Ministers (*I-cheng ta-ch'en*). The Assembly of Deliberative Princes originated in the time of Nurhaci (T'ai-tsu, 1559–1626). During the later years of his reign, the Manchu state passed from its original feudal stage to one of bureaucratic administration. The first sign of transition came in 1601, when Nurhaci set up the four "banners" (*ch'i*), governed by *pei-le* (Manchu: *beile*, deliberative princes),[2] the original number of which is unknown. In 1615 the number of banners was increased to eight. Subsequently, the number of *pei-le* was set at sixteen: thirteen sons and grandsons of Nurhaci and three sons of Surgaci, his brother.

The origin of the collective deliberation tradition was in 1622, when Nurhaci formally appointed eight of these *pei-le* as what may be termed the first deliberative princes. The *Man-chou shih-lu* records the background of this institution:

The eight . . . *pei-le* asked [Nurhaci]: "Heaven has granted you this grand empire, how should we try to consolidate it? Furthermore, in regard to all the blessings, how should we inherit them?"

Nurhaci answered: "Let no violent person succeed to my throne; because as soon as such a person becomes ruler, he will act recklessly and sin against Heaven. Moreover, one man's vision certainly cannot match that of a group. Therefore, I appoint you kings over the eight banners [*ku-shan pei-le*] so that you may rule the empire collectively with one accord and that you may avoid mistakes."

Then Nurhaci spelled out the qualifications of his successor: "Anyone among you eight *pei-le,* if he has talent and possesses virtue and is willing to accept criticism, may succeed me to the throne." [3]

The gradual shift from administration by the *pei-le* to administration by a bureaucracy also had its origin in Nurhaci's time, though bureaucratic participation in decision-making did not begin until 1626. Some have asserted that this process began in 1616, with the imperial appointment of "the five ministers" (*wu ta-ch'en*) to take charge of administration and conduct hearings on legal disputes.[4] As Franz Michael has made clear, however, the functions of these ministers were strictly technical.[5] Furthermore, the contention that "the eight ministers" (*pa ta-ch'en*) appointed by Nurhaci in 1623 constituted another stage in the evolution of the deliberative ministers cannot be sustained.[6] The functions of the eight were to watch over the eight *ku-shan pei-le* and discover any selfish motives among them, and to give advice on civil and military affairs. They seem, therefore, to have been the prototype of the censorial rather than the deliberative body in the early Manchu bureaucracy.

The bona fide Assembly of Deliberative Ministers only appeared in 1626, when the new sovereign T'ai-tsung (reigned 1627–1643) appointed eight banner commanders (*ku-shan o-chen*)[7] to be the functional commanders of the eight banners. These officers were also the first deliberative ministers. In peacetime, they were allowed to participate in deliberations on matters of state side by side with the *pei-le;* in time of the hunt or war, "they led their respective banner forces, all things being under their supervision and investigation." [8] In 1637, T'ai-tsung expanded membership of the Assembly of Deliberative Ministers by appointing three additional ministers for each of the eight banner units. This increasing tendency to deprive the *pei-le* of their power by relying on ministers should be viewed as unmistakable evidence of T'ai-tsung's intention to become a de facto emperor of the "Great Ch'ing Dynasty" which he had announced only a year before.

By 1636, the year when T'ai-tsung proclaimed himself emperor of the Great Ch'ing, he had subjugated all the contenders among his clansmen. In the same year, following Ming practice, he bureaucratized the nobility and classified the *pei-le* into nine princely ranks. Only the first two ranks were designated as king or prince (*wang*), and the term *pei-le* came to mean a prince of the third rank.[9] The imperial power was further strengthened during the Regency of Dorgon in the early Shun-chih reign with even greater curtailment of the princes' power.

In 1644, the Ch'ing capital was moved to Peking from Mukden, and the empire absorbed a great part of China proper. Prince Dorgon, who ruled as regent for the child Shun-chih Emperor, expanded membership of the Assembly of Deliberative Ministers further to include high civil officials such as the grand secretaries[10] and the presidents of the Six Boards. By the middle of the K'ang-hsi reign, censors-general and presidents of the Court of Colonial Affairs (*Li-fan yüan*) were admitted to this deliberative body.[11] By 1685, when the Ch'ing forces had conquered all China, the Manchu and Mongol banner commanders, members of the Assembly of Deliberative Ministers ex officio, were excluded from that body but allowed to participate in deliberations pertaining to military affairs. Throughout the early Ch'ing period the deliberative ministers were nearly all Manchus except for a few Mongol and Chinese banner leaders.[12]

The term *ta-ch'en* means ministers or high officials, so it is obvious that they were imperial appointees and subject to arbitrary dismissal. Yet the status of the deliberative princes vis-à-vis the sovereign reflected changes in the power structure during this formative period of the Manchu bureaucracy.

In the Ch'ing records, descriptions of deliberative council functions are very sketchy and rare. According to one Ch'ing source,[13] the council was in charge of deliberating weighty military affairs not handled by the *Nei-ko*. Based on the findings of recent studies, however, their functions can be categorized thus: (1) deliberation on affairs related to military forces, including both the banner troops and the Green Standards (*lü-ying*); (2) deliberation on nonmilitary affairs of the bannermen (the banner organization was both military and social); (3) announcement of the emperor's final decisions on military affairs; and (4) discussion of important foreign affairs.[14]

This council was "the supreme political system in [early] Ch'ing times" and the supreme deliberative body whose power was second only to that of the emperor; it was a characteristic system of the Ch'ing which stemmed from the very roots of the Manchu tradition.[15]

The Assembly of Nine Ministries and Censors. Sometimes known as the Nine Senior Ministries (*Ta chiu-ch'ing*),[16] this system was inherited from the Ming; it was composed of the heads of the Six Boards, the Censorate (*Tu-ch'a yüan*), the Transmission Office (*T'ung-cheng ssu*), and the Court of Judicature and Revision (*Ta-li ssu*). It was often supplemented by censors (*k'o-tao*) and occasionally by various other officials, depending on the nature of the subject matter under deliberation. The censor's presence in the conference was obviously for the purpose of discovering any irregularities in the deliberations.[17]

Because both Chinese and Manchu ministers were included in the council, the emperor often appointed the participants on an ethnic basis. In the *Ch'ing-shih-lu* (Veritable records of the Ch'ing dynasty) terms are often used such as the Manchu nine ministers (*Man chiu-ch'ing*), the Chinese nine ministers (*Han chiu-ch'ing*), and the Manchu and Chinese nine ministers (*Man-han chiu-ch'ing*). Sometimes only one of the two groups was called to deliberate by the emperor, depending on the subject matter.

Generally speaking, the Assembly of Nine Ministers and Censors was appointed for three purposes: (1) to propose alternatives to the emperor before he made final decisions on general policies; (2) to nominate candidates for a few special types of high official posts, mainly governor-general and governor;[18] (3) to deliberate on new governmental regulations such as those on official rank and civil examinations.[19]

Joint Sessions. Although the Assembly of Deliberative Princes and Ministers was charged mainly with deliberation on military matters and banner affairs, it was often ordered to meet in joint session with the Assembly of Nine Ministers. The subject matter of such sessions seems to have been civil affairs and in general to have pertained to the three categories mentioned above. A joint session was convened when the nature of the issues seemed important and complex or when the subject had been already deliberated by the Assembly of Nine Ministers and had been referred further along. In early times, various other groups were sometimes included in joint sessions, depending upon the nature of the subject matter; but ordinarily the basic membership consisted of the deliberating princes and ministers and the nine ministers and censors.[20]

Establishment of the Nei-ko. Although grand secretaries in the *Nei-ko* were frequently appointed to participate in deliberations in early Ch'ing times,[21] the *Nei-ko* system itself originated,[22] not as a deliberative body, but primarily as a secretarial-advisory office which facilitated communication between the Manchu rulers and their bureaucracy. One peculiar problem confronting the early Manchu rulers that did not concern the Ming emperors at all was the language barrier. The Grand Secretariat was originally established to translate documents written in Manchu into Chinese and vice versa and to keep the state records, but it was not until 1658 (the fifteenth year of the Shun-chih reign) that the name *Nei-ko* for the first time appeared in Ch'ing governmental structure. And not until 1670, the ninth year of K'ang-hsi, did this institution become firmly established. Its development underwent three phases.

In 1599, at Nurhaci's request, the Manchu script was devised from a modified form of the Mongolian alphabet,[23] and in 1614 the title of literary clerk (*pi-t'ieh-shih*) first appeared in Manchu records. The duty of a clerk was to keep the financial account in a *niru* (a banner company, the basic social and military unit in early Manchu society).[24] In 1629, when T'ai-tsung became the sovereign ruler of the Manchu tribes, he established the Literature Hall (*Wen-kuan*) in Mukden. Scholars (*ju-ch'en*) appointed to serve in the hall were to translate Chinese books and keep records of the Manchu state, in terms of both its achievements and its mistakes.[25] It should be noted that these early scholars were actually military officers temporarily assigned to serve in the hall; there were no purely civil officials in the Manchu organization at this time. In 1631, T'ai-tsung established the Six Boards superficially patterned on the structure of the Ming dynasty. In 1634, sixteen translators with the *chü-jen* degree were selected through an examination given by the Board of Rites and given offices in the Literature Hall. This marked the beginning of purely civil appointments and ended the first phase of the *Nei-ko*'s evolution.

In 1636, the Literature Hall was converted into the Three Inner Courts (*Nei san-yüan*): the Inner Court of Historiography (*Nei kuo-shih kuan*), the Inner Court of Secretariat (*Nei pi-shu yüan*), and the Inner Court of Literature (*Nei hung-wen yüan*). Two months later, grand secretaries (*ta hsüeh-shih*) and subchancellors (*hsüeh-shih*) were appointed to the Inner Courts. Their status in the Manchu bureaucratic hierarchy at this time was not high; a grand secretary was only "comparable to a colonel" [26] and a subchancellor "to a lieutenant-colonel." [27] These officials served as personal secretaries who helped T'ai-tsung to draft edicts and advised him on foreign affairs. Their official status was far inferior to the heads of the Six Boards (who were at this time all Manchu *pei-le*); they were, therefore, far from being a formal deliberative body.

After the move to Peking and during Prince Regent Dorgon's de facto rule, the Three Inner Courts remained primarily a secretarial and advisory body. The Six Boards submitted their memorials directly to the emperor, and only memorials which had nothing to do with the boards[28] were presented through the Inner Courts. Such memorials were presented by individual Chinese officials or civilians and were written in Chinese; they had to be translated into Manchu before presentation to the throne. They usually contained proposals for the conquest of China and for consolidation of the conquered areas in China proper.

By 1653, three years after the death of Dorgon, the deliberating procedure in connection with the central administrative organs was operating as follows: (1) the chiefs of the central organs presented their memorials in person and the emperor made decisions by oral instruction; (2) after returning to their respective offices the memorialists wrote the imperial oral instructions on slips of paper and sent them together with the original memorials to the Inner Courts, where the memorials were endorsed with red ink according to the slips and then sent to the Six Sections (*Liu-k'o*).[29] In other words, the emperor did not at this time personally endorse memorials presented by the central organs. It was possible for ministers to misundertstand the imperial will or make errors; in February 1653, for example, the Censorate impeached Sun Ch'eng-tse, vice-president of the Board of Personnel, and Tung Fu, secretary of the Transmission Office, the one for deafness and the other for old age. The emperor's original decision had been: "Let the Board of Personnel deliberate and memorialize in reply"; the board misunderstood it for "Let them be dismissed" (*ko-chih*). The emperor, upon learning of the mistake, realized the inadequacy of the existing procedure and asked the grand secretaries how the Ming "draft rescript" (*p'iao-ni*) system had operated. He then ordered the deliberative princes and ministers, the grand secretaries,[30] and both the Manchu and Chinese nine ministers to meet in joint session to deliberate possible improvements of the existing procedure.[31]

The result of the deliberation was approved by the emperor. The edict reads: "Hereafter, let all ministers present their memorials in person as usual. After We have read the memorials, they may withdraw. After We have written our rescripts on the memorials personally in Manchu or in Chinese, let them be sent down to the Inner Courts through which the endorsed memorials are sent to the Six Sections." Then the Six Sections will notify the boards or the departments concerned to "copy them out." [32]

All memorials were endorsed by the emperor's own hand, so that the process was a heavy burden upon him. On March 30, 1653, the Shun-chih Emperor complained to his ministers: "Now I am personally executing all state affairs. The nation is vast and affairs of state are extremely complex. I have to endorse all memorials and make decisions by myself without a minute of rest." [33]

On December 15 of that year it was decided, again based on advice of the deliberative princes and ministers, that

> a room just inside the T'ai-ho Gate is chosen in which the grand secretaries and subchancellors are to be on duty in turn. As to the memorials, they may be endorsed by the emperor himself, or [by the grand secretaries] in the presence of the emperor [based on the imperial oral instructions]. If [the grand secretaries] consider that the imperial decisions are not feasible and should be corrected, they should express their opinions to the emperor suggesting proper corrections so that improper decisions and errors may be avoided.[34]

This was indeed a significant change: although the grand secretaries had not yet been allowed the initiative in proposing draft rescripts, for the first time in Ch'ing history they were ordered not only to assist the emperor in endorsing memorials, but, most important of all, to make suggestions regarding decisions. This was the second phase.

In 1658 the Shun-chih Emperor reorganized the Inner Courts into two independent organs, the *Nei-ko* and the Hanlin Academy, indicating movement toward the copying of Chinese (mainly Ming) institutions. Another enhancement of the *Nei-ko*'s position arose in 1660. By that year, the volume of memorials from the central organs and censors had increased to such an extent that even with the assistance of the grand secretaries the Shun-chih Emperor could hardly deal with them all at the morning audience. The result was a new rule: "Hereafter all memorials from central organs and censors should be presented in person at noon so that We may read them [early]; the following day they are to be sent down [to the *Nei-ko*] for making draft rescripts . . ." [35] This implies that the system of making draft rescripts in the *Nei-ko* had become institutionalized.

Nevertheless, in 1661, only a few months after the Shun-chih Emperor's death, the four joint regents who ruled the Ch'ing government during the K'ang-hsi Emperor's minority issued an edict in the name of the emperor which abolished the *Nei-ko* and revived the former Three Inner Courts system. [36] This indicates an upsurge in the strength of the Manchu ruling elite during the regency. Only in 1670, the ninth year of the K'ang-hsi reign and two years after the K'ang-hsi Emperor had eliminated the most dominating Regent, Oboi, and taken over the reins of the government personally, was the *Nei-ko* re-established.

By the year 1690, when the first *Ch'ing Collected Statutes* were promulgated, the institutional status of the *Nei-ko* was firmly established. According to the *Statutes*:

> All memorials written in Manchu from central and provincial organs, as well as from individual officials, should be sent to the grand secretaries and the subchancellors of the *Nei-ko* in order that they might propose draft rescripts and present them to the emperor for final decisions. If they are written only in Chinese or Mongolian, they should be sent to the Imperial Patent Office [*Chung-shu-k'o*] to be translated (either the entire memorial or the *t'ieh-huang* [summaries] only) . . . They should then be sent to the grand secretaries and subchancellors who can propose draft rescripts before presentation to the emperor for decisions. [37]

This general statement is the only reference made in the *Statutes* to the processing of memorials in the *Nei-ko*. Private accounts must be relied upon for a detailed analysis of the draft rescript system (see Chapter IV).

Procedures and Problems. Before 1699, deliberative princes brought their own palace commandant (*ch'ang-shih,* rank 3A) to the Council of Deliberative Princes and Ministers; and ex-deliberative ministers (deliberative ministers at large, *hsien-san i-cheng ta-ch'en*[38]) were allowed to attend the meetings, perhaps as observers. These elements, though without the right to make decisions, functioned as gossipers, making secrecy most difficult. In 1699 the K'ang-hsi Emperor decreed that they be excluded from the meetings.

A list of 1690 shows that such factional strongmen as the Imperial Uncle T'ung Kuo-wei, Songgotu, and Mingju, as well as Sunu, were all in the ranks of deliberative ministers;[39] Prince Fu-ch'uan, the emperor's elder brother, for whom he had much respect and affection, and Prince Ch'ang-ning were among the deliberative princes.

In time of war deliberative ministers were divisible into two groups, one of which accompanied the campaigning generalissimo while the other remained in the capital. The council in either case was often dominated by strong factional leaders; hence, some of the participants simply "sat in the conference quietly just like wooden dummies," in the emperor's description, "without uttering a word." [40]

Insofar as procedures are concerned, the council was convened nearly always in response to requests of the emperor, either to give initial deliberation to matters within its jurisdiction or to review, usually jointly with another body, important matters that had already been deliberated elsewhere. If two different opinions emerged, "both were presented to the emperor for consideration" [41] (*liang-i i-wen*). During the K'ang-hsi period, council meetings were held in the Forbidden City, just outside the Middle-Left Gate.[42]

The bulky size of the Assembly of Nine Ministries and Censors suggests its own operational problems. Each of the Six Boards was represented by six ministers, and Manchu and Chinese were each represented by a president and two vice-presidents. That total was thirty-six, but, adding members from other organs and including censors, the total number of participants well exceeded fifty.

Divergent human motives and personal connections made the assembly extremely ineffective. Certain patterns of irregularity emerged constantly: (1) The proceedings were controlled by one or two influentials, usually Manchus.[43] (2) In making recommendations for high official posts (*hui-t'ui*) factional interests took precedence; members managed to recommend their own men — relatives, friends, students, fellow graduates, fellow countrymen — and sometimes compromises were reached in exchange for a deal in the next meeting.[44] (3) The emperor thus often received false recommendations from the assembly.[45] (4) Censors sometimes clashed with the dominating elements among the ministers and made their complaints known to the emperor;[46] and sometimes they, too, collaborated with these forces,[47] though in most cases they adopted passive attitudes for self-preservation.

Some middle-level bureaucrats of the board (with whom the subject matter under discussion at the time was chiefly concerned) were also allowed to participate. They were usually department directors (*lang-chung*), known as *ssu-kuan* (department officials), whose participation was based on technical knowledge of regulations. Sometimes influentials at the meeting would be forced to reckon with them in order to attain their aims.[48]

The constituents of joint sessions varied from case to case, depending upon nature of the subject matter. They shared with the assembly problems that were essentially the same but more complex. Participants had no equal rights because of built-in Manchu superiority over the Chinese. Before 1688 Chinese grand secretaries, while briefing the council on results of the deliberation, on behalf of the assembly, were made to do so kneeling before the Manchu deliberative princes in joint session.[49] Although the K'ang-hsi Emperor abolished this practice (in 1688), the Chinese did not become equals until the last decade of the K'ang-hsi reign.

When the assembly or any joint session was convened, the board with which the deliberation was most concerned was responsible for making up the "draft memorial" (*ni-kao*) and asked the other participants to "endorse the draft memorial" (*hua-t'i*) before submitting it to the emperor. Many would sign their names (*shu-ming*) without knowing the contents;[50] again, built-in Manchu-Chinese inequality was partially responsible for such behavior. Before 1704, for example, depositions recorded by the Board of Punishments were written only in Manchu — consequently, few Chinese ministers could read them, but they had to sign anyway as a formality.[51]

Formal procedures remained the same throughout the K'ang-hsi years, even though new channels of information were opened as a result of introduction of the palace memorial system.

Intragovernmental communication is one of the most crucial determinants in the decision-making process of any form of government.[1] The major institutional device for receipt of information by the emperor during the first half of the K'ang-hsi reign was the traditional memorial system, inherited along with the *Nei-ko* institution from the Ming in the Shun-chih era. The memorial system itself will be treated separately; in this chapter, four minor institutional devices that were closely related to the system will be discussed.

The face-to-face channel of communication between the K'ang-hsi Emperor and his officials was the audience system. Morning audience was held almost daily for the central government officials and special audiences occasionally for provincial officials. General features of the system will be discussed here; included in Appendix Case A is an actual account of a special audience between the K'ang-hsi Emperor and Governor Ch'en Pin that sheds much light on how the emperor met with an official, what subjects were discussed, and, most important, what information the emperor wished to gather concerning local conditions.

The morning audience (*yü-men t'ing-cheng*) performed several functions:[2] (1) heads of the central organs presented their memorials in person, and the emperor could discuss the subject matter with them if he considered it necessary; (2) the emperor could discuss with the grand secretaries memorials presented by the Six Boards, so that they could prepare proper draft rescripts according to the imperial oral instructions;[3] (3) the emperor could interview officials whose names were presented on the "green-head tablets" (*lü-t'ou-p'ai*).[4] The emperor obtained much firsthand information concerning local conditions through conversation with certain types of high provincial officials summoned to special audiences with the emperor at these hours.

Regulations governing the time and procedure of the morning audience are recorded clearly in the *Chü-i-lu,* a valuable source of the K'ang-hsi period:

The morning audience always started around 7:45 A.M. during winter and spring months, and around 8:45 A.M. during summer and autumn months. The officials of the *Nei-ko* and the central organs first gathered together at dawn in front of the Meridian Gate; then they proceeded to the Central Left Gate for a short rest before they mustered outside of the Ch'ien-ch'ing Gate [Yü-men] waiting for the emperor. After the emperor arrived at the prescribed hour and mounted his imperial throne, the Six Boards, the Censorate, and other central departments presented their memorials in prescribed order. For instance, if the Board of Personnel presented its memorials first on the first day of a certain month, the Board of Revenue would be the first to present its memorials on the following day, and so on. If, however, the officials of the Imperial Clan Court were present, they would present their memorials before the boards. After the boards, the Three Judiciaries always stood in the third place. The censors and the supervising censors always presented their memorials last. After all memorials were presented [and read by the emperor], the grand secretaries and the subchancellors of the *Nei-ko* would come to the imperial presence to receive his instructions [regarding the action to be taken on the memorials].[5]

The emperor was very serious about holding the daily morning audience. Once, in 1695, although his skin still burned after treatment with a cauterizing agent, he refused to listen to his grand secretaries' suggestions that the morning audience be temporarily suspended and memorials from the central organs presented through the *Nei-ko*. He said he would feel terribly bored if he could not see his ministers every day.[6] The conscientious attitude of the K'ang-hsi Emperor was in sharp contrast to that of the late Ming emperors, one of whom allegedly refused to see his grand secretaries at the morning audience for twenty years straight.[7]

The emperor often summoned certain types of high-ranking provincial officials to Peking for special audiences (*pi-chien or ju-chin*). Such meetings were usually initiated by the provincial officials because they implied special prestige and honor; the audiences were usually requested on the formal grounds that the officials wished to inquire personally about the emperor's well-being.

This institution probably did not become a constant practice until after 1683, only two years after the Rebellion of the Three Feudatories (1673–1681). The emperor told his grand secretaries in 1683 that the "commanders-in-chief and brigade generals in the frontier regions often become arrogant and are apt to start revolts, because they have held military power for a long period. If they are frequently summoned to the court for special audiences their hearts will learn to respect and fear [imperial authority]." [8] Undoubtedly, the rebellion caused the emperor to pay attention to such potential dangers in the frontier regions and thus led him to implement this system.

The privilege of special audience was extended only to certain high-ranking provincial officials. The financial commissioners (*pu-cheng-shih*) and judicial commissioners (*an-ch'a-shih*) were allowed to have a special audience with the emperor triennially, on the occasion of the Great Accounting (*ta-chi*).[9] The purpose was two-fold: they could express opinions on how to improve the local administration; after considering their suggestions, the emperor could make new appraisals of their talents and abilities for future reference in promotions and demotions.[10]

The top-ranking provincial authorities were summoned for special audiences irregularly. The K'ang-hsi Emperor said in 1695: "Occasionally, I summon governors-general, governors, commanders-in-chief, or brigade generals for special audiences, in order to ask them about local conditions and the livelihood of the common people and soldiers — this is an institution of great significance." [11] Reporting on local conditions honestly was obligatory. The emperor used such interviews to test the motives of the officials, revealing on one occasion that he often took notes on the conversations.[12] Before a summoned official left Peking for his provincial post he would be granted a "farewell audience" (*pi-tz'u*) with the emperor, at which he would request new instructions from the emperor.[13]

The question of how effectively special audiences broadened channels of communication and thus the emperor's awareness of local conditions cannot be answered quantitatively, since the necessary data is not available. Judging from the content of such audiences, which sometimes were very comprehensive, it is certain that the channel was a useful one. As Ch'en Pin's audience account shows, this practice, unlike other types of formalistic audiences, had several particular advantages: (1) The emperor might make inquiries and discuss any substantive problem at length; (2) the official could relate not only what he knew about local conditions under his direct jurisdiction, but also whatever he had observed on his way to

Peking; and (3) the conversation could be kept strictly secret between the emperor and the official, who could thus speak more freely than otherwise.

Censors were often called "speech officials" (*yen-kuan*) or sometimes "officials serving as ears and eyes [of the emperor]" (*erh-mu chih kuan*). One of their most important functions was to supply political information to the throne. There were two types in K'ang-hsi times, censors (*yü-shih* or *chien-ch'a yü-shih*) and supervising censors (*chi-shih-chung*). The former were officials in the Censorate under the general supervision of censors-general, but they were independently responsible to the throne for what they said. They were assigned to serve in fifteen different circuits (*tao*) with the responsibility of watching over the central organs and participating in deliberations on judicial cases in their respective provinces. Because each circuit censor was in charge of one province or one special area (for instance, the capital area), his official title was designed to fit the administrative unit to which he was assigned (for example, "censor overseeing the Honan Circuit," *Honan tao chieh-ch'a yü-shih*). The supervising censors served in the Six Sections, an independent organ with a special function in the memorial system.[14] Normally a censor's information was written in a memorial.[15] Theoretically, his right of speech was protected as long as he did not prevaricate. The censors could impeach any official on hearsay evidence, although in practice they were often reproved for their ulterior motives and false accusations.[16]

The K'ang-hsi Emperor's policy toward censors was generally quite lenient, in order to encourage them to supply information essential to his decision-making. In 1700, the supervising censor Mu-ho-lun presented a memorial attacking the luxury which he felt prevailed in the court. Since an accusation of this kind implied remonstration with the emperor himself, the *Nei-ko* proposed a rescript reprimanding Mu-ho-lun. The K'ang-hsi Emperor, though disagreeing with Mu-ho-lun's accusation, rejected the proposed rescript and said to the grand secretaries: "It is the censors' special duty that they serve as the imperial ears and eyes. If they are condemned as a result of their words, who will ever dare say anything again . . . Therefore, [Mu-ho-lun] is not [to be] reprimanded because of this memorial." He also took the occasion to reiterate his general policy: "It is most essential at this time that channels of information be broadened and censors be encouraged to give suggestions . . . If what they say is proper, I will carry it out; otherwise I will simply return their memorials. This way, officials in the capital and in the provinces will all be afraid and become watchful." [17]

Operational limitations existed in this censorial channel of communication. Few censors were sent to the provinces on special missions,[18] therefore most of them received information on conditions in the provinces through hearsay in the capital. Thus the emperor could not rely on them for accurate and useful information on what was happening in the provinces. The censors' abuses of their special privileges constituted a further reason for the emperor to seek information through other channels.

Imperial commissioners were high-ranking officials sent to the provinces on an ad hoc basis to carry out specific imperial missions. After a commissioner had returned from a certain province, the emperor would inquire about what he had learned with regard to local conditions, especially the performance of local officials. For instance, in 1690, when Chang P'eng-ko (then director-general of the Yellow River and Grand Canal) returned from an imperial mission in Shensi province, the emperor asked him: "How was the conduct of the acting governor-general Hsi-erh-ta?" He replied: "He is a very good official." The emperor asked again: "How is the present governor of Shensi Pei-ho-no compared with his predecessor Pa-hsi?" Chang answered: "Well, Pa-hsi is a very careful person, whereas Pei-ho-no manages things very skillfully without overlooking details." [19] Conversations of this sort, some of which are rather lengthy, were frequently recorded in the *Ch'ing-shih-lu*.[20] The imperial commissioners were also subject to imperial inspection. For example, after Chang P'eng-ko retired from the imperial presence, the K'ang-hsi Emperor turned to his grand secretaries and said: "While Chang P'eng-ko was in Shensi, I made careful examinations and inquiries about him. I found that he was indeed a very honest official. He is the most incorruptible official in the entire nation." [21]

The K'ang-hsi Emperor sometimes made important decisions based on, or influenced by, his own personal observations. He constantly toured the Metropolitan (capital) area, visited the imperial tombs, and traveled to various provinces, in addition to traveling regularly between Peking and his summer palace at Jehol and the hunting exercises in which he engaged on various occasions according to Manchu tradition.

He made six tours in the southern provinces,[22] the primary purpose of which was, according to the emperor himself: "to make personal observations and inquiries about the people's hardships . . . and to investigate local customs" in the Chekiang and Chiang-nan regions; on-the-spot inspection of the conservation work on the Yellow River was a secondary motivation.[23] Hsiao I-shan believes the tours had a third sociopolitical function: to impress the southern area with the power of the Manchu government because the potential for rebellion there was still high at that time.[24] Again according to the emperor, the tours were also made with the intention of training the heir apparent Yin-jeng "so that [he] might become acquainted with the local customs and the people's hardships";[25] in this respect they seem to have fallen short of their purpose, however, for the reckless and immoral acts of the heir apparent while on tour contributed largely to the emperor's disillusionment with him.

The manner in which these tours supplied the emperor with firsthand information is illustrated by four incidents. The first two show the accessibility of the emperor during his tours; the last two show the importance to the emperor's decisions of the information gathered.

There is good reason to believe that the K'ang-hsi Emperor was fairly approachable. One day in 1695, as he toured the Metropolitan area inspecting local conditions, he noticed that many soldiers were heavily loaded, traveling hastily along the road, and that all appeared very weary. When he asked them why they had to work so hard, he discovered that the Board of War had abused the use of the official seal (in affixing it on an order) to please some high officials and had thus ordered the soldiers to such strenuous work.[26] On another occasion, in 1683, the emperor was traveling to Shensi province. On his way, he saw some villagers carrying beans and rice on their shoulders, and he asked them why they were doing this. The villagers answered that they were preparing rations for the imperial visit. The emperor immediately ordered a subchancellor of the *Nei-ko* to investigate the case, since he had explicitly issued an edict that all rations for his visit would be prepared by the Imperial Household, not by local officials.[27] Sometimes the emperor called people to his chariot who had come out to welcome him on the road: "I asked them about local conditions, good or bad; they always answered my questions very honestly . . . I became familiar with all sorts of local situations and customs." [28]

The K'ang-hsi Emperor often arrived at important decisions from information gathered on imperial tours; in 1708, for example, an edict was issued to the effect that "the land-poll tax of the Chiang-nan province amounting to 4,750,400 taels, and that of Chekiang province amounting to 2,577,000 taels, be exempted." In making such a decision the emperor was greatly influenced by the impression he had of poor conditions of the area, through which he had traveled on southern tours.[29] In 1707, the emperor made the famous honest official Chang Po-hsing governor of Fukien while he was still traveling in the south because his inquiries about that official during his tour confirmed his belief that Chang was indeed incorruptible and reliable.

In the foregoing chapters, the structure of the deliberative bodies and the four minor means of communication through which the K'ang-hsi Emperor received information necessary for making decisions have been described. By studying the traditional memorial system, the procedural aspect of this communication process can be illuminated.

The memorial system was the major institutional device employed by the emperor to facilitate communication between himself and his bureaucracy. He based most of his decisions in governmental affairs on information received in memorials from the Metropolitan and provincial officials.

After the conquest of China, the Manchus adopted the traditional memorial (*pen-chang*) system from the Ming, together with the *Nei-ko* institution, the main function of which was to deal with memorials. There were basically two types of memorials: *tsou-pen* and *t'i-pen*. The former were used by officials, as well as by common people, to memorialize the throne on personal matters; the latter were used by certain high-ranking officials of governmental organs for official, or public, matters.[1]

In 1651, the official forms of *t'i-pen* and *tsou-pen* were published for the first time. They were exact copies of the Ming forms; but because the criteria for distinguishing between official and personal matters were never clearly defined, officials were often impeached by the Transmission Office for confusing the two forms. Eventually, after repeated futile reiterations of the difference between them, the *tsou-pen* form was abolished in 1747. Thereafter, memorialists used either the *t'i-pen* or a newer form, known as *tsou-che* (palace memorials), which had by then taken over some functions of the *tsou-pen*.[2]

Memorials from provincial authorities were transmitted to Peking through the postal facilities, and imperial instructions independently issued or in response to incoming memorials were transmitted to the various provinces in the same way. Thus effective functioning of the postal system had direct bearing on the successful use of memorials as a communication medium between the Emperor and his representatives.

The formal structure of the Ch'ing postal system was in general an almost exact takeover from the Ming dynasty and remained unchanged throughout the Ch'ing period until Western systems were introduced in the late nineteenth century.[3] Since the transmission of palace memorials required maximum secrecy, some more detailed regulations were set, but the basic structure of the postal system did not undergo significant changes.

Early Ch'ing postal service was supervised by the Remount Department (*Ch'e-chia ch'ing-li ssu*) of the Board of War, under which a central office called the Imperial Dispatch Office (*Hui-t'ung kuan*) was charged with means of transportation and the stations (*i*) in the provinces.[4] The stations extended through the provinces in all directions from Peking, where the central station was situated. Four main routes radiated from the central station, along which these stations were scattered: "(1) the northeastern route, from Peking to Mukden and thence to Kirin and Heilungkiang; (2) the eastern route, to Shantung and thence to (a) Anhwei, Kiangsi, and Kwangtung, or (b) Kiangsu, Chekiang, and Fukien; (3) the central route, to Honan and thence to (a) Hupeh, Hunan, and Kwangsi, or (b) Kweichow and Yunnan; (4) the western route, to Shansi and Shensi and thence to (a) Kansu and Sinkiang, or (b) Szechwan and Tibet." [5] All the stations were equipped with horses and/or other transportation for rapid transfer of memorials and other important documents.[6]

Memorials were transmitted to Peking from the provinces by one of two methods. They could be carried by post soldiers (*p'u-ping*) stationed at each of the *p'u* (a special type of station established solely for the purpose of transmitting government documents) and relay expresses;[7] the relay speed was set at three hundred *li* (about a hundred miles) per day. Alternatively, they were transmitted by special messengers (*t'i-t'ang ch'eng-ch'ai*), who were allowed to use a prescribed number of horses or other conveyances from the stations. The messengers were required to show their express tags (*huo-p'ai*) in order to use these facilities.[8]

After memorials had reached the capital, they were submitted to the Transmission Office, ordinarily through the superintendents of courier posts (*chu-ching t'i-t'ang*). The Transmission Office examined their form and contents[9] and then transferred them to the *Nei-ko* for the making of draft rescripts. Here the actual decision-making procedure started.

By the year 1733, a memorial delivered at the Transmission Office would be accompanied by at least four items (all prepared by the memorialist himself): (1) *fu-pen* (copies of the memorials); (2) *t'ieh-huang* (summary of the memorial); (3) *chieh-t'ieh* (memoranda); and (4) *yin-wen* (transmission records).[10] The *t'ieh-huang* was a very brief summary of the memorial and was attached to the back of the memorial itself.[11] The *chieh-t'ieh* were either exact copies or much more detailed summaries of the memorial, prepared in two or more copies, one for the Transmission Office for future reference [12] and one for each board or department concerned so that a preliminary study of the memorial could be made.[13] The *yin-wen* was a separate piece of paper on which the messenger's name and the date of the document's arrival at each postal station were entered in order to assure the punctuality of the transmission; the messenger was held responsible for any delay.[14]

In form, memorials had to comply with rigid regulations regarding number and honorary elevation of characters. By 1724, the maximum number of characters allowed in a memorial was three hundred and in a *t'ieh-huang* one hundred.[15] This restriction inevitably limited the content of a memorial and made it impossible to include detailed information.

After memorials and their subsidiary documents were transferred to the *Nei-ko,* the actual draft rescript (*p'iao-ni*) procedure got under way. Since the *K'ang-hsi Collected Statutes* (published 1690) and the *Yung-cheng Collected Statutes* (published 1732), are similar in general content and give an identical general statement on this procedure,[16] the prescribed method in this period (1690–1732) can be regarded as nearly constant. Both editions fail to give any further detailed description of the draft rescript procedure, but two valuable accounts are available to supplement them: the *Nei-ko hsiao-chih* (A brief sketch of the *Nei-ko*), by Yeh Feng-mao, and the *Nei-ko chih* (An account of the *Nei-ko*), by Hsi Wu-ao. Both authors served as secretaries (*chung-shu*) in the *Nei-ko* during the Yung-cheng reign. Their accounts shed much light on the subject during the period of this study.[17]

The *Nei-ko* was composed of various types of officials, each of whom was charged with prescribed duties in connection with the draft rescript procedure (its composition during the period under consideration is shown in the table below). Their major functions and relationships will be made clear after their respective roles in the draft rescript procedure is described. That procedure consisted of the eight steps that follow.

(1) After a memorial was transferred to the *Nei-ko* from the Transmission Office, the scribes in the Chinese Registry (*Han p'iao-ch'ien ch'u*)

Composition of the *Nei-ko*

Types of officials	Ranks	Man-chus	Mon-gols	Chinese Banner-men	Chinese	Total
Grand secretaries (*ta-hsüeh-shih*)	2A		Unspecified			
Subchancellors (*hsüeh-shih*)	3A	6	—	4	—	10
Readers (*shih-tu hsüeh-shih*)	4B	6	2	2	—	10
Assistant readers (*shih-tu*)	6A	11(8)[a]	2	2	(2)[b]	15
Archivists (*tien-chi*)	8B	2	—	2	2	6
Secretaries (*chung-shu,* or *she-jen*)	7B	75 (64)[a]	19 (16)[a]	13 (8)[a]	36 (32)[a]	143

Source: *Ta-Ch'ing hui-tien* (1732), chap. ii, pp. 1–2b.
[a] Figures after 1699.
[b] These two Chinese assistant readers were added only in 1726; there were no Chinese readers or assistant readers appointed before them.

made the preliminary drafts (*ts'ao-ch'ien*).[18] Then the memorial was handed to the assistant readers, who, after carefully reviewing it, sent it to the Manchu Registry (*Man p'iao-ch'ien ch'u*) for translation into Manchu. Subsequently, the draft in Chinese and Manchu was presented to the grand secretaries for final approval.

(2) After the grand secretaries had approved the preliminary drafts, the one in Manchu was handed back to the Manchu Registry and the one in Chinese to the Chinese Registry. Formal drafts (*cheng-ch'ien*) were then made in both languages by the registries.

(3) Eventually, the scribes of the Manchu Registry inserted the formal drafts in the memorial and presented them altogether to the emperor through the red memorial scribes (*hung-pen-shang*) in the Red Memorial Office (*Hung-pen fang,* or *P'i-peng ch'u,* Endorsement Copying Office).[19]

(4) In response to the draft proposals, the emperor could take one of three alternative actions: approve the draft, approve it with corrections, or retain the memorial and the draft in the palace, along with others of them, until he had accumulated a goodly number for discussion with his grand secretaries in a morning audience. Such memorials were called "retained memorials" (*liu-chung pen* or *che-pen*).[20]

(5) The approved draft proposal together with the memorial was handed back to the Red Memorial Office, where scribes copied the draft rescript in Manchu at the end of the memorial text. The memorial bearing the

endorsement was returned to the *Nei-ko,* where the Chinese subchancellors wrote the approved draft rescript onto the first page of the memorial in large Chinese characters on top of the memorial text. The memorial at this stage was called a "red memorial" because the endorsement was done in vermilion ink.

(6) The red memorial was then transferred to the Chinese Registry, where Chinese scribes recorded the imperial decision (endorsement) in the Imperial Instruction Book (*ssu-lun pu*) for later reference. The original draft rescript slips were kept in this office.

(7) The Chinese Registry then notified the Six Sections to send a supervising censor to receive the red memorial. A copy was made in the appropriate section for the appropriate board charged with its execution.[21] For example, if the decision was concerned with financial matters, the Section of Revenue (*Hu-k'o*) would make a copy of the red memorial and send it to the Board of Revenue. However, if the decision was concerned mainly with a certain board or department, but other central organs were involved, a main copy (*cheng-ch'ao*) would be made for the board or department and extra copies (*wai-ch'ao*) for the other organs. The red memorial was kept in the Six Sections until the end of the year and then returned to the *Nei-ko* for filing.[22] It should be noted that if an imperial edict was issued independently without an accompanying memorial, the board concerned would send a clerk directly to the *Nei-ko* to copy and execute it.[23]

The process summarized above normally took no more than four days, from the time when a memorial arrived at the Transmission Office until copies including the imperial rescript were made by the Six Sections for the appropriate board.[24]

(8) The imperial decision, if concerned with the provincial governments, would be made known to them through three channels. The superintendents of the Courier Posts, stationed in the capital to represent their respective provincial governments, would go to the Six Sections to make a copy of the red memorial for the provincial governments[25] unless it was a confidential memorial (*mi-pen*); these were not allowed to be copied.[26] The *Peking Gazette (Ching-pao)*, administered by the superintendents of Courier Posts, would publish the red memorials and distribute them to all provincial governments.[27] The board concerned would send a formal communication (*tzu*) to provincial authorities with whom the decision was concerned.[28]

But provincial memorials (*t'ung-pen*) were often referred to the appropriate board or department, or even the deliberative bodies, for comments or proposals before the emperor made his final decision. The organ consulted prepared its comments in a separate memorial (called *pu-pen,* if presented by a board), which was sent to the *Nei-ko* for presentation. Under such circumstances, the draft rescript procedure operated in the following fashion. (1) When matters concerned only one board or department, the *Nei-ko* would make up the draft proposal with the set phrase: "Let the board concerned deliberate and memorialize" (*kai-pu i-tsou* or *chiao-pu i-fu*).[29] After going through all the steps just described, the board received the red memorial from the Six Sections; the board would then prepare a *t'i-pen* to memorialize the throne on its deliberations. The *Nei-ko* would have to make up such draft proposals again as "Let it be as deliberated [by the board]" (*i-i*),[30] then the memorial and the draft rescript would be processed in the same fashion as before.[31] (2) Memorials dealing with weighty affairs were often handed down to one of the deliberative bodies. In such cases the draft rescript often read: "Let the nine ministers deliberate and memorialize" (*chiu-ch'ing i-tsou*) or "Let the deliberative princes and ministers deliberate and memorialize" (*i-cheng wang ta-ch'en i-tsou*), and so forth. The assembly concerned would prepare a *t'i-pen* and present their memorial through the *Nei-ko* as usual.[32]

Some of the special terminology often encountered in Ch'ing documents shows how decisions were made.[33] When an imperial utterance was preceded by the term *yü* (the emperor has instructed that . . .), the decision was made on the emperor's own initiative without a memorial. This type of document is called a *yü* or *Shang-yü* (imperial edict). Draft proposals, made in the *Nei-ko* and subsequently copied onto the memorials after they had received the imperial approval, were called *chih* (rescript). When an imperial utterance was preceded by the term *ting* (the emperor has decided that . . .), new administrative regulations were made. Presumably, such decisions were made without going through any of the deliberative bodies or the Six Boards. When the imperial utterance was preceded by the term *t'i-chun* (the request in the *t'i-pen* has been granted), the decision was based on the proposal in a *t'i-pen* from the Six Boards, the Censorate, or the Mongolian Superintendency. When the imperial utterance was proceeded by the term *fu-chun* (approved by the emperor after replying), the decision was made in response to itemized suggestions in a *t'i-pen* presented by a censor, supervising censor, governor, or governor-general. Such suggestions had been previously turned over to the board concerned for comment or deliberation. When the imperial utterance was preceded by the term *i-ting* (decided after deliberation) and *i-chun* (approved after deliberation), the decision was made after a subject had been discussed in the Assembly of Deliberative Princes and Ministers or the Assembly of the Nine Ministers.

Hsi Wo-ao, the author of the *Nei-ko-chih,* commented: "A memorial to be presented had to go through several scores of hands before the final decision was made. This is indeed [an] extremely accurate and careful [system]." [34] To be sure, such a system ensured maximum accuracy and prevented any fraudulent alteration of the imperial instructions once the final decision was made; but precisely because such a decision-making procedure involved so many people, secrecy was most difficult. Personal motives crept in, conflicts of interest arose, and tensions developed between the participants in the deliberative bodies and the emperor himself. When, in the middle of his reign, the traditional system ceased to function efficiently as a result of these problems, the K'ang-hsi Emperor began to experiment with a new memorial system.

V | Origins of the
Palace Memorial System
in the K'ang-hsi Reign

In the middle of the K'ang-hsi era, a new medium of communication originated: the palace memorial system (*tsou-che*). On the surface, the system seems to have arisen as a result of long-standing concern on the part of the K'ang-hsi Emperor about obtaining more reliable information on conditions in the provinces; but behind this obvious reason there are underlying factors that must be investigated.

First, because the decision to introduce a new system into the Ch'ing government was made by a single individual, the K'ang-hsi Emperor himself, it is important to discover the ideological basis for his decision. The role of ideology — defined as a set of political ideas functioning to preserve the imperial order — is no stranger to students of Chinese political history. The Mandate of Heaven (*t'ien-ming*) concept that originated as early as the Chou period was carried on and elaborated successively by the Han thinkers and the Sung Neo-Confucianists. According to this theory, a new dynasty was empowered by Heaven to rule China; but the rulers had to demonstrate worthiness of divine sanction. If the ruler's worthiness declined, Heaven first warned him by showing displeasure in various ways — through droughts, floods, bad harvests, and other omens. The ruler, seeing any of these signs, was supposed to examine himself and repent. If he found nothing wrong in himself, the problem probably lay in his ministers; hence he would enjoin his ministers to follow his example. This is the theory that "Heaven and men respond to each other" (*t'ien-jen kan-ying*), which became an important part of the K'ang-hsi Emperor's state ideology. He often warned his ministers that "if our administration is at fault on earth, Heaven will respond with calamities from above." [1]

But the K'ang-hsi Emperor did not simply pay lip service to the theory. Perhaps influenced by his Jesuit scientists in problem-solving, he also developed "scientific" means to detect the divine reactions. Here again he merely refined a system adopted from the Ming: in Ming times, local officials were required to present regularly to the emperor a "rain report" in prescribed forms of memorials (*tsou-pen*). [2] Whereas the Ming emperors often did not want to bother reading these scientific data, the K'ang-hsi

Emperor considered them vital means for detecting the will of Heaven. In addition, he required his provincial officials to include in their reports information on droughts, floods, and prospects of harvests.

Provincial authorities quite naturally tended to conceal these conditions, supplying either inaccurate reports or no information at all: if they truthfully reported bad signs, this was simultaneously a confession that they had failed in their administrations, incurring the displeasure of Heaven, for which they could lose the emperor's trust or even be reprimanded. The palace memorial system was introduced into the Ch'ing bureaucracy as an informal remedial device for gathering vital information which had frequently been concealed.

In the overall control system of the K'ang-hsi Emperor, the region including Chiang-nan (literally "the area south of the Yangtze River" that comprised the two provinces Kiangsu and Anhwei) and the Chekiang province occupied a special position, often referred to in Ch'ing records as the South (nan-fang). Why the K'ang-hsi Emperor began experimenting with the new information-gathering device in this area is significant. Politically, it was a dangerous spot: the potential for revolt was high by the 1690's. People in Yangchow still vividly remembered the ruthless massacre committed only a few decades earlier by invading Manchu troops. Heavy banner forces, ready to suppress any revolt, had been stationed in the area.[3] Any occurrence which might increase disaffection was of vital interest to the K'ang-hsi Emperor.

The South also had its cultural significance in the control system. It was the talent reservoir from which the K'ang-hsi Emperor recruited most of the trusted officials to staff his regular bureaucracy,[4] as well as the majority of scholar advisors serving him in the South Library. The emperor was, however, by no means unaware of the adverse effects brought about by these advisors as carriers of the Chinese culture; with them came the undesirable elements as well, thus they required some sort of surveillance.

The South was of economic significance in the imperial control system. As the chief rice-producing area, it regularly transported "tribute-rice" to Peking through the Grand Canal in order to support the gigantic imperial bureaucracy in the north. Both the tribute grains and the Grand Canal signified the indispensability of maintaining normal communications between the South and the capital. The grain transport was under administration of the director-general (ts'ao-yün tsung-tu, rank 2A);[5] every year thousands of canal barges were used to transport over a quarter million tons of tribute-rice to Peking.[6] For these reasons, the prospects of harvests, rain conditions, and problems of transport through the Grand Canal were automatically of the greatest interest to the K'ang-hsi Emperor. Information was vital for preventative measures.

The new system was not an outright invention, but rather an adaptation of an old Manchu tradition. As Kroeber says: "It is the talented and the geniuses who make inventions. But they only make them when and if their cultures permit; and they make only the specific inventions that their cultures allow, within a narrow range." [7] The palace memorial system was developed out of the Manchu tradition of the *ch'ing-an che*[8] (greetings memorials) that were ritually sent by Manchu bannermen to the imperial princess who headed the banners or to the emperor himself. This was originally a personal type of memorial, not an official document for intra-governmental communication. The K'ang-hsi Emperor converted the original Manchu institution into a secret means of communication.

Genesis of the New System. The system was initiated rather uneventfully in 1693 when Li Hsü, a bondservant of the Imperial Household who was serving his term as the textile commissioner (or superintendent of the Imperial Manufactory, *chih-tsao*) at Soochow, sent the K'ang-hsi Emperor a *ch'ing-an che* to inquire about his well-being. This time there was a significant difference: he included a little information on rain conditions and rice prices in the South. This act marked the introduction of the palace memorial system into the Ch'ing bureaucracy; the epoch-making document, together with the imperial vermilion endorsement, is worth quoting.

> Your subject Li Hsü, *yüan-wai-lang* [second class secretary in the Imperial Household], taking charge of the Imperial Manufactory at Soochow, hereby reverently memorializes Your Majesty on the matter of rainfall. During this summer, drought was prolonged, people everywhere were praying for rain, and on account of Your Majesty's blessedness, precious dew eventually fell on the eighteenth of the sixth month [July 20, 1693]. Recently the Soochow area has also been blessed by plentiful rainfall . . . At the present time, the price of rice is stable: coarse rice sells for 7 *ch'ien* [seven-tenths of a silver tael] [per picul], and fine rice for 9 *ch'ien*. The people's mood and frame of mind are relaxed, all rejoicing over the Heavenly blessing. Your subject is not charged with local administrative duties and should not have reported

on this unduly. However, seeing that Your Majesty loves your people like your own children, I, therefore, venture to report to you what I have come to know. The seventh month of the thirty-second year of K'ang-hsi [1693].

Li Hsü's admission that he had memorialized "unduly" reflects the fact that reports on local conditions had, up to this time, been uniquely within the province of the local authorities. The admission also indicates that this was Li's first secret report written in a *ch'ing-an che*.

Instead of invoking the emperor's reproof, the report pleased the sovereign. The vermilion endorsement reads:

I have completely recovered [from my malaria].[9] During the fifth month, I heard that in the area south of the Huai River and Hsü-chou, rain was delayed and drought prolonged into the summer; the people, therefore, all felt extremely uneasy and anxious, especially in Che-kiang province. I have been consumed with anxiety day and night, and have not been able to eat and sleep peacefully. Whenever I had an audience with someone who had just arrived from the South, I always inquired of him about the situation in detail.[10] Now after I have read your report, I feel relieved to some extent in my heart from my burden.

The endorsement was concluded by a secret commission which inaugurated the palace memorial system as part of the Ch'ing administration. The commission reads: "After the autumn harvest, send me again [reports in] *tsou-t'ieh* [that is, *tsou-che*]. By all means don't let anyone know whenever you prepare such reports!" [11] In addition to Li Hsü, at least three other members of the Imperial Household, Ts'ao Yin, his son Ts'ao Yung, and his adopted son (nephew) Ts'ao Fu, were charged by the emperor with the same special mission.[12]

Small wonder that palace memorials after 1693 were used more for reporting weather conditions and prospects of harvests than for any other purpose. Li Hsü regularly sent to the emperor reports on rice prices and weather conditions. Weather data were tabulated and designated as weather charts (*yin-ch'ing piao* or *ch'ing-yü lu,* literally, table of rain or shine). They seem to have been sent to the emperor monthly, at least during the last decade of the K'ang-hsi reign. The responsibility of being secret informant was shared by other superintendents of the Imperial Manufactories, at two other southern cities: Hangchow and Nanking (Chiang-ning). One of the reports submitted by Ts'ao Fu reveals the reports' frequency;

and the emperor's vermilion endorsement reveals his great concern about the information. The report, incorporated in a *ch'ing-an che,* reads:

> Your bondservant Ts'ao Fu, superintendent of the Imperial Manufactory at Chiang-ning, reverently inquires after Your Majesty's well-being. Your bondservant arrived at Chiang-ning on the seventeenth of the fifth month. The harvests of wheat and barley vary from 80 percent to 90 percent; the rice prices range from 7.8 *ch'ien* to 8.5 or 8.6 *ch'ien.* Rain has been sufficient everywhere; farmers were able to transplant their young rice plants. Therefore, the prospect for a good autumn harvest is quite good . . . The weather report for the fourth month is enclosed. Also attached are the overdue weather reports for the second and third months, as well as for the intercalary third month.

The endorsement reads: "Noted. I heard that there has been excessive rainfall in the Chekiang province; hence people are suffering from food shortage and so forth. I wonder if this is true. You may carefully investigate this matter; but you ought to carry it out secretly." [13]

Bondservants and Their Secret Palace Memorials. The choice of Li Hsü and the Ts'aos as his secret informants in the South clearly suggests that the emperor's decisions were by no means without rationale. Bondservants were the emperor's personal servants, and they served the emperor alone.[14] Both Li Hsü and Ts'ao Yin were bondservants of the Upper White Banner under the Imperial Household.

These bondservants were bannermen of a special type, with multiple status. They were simultaneously Chinese, bannermen, and personal servants of the emperor. Their language competence, their ease in establishing connections with both the Manchus and the Chinese, and their loyalty to the imperial master were their best qualifications for the secret role.

While Li Hsü's personal relationship with the emperor cannot be ascertained, the Ts'ao family had a long history of intimacy with the K'ang-hsi Emperor. Ts'ao Yin's mother, who had first served in the palace as a female attendant (*kung-nü*), was selected as Prince Hsuan-yeh's nurse (*pao-mu,* literally nursing mammy).[15] It is said that even after he had become K'ang-hsi Emperor, the prince continued to remember her with affection and showed her special favor, often referring to her as "an old lady from my family." Ts'ao Yin was said to have been the young K'ang-hsi Emperor's childhood reading companion (*pan-tu*),[16] and two of his daughters married men of princely rank. Indeed, as far as the emperor was concerned, the Ts'aos were members of his own family; they were more royal favorites than bondservants.

In the early part of the K'ang-hsi reign, Ts'ao Yin's father occupied the post of textile commissioner of Nanking for twenty-one years (1663–1684). In 1690, Ts'ao Yin was appointed textile commissioner of Soochow, and late in 1692 he was transferred to the same position at Nanking. The vacated post at Soochow was filled by Li Hsü, a cousin of Ts'ao Yin.[17] Before taking this post Li had been a secretary in the *Nei-ko;* he had also been a prefect in Kwangtung. In contrast with Ts'ao Yin, Li does not seem to have had any close relationship with the emperor; his asset probably lay in his administrative experience, obtained during his service in the regular bureaucracy.

This difference in relationship was also reflected in the emperor's attitude toward them after both had become his secret informants. In general, the vermilion endorsements noted on Ts'ao Yin's palace memorials were much more affectionate than those on Li's memorials; some overtone of "family talks" can be detected in the former.

The two bondservants had wide connections with the southern Chinese literati, and this was a great asset in playing the role of imperial informant in that area. Ts'ao Yin, for instance, during his term as Soochow textile commissioner, became associated with "scholars of considerable reputation"[18] and moved in the "upper-class" circle with the southern literati. He frequently attended their drinking parties and poetry clubs, these being perfect occasions for acquiring firsthand information.[19]

Ts'ao Yin also had a close association with the Manchu figure Mingju and his son Singde, a celebrated poet of the time. Mingju, by 1690 the most powerful grand secretary, was on friendly terms with southern Chinese literati. Singde and Ts'ao Yin both studied under the famous Hsü Ch'ien-hsüeh, whose influence in the court was paramount in this period.

Li Hsü was a man of compromise and sometimes lacked honesty — a fact well known to the emperor. Once, when he was found guilty of having cheated the emperor, he memorialized and said, "I should have reported to Your Majesty honestly about this matter; but somehow my mind was temporarily darkened and I ventured to conceal it."[20] Probably his main asset was his ability to read the emperor's mind. He procured rare objects for the emperor as personal gifts; he gathered together "a troupe of girl actresses" and sent them to Peking in order to amuse the emperor.[21] In this light, it could hardly have been pure accident for him to send the emperor a *ch'ing-an-che* in the seventh month of the thirty-second year (1693) wherein he "unduly" reported on local conditions that were strictly within the duties of provincial officials. Only in the previous month, the emperor had publicly issued an edict through the grand secretaries wherein he had expressed grave concern over the extreme lack of rain in the South; and he had sent officials from the Board of Revenue to make an on-the-spot investigation of conditions.[22] This edict had undoubtedly reached the South through the *Peking Gazette* — read with close attention by all provincial officials. The unprecedented action taken by Li Hsü in 1693 was probably motivated by his desire to seize the opportunity of pleasing the emperor; he had indeed guessed the mind of the emperor, who, after reading the report, felt "relieved to some extent" of his extreme anxieties.[23]

The significant role played by human motives in interpersonal relations and, in turn, in the change of existing institutions is thus suggested. Oddly enough, the motive of a "small man" in this instance played a decisive catalytic role in the precipitation of a major institution.

The extrabureaucratic establishment of a direct, secret, and informal line of communication between the emperor and his bondservants underwent changes corresponding to the changing roles of bondservants. It developed almost entirely along its own course until approximately the year 1700, around which time the use of palace memorials was introduced into the central administration in response to irregular activities in the court. The effects of court politics in the capital began to be felt in the provinces, especially in the South. Interactions occurred, therefore, between developments in the South and in the capital. The combined force of these processes also affected structural changes within the existing communication-decision machine. The aspect of court politics in the political process is a complex matter that will be dealt with in later chapters; concern here will be with structural change in both the extrabureaucratic and the intrabureaucratic aspects of the institution.

During the early years, roughly from 1693 to 1700, the extrabureaucratic aspect maintained its basic features. The two secret informants Li Hsü and Ts'ao Yin (the latter's earliest palace memorial can be dated 1697)[24] continued to supply the emperor with information on weather conditions, harvest prospects, and local prices. They also performed an ideological function for the emperor, and information about this role-playing was reported in palace memorials: for example, Ts'ao Yin was ordered by the emperor to distribute relief rice to the poor at low price[25] and to work in conjunction with the provincial authorities to repair the tombs of the Ming emperors[26] — gestures intended to magnify the emperor's image of benevolence and reverence toward the Ming rulers. On one occasion bondservants assumed the additional role of foreign intelligence agents, when they were ordered to send men to Japan to investigate some activities that had evoked the emperor's suspicion.[27]

After 1700, role changes allowed the two bondservants to perform more functions. Ts'ao Yin was made a salt censor in 1704.[28] Although by this time only Manchus (including Chinese bondservants) were appointed as Lianghui salt censor, the post was still within the regular bureaucracy. Unlike the textile commissioner, the salt censor was entitled to use routine memorials (*t'i-pen*) to communicate with the emperor about official matters within his jurisdiction.[29] The following year, Li Hsü was appointed to the same post. Still later, Li Hsü and Ts'ao Yin were given concurrent titles of vice-president of the Board of Revenue and commissioner of the Transmission Office, respectively. These titles sanctioned their right to send both routine and palace memorials, like other high-ranking provincial officials.

Along with these role changes, the two expanded their scope of information by including illicit activities concerning the salt trade in their messages to the emperor. When court politics so affected local conditions, robberies and scandals were so serious, and rumors were constantly flying in the South, the emperor was particularly interested in "scientific" data on weather, harvests, rain, and food prices. In the late years of his reign, monthly weather reports were sent the emperor to keep him abreast of the signs of Heaven.[30]

The emperor counted not only on his bondservants, but also on his provincial officials to supply such information. For instance, Chao Hunghsieh's surviving palace memorials, now stored in the National Palace Museum archives, amounted to 1177 pieces. (The total number of surviving palace memorials of the K'ang-hsi period is 2983.) Excluding 485 pieces of *ch'ing-an che* that were purely ritualistic, palace memorials that Chao sent to report on this information amounted to 268 pieces, nearly half of the substantive memorials.[31] In short, it may be said that it was through the use of bondservants who performed both "personal" and "official" roles that the line between the two aspects of the imperial bureaucracy became blurred. It was indeed a subtle amalgamation.

Development of the New System within the Formal Bureaucracy. After 1700, the palace memorial system within the formal bureaucracy also underwent significant structural changes; the changes themselves will be considered here, the factors of both the political process and the human motivation involved in later chapters.

Development of the system after 1700 can be divided generally into two stages, one extending roughly from 1701 to 1712 and the other from 1712 to 1722. The palace memorial system could be described in its original form as a bipolar system with the southern pole in the Chiang-nan area and northern pole in Peking. At each pole the privilege was extended to include top-echelon bureaucrats. Surviving palace memorials seem to suggest that from 1701 at the latest, provincial officials were authorized to send palace memorials. At first permission to do so seems to have been given on an individual basis; but during the ensuing decade, somewhere around 1705, all provincial authorities were ordered to send memorials.

The earliest surviving palace memorial presented by a local official is in the National Palace Museum archives. It was sent by Li Lin-sheng on November 19, 1701. This memorial deserves comment because it reflects some of the confusion encountered by provincial officials, especially the Manchus. Owing to their emphasis on military competence, Manchu military officials were versed neither in Chinese nor in their own language; consequently, to write secret palace memorials themselves constituted a real problem for some. Since Manchu local officials usually relied on their Chinese secretaries to handle their documents, they had no idea how to write memorials, as Li Lin-sheng's case will show.

Li Lin-sheng was at the time commander-in-chief of the Shensi and Kansu region. Earlier, he had dispatched his men to escort some messengers sent by the chief of Galdan to Peking. Upon the messengers' return, the emperor ordered his bodyguards to grant Li some gifts; in addition, an imperial decree written in Manchu was transmitted to him through the imperial bodyguards. The decree was written in somewhat the same form as the later "court letter":

Wu Ta-ch'an hereby transmits this imperial decree [*ch'uan-feng chih-i*] to commander-in-chief Li Lin-sheng. The emperor told us to inquire after your physical well-being [*shen-shang hao-mo*] and to ask how the officials under your command are doing. The emperor also remarked that you frequently reported on local affairs [*ti-fang shih-i*] and rain conditions [*yü-shui ch'ing-hsing*] while you were commander-in-chief elsewhere. The emperor wondered why you have not sent any information in memorials since you took this new post. Hereafter, you should frequently memorialize the emperor on local affairs.[32]

Despite the fact that this decree was quoted in a *tsou-che*, Li marked his memorial as *t'i-pen*. In closing, after reporting on rain conditions, he said, "I hereby reverently submit this *t'i-pen*" [*chü-pen chin-t'i*]. The vermilion endorsement reads: "Noted. Hereafter whenever you prepare a *tsou-che*, you ought to write it in Manchu (*ch'ing-tzu*). It is not necessary to stamp your official seal on it." [33]

Curiously, Li prepared a separate *t'i-pen* that reported the same thing but in simpler form.[34] Upon receiving his memorial back, Li presented a palace memorial (this time he properly addressed it as *tsou-che* and did not apply his official seal). He first acknowledged the emperor's instructions and then included a report on recent weather conditions and harvest prospects. The memorial ended with a request, which reads:

> Moreover, your subject [*ch'en*] ought to obey Your Majesty's injunction to write my palace memorials [*che*] in Manchu language. However, although I had some knowledge in Manchu, my eyes are too dim to write them because of my old age. On top of this, my Manchu grammar is very bad. If I ask someone else to write it for me, I am afraid that the wording may not be in accordance with the proprieties because I myself cannot tell whether the language is proper or not. I therefore ask your gracious permission to continue the use of Chinese in my *tsou-che* in order to avoid mistakes. I hereby reverently present this palace memorial.

The emperor, instead of placing his endorsement on the memorial proper, wrote some blunt words on the envelope: "Noted. I am afraid that even this Chinese was not composed by yourself." [35]

Sung Lao, the governor of Kiangsu, was the first civil official in the regular provincial administration to whom the privilege of sending palace memorials was extended. In one of Li Hsü's palace memorials submitted in 1703, the endorsement reads: "During the last two visits of mine to the South [in 1699 and 1703], Governor Sung Lao was very meticulous in handling things; I therefore want to grant him two fans upon which

I have written some verses in my own hand . . . You are to transfer my gifts to Sung Lao. It will be unnecessary for him to prepare a memorial to express his gratitude." More significantly, the endorsement ended with an instruction: "Hereafter, if he has anything to memorialize, let him use secret palace memorials [*mi-che*] to do so; such memorials ought to be submitted through you." [36]

It must be added that palace memorials sent from Sung Lao during the year following the reception of the emperor's secret commission did not contain information that we might consider secret in the general sense. In his first memorial, he thanked the emperor for having extended the privilege to him; then he reported that the final proof of some imperial literary works had not yet been completed because of Kao Shih-ch'i's illness.[37] In the next memorial, he first inquired about the well-being of both the emperor and the heir apparent;[38] he then reported on the drought in the South and the death of Kao Shih-ch'i, finally asking further instruction as to how the printed book proofs should be sent to the emperor.[39] His palace memorials submitted from that time until 1713 totaled forty-four pieces, largely dealing with similar information: weather, harvest, presents to the emperor, food prices, and so on.[40]

During the ensuing few years, many provincial authorities submitted palace memorials in considerable numbers — a fact suggesting that the privilege was extended to all provincial authorities within this period, although the exact date of authorization has not been found.[41] These officials included generals-in-chief, governors-general, governors, commanders-in-chief, and brigade generals. The emperor ordered them to enclose their secret reports in their *ch'ing-an che*.[42]

The system in the northern pole underwent a similar process. It started with Wang Hung-hsü, a personal adviser of the emperor in the South Library within the palace precincts; from there it grew until all court ministers of the third rank or higher were included.[43] The rationale for choosing Wang Hung-hsü as the first informant in the central bureaucracy can be understood by tracing his relationship with the emperor, as well as considering the unique functions of the South Library in the imperial court.[44]

The origins of the library stemmed from a major policy of the K'ang-hsi Emperor: rule the Chinese by using the Chinese. To help form the sage ruler image, the K'ang-hsi Emperor began his self-imposed Confucian education early in life. The South Library was his private study. It was so called because it was located on the south side of the imperial living quarters. Throughout the K'ang-hsi reign, officials who were called upon to serve in the library were learned scholars or good calligraphers. Chief among the library's functions was that these scholars expounded Confucian Classics to the emperor there as frequently as the emperor deemed necessary during the day. Some trusted scholars in the library were asked to accompany the emperor in his tours to the South and other parts of the country.

During the first half of the K'ang-hsi reign, three southerners were most influential in the library, Kao Shih-ch'i, Hsü Ch'ien-hsüeh, and Wang Hung-hsü. Hsü died in 1694 and Kao retired from active court service in 1697; thereafter, Wang was the only one who remained in active service in the court and concurrently served the emperor as a personal adviser.

Wang's role in the expansion of the palace memorial system in the North contrasts with that of Li Hsü in the South. Li was a bondservant in the Imperial Household and Wang his personal adviser. Both stood between two worlds: Li between Manchu and Chinese, Wang between inner court and the out court in Peking. Wang was a high official, well acquainted with the complex administrative regulations, and he had been known by the emperor through his long-time personal association as adviser in the library. He served from 1684 to 1705 in the capacities of sub-chancellor in the *Nei-ko,* vice-president of the Board of Revenue, censor-general, president of the Board of Revenue, and president of the Board of Works. It was while he served in the last capacity, and was concurrently a senior and trusted member in the library, that he was chosen as the informant; this clearly was no arbitrary choice, but rather a recognition of his special qualifications.

The initial process in the capital began with a secret instruction (*mi-yü*) sent by the emperor to Wang Hung-hsü while the emperor was on his fifth tour of the South (1705). The instruction reads: "Whenever something in the capital is worth reporting to me, you ought to write a secret palace memorial and enclose it in your *ch'ing-an che.* Don't let any one know it. In the event that it should be divulged, there would be serious consequences. Be careful! Be careful!" [45]

In response to this secret instruction, Wang submitted his first secret palace memorial:

> Your subject Wang Hung-hsü reverently submits this secret palace memorial . . . on the thirteenth day [of this second month] at the

> hour of *mao* [5–7 A.M.], I went to the inner court [the South Library] to be on duty. At that time the other two ministers Ch'a [Shen-hsing] and Ts'ai [T'ing] had not come to the library. Your subject opened [the secret instruction] and read it and felt extremely grateful for your secret commission . . . You have instructed me kindly and earnestly, worrying that I might not be watchful enough, and that your secret instruction might be carelessly divulged and hence serious results might be evoked . . . Perhaps I could only ask Heaven in trembling and lowliness of heart to seal up my lips so that even among my kindred, I will not dare to tell any one of them.

Then he assured the emperor, "I will be very careful so that I will not fail your gracious charge. Hereafter if I find anything worth reporting to Your Majesty, I will immediately prepare a small [secret] palace memorial and present it to Your Majesty." [46] The emperor endorsed his memorial with only one character *shih* (yes).

After the K'ang-hsi Emperor returned to the capital from his tour, he again left Peking for Jehol and his summer palace.[47] He left similar instructions to those quoted above on a routine *ch'ing-an che* presented by Wang.[48] They read: "Hereafter if you have a palace memorial to present, follow the same channel that you did while I was touring the South. But when I return to the capital, you need not present any [more] palace memorials because there are too many people around." [49]

During his sixth and last tour of the South in 1707, the emperor ordered Wang to accompany him; Wang was an active agent for the emperor and engaged in secret investigations. He continued his mission in the South even after the emperor had returned to Peking, later returning to the capital himself.[50] His reports dealt with irregular activities in the central bureaucracy and their local effects. Great pains were taken to preserve the highly confidential nature of these communications due to the sensitive nature of the subject matter. For example, in connection with a report on an unfair trial conducted by the joint session of deliberative princes and the nine ministers, Wang wrote: "This palace memorial of mine may cause serious consequences to my own life as well as to the lives of my whole family; I therefore humbly beg that Your Majesty secretly read it and secretly endorse it and secretly return it to me in order to prevent its contents from being divulged." The vermilion endorsement reads: "I have very secretly read it; not a single soul knows of it. I understand what you mean." [51] In order to conceal Wang's name, the emperor and Wang always used two envelopes when sending and returning the endorsed memorial. Wang wrote the phrase *"Nan-shu-fang chin-feng"* (reverently sealed by the South Library) on the outside of the envelope, and the emperor sealed the outer envelope by affixing the character *"feng"* (sealed).[52]

The emperor in 1712 charged all the ministers of the third rank or higher at the capital to present palace memorials to him secretly, following the example of the provincial authorities. These officials included imperial chamberlains of the guards (*ling shih-wei nei-ta-ch'en*), grand secretaries, lieutenants-general, presidents and vice-presidents of the boards, secretaries of the Grand Secretariat, and associate censors-general and others. The emperor justified this expansion of the system on the grounds that there were many matters concerning which he had no other direct sources of information.[53]

Operation of the New System. According to rule, palace memorials had to be prepared by the memorialists themselves (although there were exceptions, as the case of Li Lin-sheng has shown). For example, one of the palace memorials submitted by Wang Hung-hsü reads:

> Your subject Wang Hung-hsü hereby reverently memorializes: On the seventeenth day of the third month your subject received respectfully Your Majesty's sealed endorsement. I returned to my lodge and opened the envelope secretly to read it. I was deeply grateful for having been charged with this responsibility. I felt even more grateful for receiving Your Majesty's instruction, saying, "You ought to write your report secretly with your own hand; you must not let anyone know of your report; otherwise, it will be unfortunate for you . . ."[54]

The same rule applied to Li Hsü. In response to one of his palace memorials, the emperor noted: "I am well. Recently I heard that there was a great deal of gossip in the South: people fabricating stories and criticizing important state affairs and trivial matters. Since I do not have any one trustworthy from whom to inquire about this situation, and I have bestowed many profound favors upon you, you therefore ought to prepare palace memorials with your own hand so as to keep me informed of whatever you happen to find." The emperor then warned Li: "You should never tell anyone about this injunction of mine. If anyone should come to know of it, the consequences would be most disastrous for you!" [55]

The injunction to Ts'ao Yin was even more emphatic: "If you encounter anything which would cause doubt or perplexity, you may send me secret palace memorials to secure my instructions. Whenever you prepare a palace memorial you may not ask any one else to write it for you. There would be most serious consequences once people came to know of this [matter]." Then followed the most emphatic warning of all: "Be careful! Be careful! Be careful! Be careful!" [56]

A palace memorial was either enclosed in a separate *ch'ing-an che* or included in the text of the latter. Wang Hung-hsü's palace memorials were often enclosed in his greetings memorials. His secret reports thus enclosed were very small in size: only eight centimeters long and four wide.[57] Palace memorials from provincial authorities were also separate enclosures. The capital officials and agents of the Imperial Household, such as Li Hsü and Ts'ao Yin, usually used the joint form.[58]

Secret palace memorials were contained in securely sealed envelopes. Wang Hung-hsü submitted his palace memorials at the South Library; while the emperor was in the South and Wang remained in Peking, they were mixed with routine palace reports when dispatched. When Wang accompanied the emperor on tour, he presented them through the director of eunuchs at the imperial traveling lodge.[59] Capital officials submitted their palace memorials in person at the morning audiences.[60]

Palace memorials from the provinces, especially the Chiang-nan and Chekiang area, were transmitted in a more complicated fashion, since messengers had to be dispatched to transmit the documents to Peking. Provincial officials often sent their house servants or military officers of a lower rank to carry out the mission.[61] Li Hsü and other superintendents of the imperial manufactories sent only their servants because there were no military units under their command. Sometimes a provincial memorialist of lower rank would request an official of higher rank to transmit his palace memorials to Peking.[62] On other occasions, the emperor instructed a provincial governor to submit his palace memorials through Li Hsü, who would in turn send a servant to transmit them along with his own to Peking.[63]

The idea of sending private messengers instead of relying on the postal express facilities is significant for several reasons. First, palace memorials only supplied secret reports on local conditions or on mutual surveillance and were usually not urgent in nature, hence there was no need to rush. Second, memorialists without local administrative duties, such as Li Hsü, did not have the right to use official facilities. Third, and perhaps most important, private messengers assured absolute secrecy — as far as the memorialists were concerned, their servants were more trustworthy than the public postal system.

The messengers themselves also performed some intelligence functions while transmitting palace memorials. As the K'ang-hsi Emperor once revealed: "[Whenever] messengers [*tsou-shih chih-jen*] from the various provinces [arrived], I always inquired of them about the harvest prospects and the prices of rice in the localities through which they had passed. Therefore, the governors-general, governors, commanders-in-chief, and brigade generals dared not conceal the truth; if they did I would find it out through these messengers." [64] In the very late years of the K'ang-hsi reign, campaigning generals in the frontier regions presumably were allowed to use post express horses, although they still had to provide their own messengers.[65]

After messengers had arrived at Peking, they submitted their palace memorials at the palace gate (*kung-men*), that is, the Ch'ien-ch'ing Gate. Palace guards at the gate (*Ch'ien-ch'ing men shih-wei*) were in charge of accepting palace memorials.[66] The guard office at the gate was often referred to as the Outer Chancery of Memorials (*Wai tsou-shih ch'u*).[67] The palace guards then transferred the incoming palace memorials to the chancery eunuchs (*tsou-shih t'ai-chien*),[68] whose office was often referred to as the Inner Chancery of Memorials (*Nei tsou-shih ch'u*).[69] The eunuchs presented the palace memorials immediately to the emperor.

As a general principle, all palace memorials were handled in a most secret fashion once they had reached the hands of the emperor. In an edict of 1712 the emperor said: "All officials in the court know that I am very cautious in handling things. When I receive secret palace memorials, none of their contents are ever divulged." [70] He read them all by himself very quickly and could remember their contents for a long time. He always acted on them promptly and endorsed them with his own hand. As he testified in an edict: "All the vermilion endorsements on the incoming palace memorials from the provinces were done by my own hand; no one ever endorsed them for me." He then referred to an interesting incident: "[Even] when my right hand was ailing and I could not hold my brush, I simply used my left hand to make the endorsements — never have I relied on any one else to assist me."

After endorsing the memorials, he also sealed the envelopes with his own hands. Therefore, even his "palace attendants who were always around could not know a single word of the endorsements." Furthermore, he never left any records or duplicates for later reference. All palace memorials bearing the imperial endorsements were returned to the memorialists and kept in their hands. Despite all these precautions, however, the emperor admitted that sometimes "there might have been some mean characters who dared to risk capital punishment and opened the sealed container of palace memorials," or "sometimes the memorialist himself might have carelessly disclosed the content of his secret memorial to his friends." [71]

When palace memorials were presented merely for supplying secret information, the most common vermilion endorsement read: "I have understood" (*chih-tao-le* or *ming-pai-le*); sometimes the emperor showed his concurrence with the memorialist's view and noted "Yes" (*shih*). The response to a greetings palace memorial often read: "I am well" (*chen-an*). On one occasion, the emperor showed his reaction toward irregular incidents reported in a secret palace memorial by simply noting: "Ridiculous!" (*k'o-hsiao*).[72] Sometimes he assured the memorialist: "I have read [your report] in an extremely secret fashion. Not a single soul knows of it. I understand what you mean." [73] Palace memorials of this sort, of course, resulted in no overt action on the part of the emperor.

At times the emperor would give further instructions to the memorialists such as: "Continue your secret investigation" (*tsai mi-fang*), or "You ought to present secret palace memorials as before whenever you come to know anything worthwhile reporting." [74]

With provincial authorities, for example in the case of Nien Keng-yao, the governor-general of Szechwan, the emperor often endorsed his palace memorials item by item. When a certain item fell within his official jurisdiction, the emperor would note "For this item, you ought to submit a *t'i-pen*" (*chü-t'i*), or "For this item, you ought to submit an impeachment memorial [still a *t'i-pen*]" (*tz'u-chien tang-ts'an*), or "You ought to discuss this matter with the governor-general," and so forth.[75]

The breadth of topics covered in palace memorials was very comprehensive. Almost anything might be reported in them. In general, those from the provinces were presented to keep the emperor informed of any events indicative of a possible local disturbance or insurrection. The information might be mere rumor, but if they so indicated in their reports, the memorialists were not held responsible for the degree of accuracy.[76] Contents also included such matters as natural calamities, weather conditions, food supplies and harvest prospects, wonders and prodigies, and local rumors, local robbery and murder cases (matters local officials often tended to conceal) and irregularities in local administrations.[77]

Because the K'ang-hsi Emperor's main purpose in ordering officials to present palace memorials secretly was to obtain information, the system remained largely informal and secret in nature. There is much evidence that the emperor ordered memorialists to use traditional memorials (*t'i-pen*) as much as possible in order not to disrupt existing decision-making institutions.[78] Toward the end of his reign, however, the K'ang-hsi Emperor, for reasons yet to be studied, occasionally allowed General Nien Keng-yao to use palace memorials to secure approval of official appointments, as well as for the transmission of secret information. The endorsement under such circumstances often reads: "I have already issued an instruction [to the central office concerned] to do it" (*i-yu-chih-le*). This meant that the emperor had taken the initiative in making appointments without mentioning the memorialist who made the request.[79] But existing documents suggest that this was isolated practice; only in the Yung-cheng era was it institutionalized.

In investigating a political process such as, here, the one that was essentially responsible for structural changes in the palace memorial system, it must be remembered that process analysis concerns behavioral events in terms of interpersonal relations and their changes in time. Factionalism, a special type of human relationship formed in a group of people on the basis of a common goal, has been found by historians to have been a conspicuous political phenomenon in the K'ang-hsi bureaucracy.[1] Factional relationships were formed by major historical agents around the key actor, the K'ang-hsi Emperor. Since it was he who invented the system, through a series of decisions, and developed it to its full-fledged stage in 1712, obviously attention should be focused upon the relationships between him and those historical agents who were closest to him and, hence, most likely to influence and spur him to decisions.

During the pre-1712 years, there was no succession struggle simply because there was always a legitimate heir apparent, except for a very short time. Factional activities that threatened the imperial power were mainly centered around Yin-jeng, the heir apparent, who attempted to press the emperor for abdication in his favor. The emperor's responses to this threat constitute the major subject for process analysis. The only other faction with a significant role in the period was headed by Yin-ssu, the eighth son of the emperor; but its role was primarily a catalytic one, which affected the emperor's final decision to depose Yin-jeng.

Once Yin-jeng was deposed in 1712, the post he left became the objective for several hopefuls among the emperor's children. Thereafter, succession first emerged as a crucial issue. Meanwhile, interpersonal relations also underwent changes: before 1712 the major struggle was between the emperor and Yin-jeng, whereas after that date interactions occurred among the various aspirants to the heir apparentship. Along with changing relationships, there were changes of motives. Further alteration of the palace memorial system made by Yin-chen after he became the Yung-cheng Emperor must be understood against this background; for this reason, discussion in this chapter will be confined to the pre-1712 period, with a view to correlating events and relationship changes between the two key actors, emperor and heir apparent, and the growth of the palace memorial system.

The Emperor's Attitude and Court Behavior. Among the rivals for the throne in the K'ang-hsi period the heir apparent, Yin-jeng (1674–1725), was long the strongest contender. Before 1708, when he was deposed for the first time, factional forces centered largely around him.[2] The Yin-ssu group began to bring increasing pressure on the emperor after this incident. It was largely these factional forces that spurred the K'ang-hsi Emperor to expand the use of the palace memorial system, which had been fully developed by 1712 when Yin-jeng was deposed again for the final time.

Among the adherents of Yin-jeng, two stood out as most influential. Songgotu, grand secretary and the granduncle of the heir apparent, and T'o-ho-ch'i,[3] commandant of the Gendarmerie of the Capital City, were high officials in the capital. In addition, Asan and Gali,[4] two successive governors-general of Chiang-nan and Kiangsi, collaborated with Yin-jeng on occasion.[5] Others occupied many of the strategic positions in the central bureaucracy and were in practical control of the deliberative machinery. In 1712, for example, when the famous mutual impeachment incident between Governor-general Gali and Governor Chang Po-hsing caused one of the greatest disturbances within the bureaucracy during the entire K'ang-hsi reign,[6] the clique included both Manchu and Chinese chief grand secretaries and presidents of the Boards of Rites, War, Punishments, Personnel, and Revenue.[7] In addition to the notorious T'o-ho-ch'i, who was then the leader of the Yin-jeng clique,[8] O-shan, lieutenant general of the banner forces at Peking[9] and possibly Ma-san-ch'i, the Tartar general-in-chief of the banner garrisons in the Chiang-nan area, were among the many military officials within the Yin-jeng faction.[10]

The K'ang-hsi Emperor told Yin-jeng of his desire to abdicate in the latter's favor perhaps as early as the 1690's.[11] In the years 1696 and 1697, when the K'ang-hsi Emperor was still in his early forties, he left the capital twice to command his forces campaigning against the Eleuth; Yin-jeng, a talented young prince in his early twenties, was made regent both times. The emperor invested him with final decision-making powers in an edict which stipulated that "memorials from all the central offices should not be transferred to me at the battle front as usual; the heir apparent is vested with the power to make decisions on all state affairs. For weighty matters, let the court ministers deliberate on them first, then memorialize the heir apparent." [12] But even before the K'ang-hsi Emperor returned to Peking in 1697, he had been informed that Yin-jeng was associating with evil characters in the court and indulging in immoral acts. Upon his return, the emperor ordered the execution of several of the officials involved.[13] The emperor later testified:

> Although his iniquities multiplied day by day, I still hoped that one day he might be able to awake to his evil acts and become a new man. Whenever I toured the South and the West, I always took Yin-jeng along with me. My original purpose was that he might use these opportunities to get acquainted with the local customs and know the hardships of the common people. But Yin-jeng utilized those opportunities to extort money from the governors-general, governors, and the local officials. The mean characters and evil rascals in his employ acted even more recklessly, blackmailing and plundering in the localities.[14]

Although Yin-jeng probably never dared to change the emperor's vermilion endorsements, he was discovered to have been very active in exerting influence on court officials deliberating on decisions; he often tried to influence such decisions regarding the punishment of officials.[16] He succeeded in influencing even the emperor himself, who later testified: "I blamed whomsoever he told me to blame, punished whomsoever he told me to punish, dismissed [literally, "drove away"] whomsoever he told me to dismiss." But the emperor pointed out one exception: "Only when he told me to put someone to death, I did not listen to him — because I am not fond of killing by my own nature. I complied with his wishes whatever they might be in order to please his heart, hoping that he might eventually change from evil to good." The emperor lamented the result: "Despite my submission to his wishes, he clung to his wicked deeds forever. Therefore, I became sorely disappointed, and gave up all hope for him." [16]

This almost unlimited power of Yin-jeng in the court as a result of the K'ang-hsi Emperor's partiality toward him explains at least somewhat why the emperor operated the palace memorial system secretly and why even a memorialist such as Wang Hung-hsü, one of the emperor's most trusted confidants, was so fearful — for his life — that he begged the emperor to conceal his name in sending palace memorials reporting on factional activities, particularly involving Yin-jeng, to him. An atmosphere of fear prevailed throughout much of the bureaucracy; this fear resulted from the contradiction within the emperor's attitude, which mixed his high hopes for and deep affection toward his son with a sense of responsibility for the bureaucracy.

The K'ang-hsi Emperor's continued appeasement of the heir apparent put the entire bureaucracy in a most difficult position. Yin-jeng's clique dominated and terrified all officialdom; even the emperor's protection of officials was circumscribed by it. The emperor could not protect an official and simultaneously maintain his excessive and undifferentiated affection for his heir apparent. Court officials lamented their perilous position and said: "We will die no matter with which of the two we take our stand!" [17] The emperor later observed that he himself had been fully aware of their difficult situation, and he even explained why the saying was true: "There may be some officials who incline their hearts toward their master [the emperor] and are not willing to obey him [Yin-jeng]; and this may mean they are to be slaughtered by him in the future when he becomes the emperor. On the other hand, however, there may be some mean, unworthy persons, who have flattered him and joined his faction solely for expediency. They will be put to death when their evil deeds are discovered by me. Isn't it very true that they will die no matter with which [of us] they take their stand?!" [18]

Factionalism and the Second Stage of the System. By the year 1703, Yin-jeng's clique, headed by the powerful Songgotu, had begun to plot against the emperor's life. Songgotu and his clique had dominated state affairs for a long time, threatening court officials with death if they resisted. Fear of Songgotu's threats enhanced his influence with officialdom. A household servant of Songgotu secretly reported to the emperor the conspiracy against him,[19] and it was only then that the emperor ordered the grand secretary's arrest. He died in confinement, probably in the same year.

The emperor also ordered the arrest and execution of several important Manchu henchmen of Songgotu.[20] On the other hand only one Chinese official, by the name of Chiang Huang, was sentenced to death because seditious correspondence between Songgotu and himself was discovered in his house.[21] Although many other Chinese officials were involved, the emperor preferred simply to warn them to sever their relationship with Songgotu in order to avoid possible capital punishment.[22] But the followers of the late grand secretary continued to dominate affairs until the final deposition of the heir apparent in 1712. The clique also retained the allegiance of court ministers, palace guards, and banner officials, as well as banner soldiers. The emperor revealed in an edict that nearly all the eunuchs in the palace were also on Yin-jeng's side.[23]

It may be significant that the emperor's first transmission of a secret edict to a regular member of the provincial administration occurred only a few months earlier in the year in which Songgotu and others were arrested. As mentioned earlier, the emperor ordered Sung Lao to send him secret palace memorials through Li Hsü whenever there was something to report concerning the South.[24] The second secret palace memorial from Sung Lao was sent to report the death of Kao Shih-ch'i, who had been the household servant of Songgotu and who, according to another contemporary record, was the one who discovered Songgotu's conspiracy against the emperor.[25] This evidence, scanty though it may be, points to the possibility that extension of the secret memorial system may have been connected with the emperor's concern over factional activities in the South, especially those of the Songgotu clique.

The Songgotu incident was, naturally, a great setback for the heir apparent faction and undoubtedly encouraged other factions among the emperor's children.[26] This served to increase the potential for factional influence later, though at this time the heir apparent remained the greatest influence on the emperor's decision-making.

During the emperor's fifth tour of the South in 1705, he still felt heavily the threat of factional influence in the capital. The secret correspondence received from Wang Hung-hsü only served to strengthen his concern. During the two and a half months of the emperor's Southern tour, Wang reported in detail the unfair trial of Ch'en Ju-pi by the joint session of Assemblies of the Deliberative Princes and the Nine Ministers and Censors.[27] Wang Shan, president of the Board of Punishments and a member of Yin-jeng's clique, had recommended that Ch'en be punished immediately by strangulation. In his palace memorials, Wang Hung-hsü revealed that the censor-general Shu-lu played the dominant role in forcing the entire tribunal to endorse this recommendation. According to Wang's report, neither the Chinese nor the Manchu ministers dared to express a contrary opinion.[28]

In the same year that members of the Yin-jeng clique were attempting to sentence Ch'en Ju-pi to death, Asan, governor-general of Chiang-nan and

Kiangsi, with the apparent collaboration of Yin-jeng, was trying to take the life of another honest official, Ch'en P'eng-nien, the prefect of Chiang-ning (Nanking).[29] In this incident the K'ang-hsi Emperor's conciliation policy toward Yin-jeng and the degree of influence of the heir apparent on the emperor's decision-making were clearly shown. The dramatic episode, a portion of which follows, is vividly described in the biography of Ch'en written by Sung Ho:

> In the year *i-yu* [1705], the emperor was on his [fifth] tour of the South. The governor-general [Asan] summoned all the provincial officials to discuss the matter of engaging in elaborate preparations for the emperor's visit, by means of increasing the surtax to thirty percent [which was not legal]. All the officials approved Asan's proposal because they feared him. Only P'eng-nien was unwilling to agree with him and strongly opposed the measure. Asan was very much displeased. He withdrew his proposal, and became determined to eliminate P'eng-nien.[30]

The connection between Asan and the heir apparent was made implicit by the record when it goes on to describe how the heir apparent insisted on killing Ch'en P'eng-nien:

> Subsequently when the imperial chariots arrived at Nanking [prefecture] from Lung-t'an, the lodging facilities prepared for the emperor's visit were very shabby. Those who had plotted against P'eng-nien seized this opportunity to provoke the emperor's anger. At the same time, the heir apparent Yin-jeng, who was accompanying the emperor, felt even more furious; he insisted that P'eng-nien be put to death. After the emperor arrived at Nanking, he stayed in the residence of the superintendent of the imperial manufactory [Ts'ao-Yin].

The source continues to describe how Ch'en narrowly escaped execution despite Yin-jeng's determination to eliminate him:

> One day the young son of Ts'ao Yin was playing in the courtyard. The emperor thought he was merely an innocent child who probably did not know anything; but he asked the child a question anyway. "My son," he said, "do you happen to know any good official in Nanking prefecture?" "Yes," the child replied, "I know one good official whose name is Ch'en P'eng-nien." Meanwhile, the retired grand secretary Chang Ying[31] came to pay homage to the emperor . . . The emperor asked him about Ch'en, and Chang recommended him most highly. Chang had been the tutor of the heir apparent. The emperor therefore [trusted his words] and turned to the heir apparent:

"You see, even your own teacher thought of him very highly, why should I put him to death?" But the heir apparent insisted.

It was at this critical juncture that Ts'ao Yin, the most trusted secret memorialist, intervened. The record continues:

> The superintendent Ts'ao Yin was present at that time. He took off his hat and begged the emperor, by knocking his head reverently against the ground upon which he was kneeling, to pardon P'eng-nien. Li Hsü, the superintendent of the Imperial Manufactory at Soochow and Ts'ao Yin's brother-in-law, knelt behind Ts'ao Yin. When Li Hsü noticed that Ts'ao Yin's forehead was bleeding because he knocked it too heavily against the ground, he warned Ts'ao Yin by pulling his garment lest he should anger the emperor. Ts'ao turned his head back to Li angrily and rebuked him: "What are you talking about!" Then he continued to knock his head reverently against the stony ground. People about him could hear the bumping sound of his knocking. Because of Ts'ao Yin's earnest request, the emperor eventually pardoned Ch'en. Governor Sung Lao, after retreating from the imperial presence, showed his admiration of Ts'ao and said: "You are indeed the contemporary Chu Yun [a famous unrelenting official in the former Han times]." [32]

Factionalism and the Third Stage of the System. On October 17, 1708, the heir apparent, at the age of thirty-five (*sui*), was publicly deprived of his title and put under house confinement. The immediate cause for this drastic measure was the heir apparent's attempt to assassinate the emperor to avenge the death of Songgotu. His clique made the sovereign nervous day and night, since he never knew, in his own words, "whether I would be poisoned today or be slain tomorrow!" [33] The step was also a long-delayed retribution for Yin-jeng's other crimes, which the emperor "had tolerated for twenty years." [34] These were: (1) assaulting princes, *pei-le,* ministers, and other officials of the court, as well as banner soldiers under his control; (2) having members of his clique spy on the emperor's daily movements; (3) illegally appropriating reserve funds in the government treasury; (4) interfering in state affairs.[35]

In addition, the emperor had only recently received reports on various sexual aberrations committed by the heir apparent while accompanying the emperor on his tour of the West and South. These acts were so shocking, the emperor declared, that he could not sleep peacefully for six consecutive days. Yin-jeng not only committed fornication with women he brought from outside, but he was also addicted to sodomy with "fair young boys";[36] and all of these instruments for his pleasure were most likely purchased or even kidnapped from the South by his agents during the southern tours.[37] The charge of sodomy appears quite certain to be that "atrocious offence" which Father Ripa described in his *Memoirs* when commenting in the usual missionary tone that such an offence was held to be "the greatest abomination" by "the law of China," though promulgated by "heathens." [38]

This crucial event can also be found in the official records of Korea. The Korean source records a conversation between the king and three Korean envoys in China when the latter returned to Korea at the end of the year of Yin-jeng's deposition. At the audience, the envoys reported on the situation in China, first describing the serious threat of pirates in the Chinese coastal regions, then giving some general impressions on the deteriorating political situation in China with particular reference to the heir apparent incident.

> The interpreters [the Korean envoys obviously could not speak Chinese] all told us that the political situation among the barbarians [Manchus] is deteriorating. The barbarians spread secret affairs of the emperor to outsiders without any reservation. They spread news [for instance] as to [how the emperor] suddenly deposed the heir apparent and soon reinstated him; beating up Maci, yet still retaining his son in his post. The emperor appeared quite topsy-turvy in handling things and was regarded as a lover of money and treasures. All the people in that country called him "the money-loving emperor."

Then the envoys reported what they had heard about the heir apparent and the imperial children: "Furthermore, the heir apparent is a cruel man by nature. The common people all spread the words, saying, '[he] is disloyal, unfilial; he secretly committed adultery with [outside] women.' Whereas the other children of the emperor are even more tyrannical and violent than the heir apparent. From all these, we know the mandate of the barbarians will not last too long." [39] The Korean document not only provides some of the Korean reaction toward the incident, but it also confirms the high degree of reliability of the *Ch'ing-shih-lu*.

After the deposition of Yin-jeng, the adherents of Yin-ssu, the eighth son of the emperor, tried to induce the emperor to establish him as the new heir apparent. Yin-t'i, the eldest son, was instrumental in this plot. He told the emperor that "Chang Ming-te [the physiognomist] has said: 'Yin-ssu the eighth son of the emperor will undoubtedly receive the highest honor' "; by saying this he meant to test the emperor's intention. The emperor also discovered that Chang had hired sixteen hoodlums to assassinate Yin-jeng. Angry and alarmed at this evidence of new intrigue, the emperor ordered the arrest of Chang Ming-te. In order to reduce the pressure in favor of Yin-ssu, the emperor requested the Manchu princes and dignitaries, in conjunction with some Chinese ministers, to nominate a candidate for succession to the throne. On the suggestion of the influential Manchu grand secretary Maci, three Manchu ministers and the secret memorialist Wang Hung-hsü collectively recommended Yin-ssu for the position. The K'ang-hsi Emperor was greatly displeased by their recommendation. Later, it was discovered that Yin-t'i had employed lamas to cast evil spells on Yin-jeng. The emperor was most seriously concerned about a possible revolt because Yin-t'i had succeeded in gaining support from the younger members of the "five inferior banner units." He thus pardoned Yin-jeng on the ground that his insane acts were caused by Yin-t'i's evil spells; but the real reason for the emperor's re-establishing Yin-jeng, as he later declared, was to stop a possible coup led by the Yin-ssu clique.[40] Once the emperor had restored Yin-jeng as heir apparent, he treated him more kindly than ever in order to transform him by "love." But when at the end of three years the emperor saw no sign of change in Yin-jeng, he deposed him permanently.

Events leading to the important edict of March 5, 1712 (KH 51/1/28), ordering all court officials to present secret palace memorials directly to the emperor himself, then to the arrest of T'o-ho-ch'i on May 14 (KH 51/4/10), and eventually to the deposition of the heir apparent on October 30 (KH 51/10/1) should be outlined. The immediate cause of Yin-jeng's deposition was another attempted coup engineered by the heir apparent and his chief henchman T'o-ho-ch'i. The *Ch'ing-shih-lu* used rather mild and ambiguous terms to describe their crimes, saying that T'o-ho-ch'i had gathered people together to attend a drinking party and form a clique in order to present a recommendation for Yin-jeng.[41] Actually, in an ensuing edict,[42] the emperor described this attempt to "recommend" Yin-jeng to him as an act of "sedition" (or "rebellion"), which was committed only by "seditious officials" (*luan-ch'en tse-tzu*) in Chinese history and therefore, must be "promptly quelled before it broke into open action." This act beyond any doubt constituted an attempted coup to force the emperor to abdicate in favor of Yin-jeng: the throne was the sole position to which an heir apparent could be "recommended." [43]

It is important to note the emperor's steps prior to this final confrontation. On November 29, 1711 (KH 50/10/20), T'o-ho-ch'i was dismissed from office, although the *Ch'ing-shih-lu* recorded his dismissal in the usual polite terms: "released from his office due to sickness." [44] The famous Lungkodo[45] was appointed to take his position, first on an acting basis and later as a permanent appointee.[46]

On December 4, 1711 (KH 50/10/25), the emperor ordered the eight banner units and all court ministers to recommend officials renowned for their filial piety [47] He made special reference to three good possibilities, including Wen-ta, then grand secretary, and Mu-ho-lun, president of the Board of Revenue. This injunction was undoubtedly aimed at encouraging the heir apparent's repentance, because when the emperor severely denounced him a year later at the time of his deposition, he was described as "unfilial." [48]

Next, the emperor began to act more strictly toward the adherents of the Yin-jeng clique. In a morning audience on December 6, 1711 (KH 50/10/27), he denounced those high officials who "had formed a clique for the sake of the heir apparent." [49] Then he rebuked several incumbent Manchu ministers as the obstinate adherents of the former Songgotu clique. He pointed out a few notorious plotters, such as Keng-o, president of the Board of War,[50] and angrily scolded him: "Keng-o is the household slave in the house of Songgotu; this is why he has been so loyal to his master." Then the emperor sarcastically denounced all the others involved, asking, "Are you all Songgotu's household slaves?" In front of princes, nobles of all ranks, and civil and military high officials, the emperor ordered the arrest of Keng-o and several others, including Ch'i-shih-wu, president of the Board of Punishments, and O-shan, lieutenant general of the banner troops at Peking.[51] Three months later, on March 5, 1712 (KH 51/1/28), the emperor announced his major edict inaugurating the third stage of the palace memorial system.

The document is crucial because it not only establishes the relation between factionalism and the expansion of the system, but it reveals that the emperor was now using palace memorials not simply as an information-gathering device but also as a self-defense weapon. It is therefore helpful to quote the edict in full. It was addressed to all central high-ranking officials,

Manchu as well as Chinese, military as well as civil; it first spelled out its own theoretical raison d'être:

> Ever since ancient times, emperors were able to rule their nations in good order and great harmony whenever the ruler and his subjects were of one accord without divergent interests. But they found that abuses would arise in all things if the ruler and his subjects could not maintain good communications and thus each possessed divergent interests. This is always so according to the universal law.

Then the edict points out the specific problems confronting the emperor. It mentions in particular the heir apparent's clique and its factional activities headed by T'o-ho-ch'i.

> Although we have censors, they have often been hesitant to speak out; they keep their mouths shut all the time. For if they reported to me on things which could not be made public, their lives would certainly be endangered. How many censors could one find who are not afraid of this serious consequence? [52] This is why T'o-ho-ch'i and those small men under him have constantly mustered members in their clique without any fear of the imperial authority; but now their activities have been discovered by me.

Then the emperor stated the new policy and explained why he had, previously, authorized the provincial authorities to present palace memorials. He now wished all high-ranking central officials to follow this example.

> Rulers of past dynasties all discovered seditious and treacherous ministers. If the ruler detected their activities early, they could be quelled quietly, but if a ruler allowed such activities to spread, the harmful consequences became most serious later. It is indeed my own prescribed duty as the emperor to labor day and night for the country and for the people but there are many things about which I have no means of obtaining information. Because of this, I have ordered the generals-in-chief, governors-general, governors, commanders-in-chief, and brigade generals to enclose their secret reports in their greetings palace memorials. Therefore all the affairs in the provinces can not be concealed deceitfully. This practice has been shown to be very beneficial and effective to the people's life and welfare. Since all of you are ministers whom I trust, you therefore ought to join the high provincial officials in presenting your reports on things which ought to be memorialized by enclosing them in your greetings palace memorials.

Then the emperor described how discreetly he had handled the secret palace memorials and assured his ministers that he would continue to do so to insure the protection of the memorialists.

> All court officials know that I am very cautious in handling things. Whenever I have received secret palace memorials, none of their contents were ever divulged. There might have been, however, some worthless characters, who dared to risk capital punishment and who opened the sealed containers of the palace memorials to read them. Sometimes the memorialist himself might have too many friends and might not himself have set a watchman on his mouth, and thus care- lessly disclosed the contents of his secret palace memorial. This could possibly happen. Furthermore, in handling palace memorials, I acted on them promptly without any records or duplicates. After having been endorsed by my own hand, they were returned promptly to the memorialists. All of the memorialists have received my personal en- dorsements. Thus [if one wants to find evidence], evidence may be found in their hands, not mine!

The edict ends with the emperor's expectations for the expanded palace memorial system:

> If you [court ministers] could indeed report secretly according to the truth, then notoriously corrupt officials and notorious traitors would naturally become afraid of [being discovered], because they would not be able to know who has reported on them. Those rascals who attempt to deceive their master [the emperor] and wield power ille- gally will naturally restrain themselves. I therefore have issued this special edict to you all! [53]

Although the emperor made reference to the heir apparent in his repeated denunciations of the Yin-jeng clique, he did not give up hope of avoiding a confrontation with him. But immediately after the promulgation of the above edict he received a secret report, presumably in response to the im- perial injunction, on a conspiracy of the Yin-jeng clique. This report must have indicated that the latter were preparing a coup[54] — the nature of which has been described briefly before — which the emperor quashed before deposing the heir apparent finally.

Within the three months following receipt of the secret report, the em- peror undoubtedly pursued his investigation of the facts exposed therein. At the same time Wang I, a supervising censor, presented a memorial to impeach T'o-ho-ch'i for having accepted bribes.[55] On May 14, 1712 (KH 51/4/10), the impeachment memorial was referred to the Assembly of Nine Ministers and Censors for deliberation. Two days later the assembly submitted a joint memorial, endorsed by all the ministers who participated in the deliberation. The emperor was not satisfied with their report because T'o-ho-ch'i's confession was not included in it,[56] and the case was therefore referred to a joint tribunal composed of the president of the Imperial Clan Court and the grand secretaries, as well as the president of the Board of Punishments. The next day, the joint tribunal memorialized the emperor on what T'o-ho-ch'i and Ch'i-shih-wu had confessed regarding the "drinking party" charge. The emperor severely denounced both T'o-ho-ch'i and the heir apparent. He blamed Yin-jeng for asking T'o-ho-ch'i to recommend him to the emperor, calling T'o-ho-ch'i "the most shameless and unworthy one," and rebuking Ch'i-shih-wu, the former president of the Board of Punishments, for his "having constantly associated from childhood with gangsters." [57] The emperor ordered that the punishments due to T'o-ho-ch'i and Ch'i-shih-wu be decided after their trial for the bribery charge. However, he did not take any clear stand against the heir apparent except to denounce him as the cause of these irregular activities.[58] Seven days later, the tribunal memorialized the emperor that both T'o-ho-ch'i and Ch'i-shih-wu had been found guilty of accepting bribes; the former had received 2,400 silver taels and the latter 3,000 taels. They recommended that both be strangled. The emperor approved the recommendation and instructed that they be confined pending execution in the autumn.[59]

The heir apparent Yin-jeng, however, was left alone for another six months. On October 30, 1712 (KH 51/10/1), the K'ang-hsi Emperor, at the age of fifty-nine (*sui*), decided to permanently depose his heir apparent, who was then nearly forty; it was, nevertheless, the final coup attempt that forced the emperor to give up all hope for Yin-jeng because he had "exhausted the energy of his mind." At this juncture the emperor admitted how difficult the position was in which he had placed his ministers and testified how true it had been that "they had to die no matter with which of the two they take their stand!"

The permanent deposition of the heir apparent Yin-jeng, as mentioned earlier, only intensified the factional rivalries of the several aspirants to the throne among the children of the K'ang-hsi Emperor. The succession struggle in the post-1712 years of the K'ang-hsi reign built up enormous momentum, so great that it affected important changes in the palace memorial system after one of the major contenders, Yin-chen, had assumed the throne and become the new Yung-cheng Emperor.

VII | Changes in the
Palace Memorial System
in the Yung-cheng Reign

The palace memorial system in the Yung-cheng period underwent important changes. In general, this system was applied to gain two objectives: to crush antagonistic forces and to rehabilitate the bureaucracy. The problems inherent in both objectives were rooted in the late years of the K'ang-hsi reign; in order to understand the changes that occurred later, the bare essentials of the background against which they took place must be explored.

Antagonism was generated mainly from some of Yin-chen's brothers as a result of the succession struggle during the last decade of the K'ang-hsi period. After Yin-jeng was deposed in 1712, fraternal rivalries among the princes were further intensified. Some of his supporters continued their attempts to influence the emperor to restore Yin-jeng's heir apparentship. This "restoration faction" was apparently pursuing a hopeless cause based on wishful thinking. The emperor's determination against restoration can be perceived from the extremely severe punishments that he inflicted on Yin-jeng's chief representatives in the bureaucracy. T'o-ho-ch'i, having died in confinement, was further punished through "cutting his corpse into pieces and spreading the dust of his tomb-ground into the air and forbidding the burial of his remains." [1] Ch'i-shih-wu was said to have been put to death by having his head and limbs nailed to a wall.[2] These actions all reflected the deep hatred of the "benevolent despot" against the Yin-jeng adherents.

Early in 1713, Chao Shen-ch'iao, Chinese censor-general, presented a memorial urging the emperor to designate an heir apparent; the request was turned down.[3] In 1715, P'u-ch'i, a lieutenant general of the Plain Red Banner, was found to have engaged in secret communications with Yin-jeng through a physician and by the use of invisible ink; both P'u-ch'i and the physician were sentenced to "beheading after the autumn assizes" (*chan chien-hou*).[4] In 1718, Chu T'ien-pao, a corrector of the Hanlin Academy, memorialized the emperor, requesting that Yin-jeng be reinstated as the imperial heir because Yin-jeng, he thought, "was both benevolent and filial." Chu was condemned to death when the emperor discovered that

Yin-jeng had asked Chu's father to prevail upon him to present the memorial.[5] In 1721, the grand secretary Wang Shan strongly recommended that Yin-jeng be released and restored to his position; Wang was subsequently condemned to serve as a soldier in the Tibetan frontier in order to redeem himself, though in view of his old age Wang's son was permitted to go as his substitute.[6]

The most influential faction was still the one under the leadership of Yin-ssu, the eighth son of the emperor. This faction was most activistic in the post-1712 period and tried to win the struggle through a cooperative effort among four brothers, Yin-t'i (the eldest), Yin-ssu, Yin-t'ang, and Yin-t'i (the fourteenth). In this faction were included high Manchu and Chinese ministers, as well as people from all walks of life: Buddhists, Taoists, lamas, physicians, fortune-tellers, astrologers actors and actresses, slaves, household servants, court ministers, and even European missionaries.[7] Before 1718, this clique, though as active as ever, failed to select a strong candidate. Among the four brothers, Yin-t'i the eldest and Yin-ssu were definitely ruled out by the emperor for candidacy; Yin-t'ang, a very rich prince, was fond of "wine and women" and other "good enjoyments of life," [8] hence he was not particularly interested in the post. Not until late 1718 did this cooperative faction find a leader when Yin-t'i, the fourteenth son and the youngest in the group, was suddenly made the generalissimo to lead the expedition forces against the Eleuths.[9] His adherents all interpreted this event as an indication that the emperor intended to make Yin-t'i the heir apparent but wanted to give him a chance to show his worthiness.[10] Despite their optimism, there was much evidence to suggest that they were not at all sure about the emperor's true intention. Yin-t'ang lavishly bought off influential eunuchs to "spy on the emperor's daily mood" [11] and Generalissimo Yin-t'i turned to a fortune-teller for a forecast of his future.[12]

Yin-chih, the third son of the K'ang-hsi Emperor, may be described as an "independent" in the succession race. Before 1712, he was on good terms with Yin-jeng; he therefore had no part in effecting the latter's downfall. After that year, Yin-chih soon became the prime target of court speculation as the most hopeful for heir apparentship and thus attracted a handful of adherents.[13] His prestige was more apparent than real, because the emperor remained silent as to his choice of an heir. After Yin-t'i (the fourteenth brother) had been made generalissimo in 1718, Yin-chih was no longer considered the most hopeful, and it was Yin-t'i who attracted the greatest attention among the court ministers.

On December 20, 1722, the K'ang-hsi Emperor took the whole court by surprise when he designated Yin-chen instead of Yin-t'i as heir to the throne. Immediately rumors began to spread accusing Yin-chen of having obtained the throne by illegal means; there were several versions of the story, some fictitious.[14] Contemporary historians, too, have attempted to "prove" illegality in Yin-chen's succession.[15]

The most popular thesis asserted that Yin-t'i, the fourteenth son, was actually the legitimate heir, but that Lungkodo, commandant of the Capital City, had altered the imperial will in favor of Yin-chen. Such an assumption is quite doubtful; furthermore, there is not sufficient evidence to show that Yin-chen had engaged in any factional activities before Yin-jeng's final deposition in 1712. Even after that year, Yin-chen's influence was never strong enough to cause suspicions in the court. In general, his relationship with his brothers was fairly congenial. During those hectic junctures when Yin-jeng was twice deposed from his post, Yin-chen always behaved nobly and was praised by his fathers as a "great man." [16] Among all the brothers, he was probably the most moralistic and the most learned; it was said, for example, that many of the scrolls assumed to have been written in the emperor's own hand were actually done by Yin-chen.[17]

Legal or not, it is important to note how Yin-chen's accession brought about changes, both in relationships and motives. He was no longer a mere prince, but the emperor. Psychological frustration among his brothers led them to project complaints they had about their deceased father's choice to their victorious brother. In the early years of the Yung-chung reign, hostile forces, notably those centering around the members of the cooperative faction, continued the effort to frustrate the new emperor and aimed at his overthrow. Yin-chen had entered into a situation in which he found few friends; for this reason, he badly needed to recruit reliable men to fill his bureaucracy, otherwise he would have to find a means to re-educate the incumbents. The hostile forces posed a constant threat both to his rule and to his own life. Assassination was not uncommon during this time and as shown earlier, both the Yin-jeng and Yin-ssu factions did make attempts on the K'ang-hsi Emperor's life. When the succession struggle was at its severest, Yin-t'i the eldest so feared assassins that he felt it necessary to lock all his doors at night.[18] His own bodyguard, K'ua-se, sealed all the windows of his own quarters with boards and nails. It is not difficult to understand Yin-chen's need for some sort of defense as a control mechanism to protect himself and consolidate his rule.

In addition to the antagonism of his brothers, Yin-chen also inherited from his late father an inefficient bureaucracy, which resulted from a general disintegration of standards of administration due to his late father's appeasement attitude toward the Yin-jeng and other factions. The situation in both the central government and the provincial administrations was specially bad due to uncontrolled corruption. For instance, when Yin-chen appointed Prince I (Yin-hsiang) to investigate the actual reserve in the treasury of the Board of Revenue, he found that nearly 3,000,000 silver taels had been stolen.[19] In Shantung province alone the illegally appropriated public funds in the provincial treasury amounted to over 2,000,000 taels, while the illegally appropriated funds of the various local governments came to 600,000 taels.[20] One source relates that when Man-p'ei, a confidant of Yin-t'ang, sought the post of acting governor-general of Hu-Kuang, he paid Yin-t'ang a price of 300,000 taels for the latter's help.[21] The only way to rehabilitate this sick administration was, in Yin-chen's own words, by "putting officials under surveillance" (*ch'a-li*).[22] It was against such a background that the Yung-cheng Emperor used the palace memorial system not only as a device for secret communication, but also to achieve positive bureaucratic control.

The Expanded Structure. From the beginning of the Yung-cheng era, palace memorials were used in the recruitment of officials. As soon as Yin-chen had ascended the throne in 1722, he issued an edict urging the grand secretaries to nominate qualified candidates either as prospective officials or as officials to be promoted to higher positions if they were already in the government. The nominations were to be made in the form of secret palace memorials written by the memorialist's own hand; those who could not write were allowed to report to the emperor in a personal audience.[23] There were no regulations on calligraphy, number of characters, or form or style. Palace memorials were also utilized by the Yung-cheng Emperor to perform certain important social functions such as indoctrination and mutual surveillance, and as a means of strengthening his ties of affection with the bureaucracy. Later, with the development of the court letter system and the ad hoc committees, palace memorials came to be used to deal with nonroutine civil and military administrative affairs as well (see Chapter VIII).

Furthermore, the new emperor urged censors to take an active part in presenting secret palace memorials. An edict of 1723 reveals the background of his action: during the late years of the K'ang-hsi reign, censors seldom presented memorials because they felt the emperor would not be interested in their opinions; the Yung-cheng Emperor, while defending his late father's policy, ordered them in this edict to present secret palace memorials daily. Censors were allowed to report on anything, great or small, but they were not permitted to discuss the substance of the reports with their colleagues. If they violated this injunction, their colleagues were to secretly report on them for the violation.[24] The censorial privilege of presenting palace memorials was withdrawn in 1726 because it had been abused.[25]

The palace memorial privilege was also extended to include more provincial officials. Financial commissioners, judicial commissioners, and occasionally circuit intendants or even military officers of lower ranks were all admitted to the group. This was actually a remedial measure, to prevent high ranking provincial authorities from concealing matters.[26]

Palace memorials in the Yung-cheng period were transmitted in an even more secure fashion than before. Qualified high provincial memorialists were each issued a certain number of palace memorial boxes (che-hsia) (usually four) with locks and keys.[27] This system assured maximum secrecy; only the emperor and the memorialist possessed the same keys. Locks and keys were all imported from Europe and were not easy to reproduce; the punishment for unauthorized reproduction of keys was death.[28] The size of the palace memorial boxes was ten and nine-tenths inches long, five and four-tenths inches wide, and one and eight-tenths inches high. The boxes were made of leather, painted yellow on the outside, and lined with yellow silk inside.[29] Palace memorials were transmitted by dispatching special messengers, just as in the K'ang-hsi period.

Upon a messenger's arrival in Peking, he submitted the palace memorial box as usual to the Chancery of Memorials, where the palace guards on duty handed them to the chancery eunuchs who, in turn, would present them to the emperor immediately. No red tape whatsoever was involved in this presentation process. Sometimes local officials of lower ranks, such as financial and judicial commissioners, submitted their palace memorials through Prince I or some grand secretary; but the latter's responsibility consisted of no more than to hand over memorials to the Inner Chancery of Memorials.[30] Such a practice was merely intended to uphold the formal hierarchical order because local officials of lower rank were not qualified to present *pen-chang* (traditional memorials) directly; their *pen-chang* were presented through their immediate superiors, the governors-general and the governors.[31]

The Yung-cheng Emperor, following the practice of his late father, read all incoming palace memorials by himself. In an edict issued on August 20, 1730 (YC 8/7/7), the emperor declared:

> Palace memorials from the high provincial civil and military officials sometimes amounted to twenty to thirty in number every day, or sometimes even as many as fifty to sixty pieces. I always read them by myself and, having endorsed them, returned them to the memorialists. Never was there anyone who assisted me in handling these memorials in the palace. I do not have any archival records in the palace for reference, nor have I anyone who is charged with making any records for me. This is unlike the boards where one finds secretaries (*pi-t'ieh-shih*) and many other clerks who take charge of records and books, look up regulations and trace and investigate details. My practice has been simply this: I read the secret palace memorials and make notes on them on the basis of my judgment at that particular moment. Most of the notations are exhortations and teachings.[32]

In the same edict the Yung-cheng Emperor describes how he responded to incoming palace memorials. The following generalizations are based on this major imperial treatise: (1) If it were both feasible and imperative that requests made in a palace memorial be carried out at once, the emperor would instruct the board in question to carry them out without delay.[33] (2) If the requests made in a palace memorial seemed justifiable but the emperor was not quite sure what action should be taken, he would refer them to the proper deliberative bodies[34] for comments before he made his final decisions (technically, *ch'a-i*). (3) If requests made in a palace memorial from the provincial governors-general and governors concerned routine administrative matters, the emperor would order the memorialists to prepare a separate *t'i-pen* instead and present it again through the *Nei-ko* channel. (4) If the requests made in a palace memorial were from a provincial financial commissioner or a judicial commissioner, the emperor would instruct him to present a petition to his superiors (governor-general and governor) so that the latter could transmit his request by presenting a *t'i-pen* through the *Nei-ko*.[35] (5) It was positively forbidden for provincial officials to use palace memorials to settle routine local administrative matters which were governed by administrative regulations under supervision of the Six Boards. They could, however, send up palace memorials for imperial advice before submitting a *t'i-pen* through the regular channels; in these cases the vermilion endorsement was not, of course, taken as the final decision on the matter.

On December 30, 1722, only ten days after his enthronement, the Yung-cheng Emperor decreed that all palace memorials dispatched from the provinces before his father's death must be presented to the throne. Severe punishment would be imposed on anyone who dared to withhold them.[36] This decree was apparently issued to prevent the concealment of any palace memorial of an unfriendly nature, written by the emperor's enemies. Four days later, on January 3, 1723, another edict stipulated that memorialists who possessed palace memorials bearing the late emperor's vermilion endorsements should return them to the new emperor. The motivation behind this injunction was to prevent memorialists from retaining written evidence of their secret correspondence with the late emperor lest, as the new emperor explained, they should later "fabricate [stories] and initiate actions under the pretext that they are acting according to my late father's instructions." [37] By this the Yung-cheng Emperor hoped to conceal any evidence of differences between his late father's policies and his own and thus to protect himself against charges of filial impiety.

In the same edict, the emperor also ordered that this injunction be applied to his own vermilion endorsements: "Hereafter palace memorials which receive my personal secret instructions [*mi-chih*] should be returned in the same fashion. You are not allowed to make duplicates or to retain them for yourselves." From this time onward, this regulation became an important feature in the palace memorial system, and it was later recorded in the *Collected Statutes*.[38]

Social Functions. The Yung-cheng Emperor also seems to have quite consciously utilized palace memorials to fulfill certain social functions. In contrast, the palace memorial system in the K'ang-hsi period had functioned mainly as a communication device that greatly increased the emperor's knowledge of local political conditions; but the emperor seldom took any drastic action as a result of the memorials, with the exception of his destruction of the Yin-jeng clique. In general the K'ang-hsi Emperor seems to have often relied on this system mainly for its psychological effects. In an edict of 1716, he concisely illustrated these two points, first stating: "The fact that I have ordered all high officials to present secret palace memorials to me is something of great importance. By doing so I have meant to broaden my own knowledge [of affairs; literally, to brighten the vision of my eyes and sharpen the hearing ability of my ears]. I know very well whether a man has presented a palace memorial for a selfish purpose or for the public good." The edict then stated the psychological function of the system: "All palace memorials have always been endorsed by my own hand. Therefore, although princes and civil and military high officials know that some secret palace memorial has arrived, they can never guess what has been reported in it. Naturally, they become watchful and fearful, and hence examine themselves to see whether they have done anything wrong." [39] His failure to take action, of course, had a great deal to do with this emperor's own status quo policy, to be discussed in Chapter IX.

When the Yung-cheng Emperor took over this political device from his late father, the system acquired at least three social functions which became important features of the Yung-cheng bureaucracy.[40] First, palace memorials began to be used as media for massive moral indoctrination and administrative rehabilitation of local officials[41] — a practice obviously dictated by the chaotic condition of officialdom at the time. In the Preface to the *Chu-p'i yü-chih* (Vermilion Endorsements of the Yung-cheng Emperor),[42] the emperor particularly stressed that, in addition to the function of broadening his knowledge of political affairs, he used palace memorials to "teach people how to practice good" and "admonish people to shun evil." The total number of palace memorials bearing the vermilion endorsements of the Yung-cheng Emperor amounts to about fifty thousand.[43] In his own words, "the great majority of these vermilion endorsements concerned teachings and exhortations";[44] This shows how important a role the palace memorials played in the moral education of the bureaucracy during this period.

In general, the Yung-cheng Emperor's didactic and educational endorsements covered three major areas: (1) "to teach them to do good and admonish them to shun evil"; (2) "to show them the concrete methods of examining their subordinate officials and ruling the people"; (3) "to enlighten them in the principles of receiving blessings and avoiding misfortunes." [45] The following three cases will serve as illustrations.

In response to a palace memorial submitted by Governor-general Yang Lin, the emperor noted:

> I have earnestly and repeatedly exhorted you and taught you . . . If you could treat local affairs as if they were the business of your own family, and try to manage them tirelessly all the time, how could it be possible that you would not see any results? After three years, I want you to tell me that every thing is all right. How could you expect me to trust what you have to say at the present time? After the three-year deadline is over, if I should find that your deeds are not in accordance with your words, you will certainly regret the consequences forever! Be very careful about this.[46]

In response to a palace memorial submitted by the financial commissioner Li Wei, the emperor warned Li how to behave himself before his superiors. The vermilion endorsement reads:

> Last time when I endorsed your palace memorial, I earnestly warned you that you ought to avoid impetuousness and ill temper. Recently someone has reported that you have behaved rather recklessly on account of my trust in you and my favor shown you. I heard that you have been very rude and have shown a lack of deference toward your superiors. For instance, when you addressed the governor-general Kao Ch'i-cho and the governor Yang Ming-shih you simply called them: "Old Kao!" or "Old Yang!" [47]

Fan Shih-i, the acting governor-general of Chiang-nan and Kiangsi, once submitted a palace memorial reporting on unfavorable prospects for the autumn harvest because of too much rain. The Yung-cheng Emperor took this opportunity to teach him what "blessing" (fu) meant. His interpretation was rather pragmatic, yet it fell into the general Neo-Confucian belief that men (ruler as well as officials) would be blessed by Heaven if they just carried out their responsibilities according to the law of Heaven. The vermilion endorsement reads:

> Last time [when you told me about the optimistic prospect of the autumn harvest], I told you that I could not be sure about that until the autumn harvest. Now my prediction has been proven true. How could I expect seasonable rains and good harvest since I have mis-

takenly appointed Chang K'ai [to be the governor of Chiang-nan]. Last time, you said the harvest prospect would be good because of the immense blessings I have received from Heaven; now will you consider that I am not blessed at all? . . . I have repeatedly issued public edicts praising T'ien Wen-ching, Li Wei, and Yang Wen-ch'ien. Now you can see how fruitful the harvest results are in the three provinces under their administrations. Therefore, if you provincial governors and governors-general always use proper officials, this will be the greatest blessing I can ever have; otherwise, I am not blessed at all. Interpreting "blessing" in this fashion is supported by undeniable evidence . . . Therefore, the best way to receive blessing, I think, is to influence Heaven by your sincerity.

The endorsement ends with a rather interesting interpretation of the *Book of History*: "Last time, when I read your palace memorial, I felt that you seemed very excited about the harvest prospect. The *Book of History* says: 'The rainfall is given in proportion to your excitedness.' If this is true, the excessive rainfall may have been invoked by you [your excessive joy] — this is possible. One should never let cautiousness and watchfulness leave his own heart. Be watchful and respectful!" [48]

The Yung-cheng Emperor often used vulgar language to exhort his memorialists, a habit that could be traced back to the time before he assumed the throne;[49] a few examples give the flavor.

Bosh! You are talking complete nonsense! [50]

You are as dumb as wood and stone! I don't think you are a human being at all! [51]

You are not worthy to be compared with the wild beasts! [52]

You are extremely ignorant and stupid! [53]

One of the interesting features of the Yung-cheng Emperor's vermilion endorsements is his frequent noting of these vulgar comments interlinearly on palace memorials (the text was always written from right to left) so that he could rebuke the memorialist phrase by phrase. For instance, beside the phrase "on account of Your Majesty's immense blessedness" the emperor noted, "I am deeply disgusted with this type of empty flattering language!" [54] Such interlinear endorsements sometimes run through a whole page, depending on the subject and the emperor's mood.[55]

In striking contrast with the practice of the K'ang-hsi Emperor, the Yung-cheng Emperor often made lengthy endorsements either interlinearly or at the end of the palace memorial. Such endorsements ran from a few score to hundreds or even a thousand or more words. Although he forbade the memorialists to show their palace memorials to others, he often sent a certain official's palace memorial to another official in order to teach the latter to follow the memorialist's example.[56] In 1732, when he published his famous *Chu-p'i yü-chih*, he intended to educate not only his officialdom, but all of Chinese society. He sincerely hoped that his vermilion endorsements might be of help in improving "the human heart and social customs," and that readers "might be moved" by their moralizing power and thus "become enthusiastic about the common good." [57]

The second function of the palace memorials under the Yung-cheng Emperor was as a device for mutual surveillance of officials. Many anecdotes describe how effectively this "spy system" operated;[58] for instance, as soon as Li Wei arrived at his post as salt censor in Yunnan province, he reported on all the provincial officials. It was due partly to his boldness and honesty in reporting on others that Li advanced so rapidly along the bureaucratic ladder.[59]

When Nien Keng-yao was still in imperial favor, the Yung-cheng Emperor urged him to keep an eye on the rebellious prince Yin-t'ang, the ninth son of the K'ang-hsi Emperor. The vermilion endorsement on Nien's palace memorial reads:

> I have understood. Yin-t'ang sent me a palace memorial requesting that I grant him permission to return to Peking. I didn't give him any definite answer. I simply endorsed his palace memorial with an ambiguous phrase: "I have understood." But if he wants to return to the capital on the basis of this ambiguous endorsement of mine, you must not let him. You just have to tell him that the emperor did not give you any order to release him. So do not let him come here.[60]

But when Nien Keng-yao was transferred to Hangchow as a general-in-chief, the Yung-cheng Emperor instructed all the governors-general and governors through whose provinces Nien would pass on his way to Hangchow from Shensi to keep an eye on him. Nien's every movement was constantly reported to the emperor through palace memorials. In order to see how minute the reports were, it is necessary only to quote one portion of a memorial submitted by T'ien Wen-ching, governor of Honan:

T'ien Wen-ching, governor of Honan, reverently memorializes. This secret report is submitted in accordance with Your Majesty's personal instruction. On the twenty-ninth day of the fourth month of the third year [June 9, 1725], I received Your Majesty's personal instruction which reads: "I have heard that Nien Keng-yao sent twenty wagons containing his personal belongings through the T'ung Pass heading toward Honan. The final destination was unknown. You ought to make accurate inquiries secretly and report to me." I then secretly dispatched Po Ch'i under the disguise of a wagon owner, in order to make inquiries all along the way. (He was an imperial guard who had been sent to Honan province as an expectant official.) I have already reported on the results of his inquiries on the twenty-sixth day of the fifth month of this year.

Now Po Ch'i further reports that when he arrived at Pao-ting prefecture, he discovered that Nien had a house there which he had bought from Wang Tung, the director-general of grain transport. On the eighteenth day of the second month of this year, he unloaded nineteen wagons of personal effects at this house. The house was under the management of his house servant Yen Erh; all the goods were unloaded here . . .

Moreover, I am informed that during the third month of this year two teams of seventeen wagons and fourteen wagons [belonging to Nien] respectively passed through Honan province heading toward the north. Then during the fifth month of this year, 155 members of Nien Keng-yao's household, 142 domestic beasts, 60 wagons, 22 sedan chairs, and 79 camels left Honan territory, passing through the Meng-chin district — all belonged to Nien Keng-yao. No luggage was left in Honan.[61]

Thirdly, palace memorials in the Yung-cheng period were sometimes used as media for furthering personal relations between the memorialists and the emperor. The kind of language used for this purpose was rather unique, as far as documentary style is concerned: sometimes it is difficult to know whether one is reading memorials or affectionate letters. The emperor and his memorialists sometimes became quite sentimental; they might "shed tears," or express the longing to see each other again. The emperor frequently sent valuable gifts to his secret memorialists.[62] The K'ang-hsi Emperor had also been in the habit of giving gifts, but not nearly to the same extent.

In a further variation of the same phenomenon, sometimes the vermilion endorsements sent to Nien Keng-yao dealt with family affairs. Indeed, they often sounded like family letters, their language being so personal that one would normally expect to receive such a letter only from a close relative.[63] Irrelevancies to the subject matter dealt with in palace memorials were also common.[64] Although the correspondence with Nien certainly represents an extreme case because of the special relationship between him and the emperor, sentimentality was rather conspicuous in the system as a whole during the Yung-cheng period. For example, when the emperor endorsed a palace memorial submitted from O-erh-t'ai, governor-general of Yunnan and Kweichow, he noted: "Again I am now endorsing these words under the lamp [late at night]. I read your palace memorial with tears." [65] When O-erh-t'ai read this touching endorsement, he also, according to his memorial, "sobbed and snivelled so badly" that he completely lost his composure. The emperor was moved by the governor-general's loyalty and conscientiousness and the governor-general by the emperor's diligent, hardworking spirit as a ruler.[66]

It was not uncommon for the Yung-cheng Emperor to send gifts to trusted provincial high officials; on one occasion, he even dispatched an imperial commissioner with some lichees to T'ien Wen-ching (governor of Honan).[67] Such emotional elements in his palace memorial system had a great deal to do with his own temperament and ideology. In the endorsements of the Yung-cheng Emperor, the reader is often struck by his display of naked emotion, which, as his late father had once commented, was "sometimes slightly unstable." [68]

The tremendous expansion of the palace memorial system in the early years of the Yung-cheng reign slowed down gradually from 1728, by which year antagonistic forces had been largely suppressed and the Yung-cheng administration greatly revitalized on both the central and the provincial levels. Along with the expansion, an overwhelming amount of raw information poured in through the new channel of communication, and eventually it also affected structural changes within the existing communication-decision network, thereby affecting the decision-making procedure. In response to the influx of information, paper work was multiplied and additional secretarial assistance became absolutely inevitable.

When such information became the basis for imperial decisions, complexities of administration and policy made it imperative for the emperor to seek technical advice; he did so at first within the existing decision-making structure. During the first three years of the Yung-cheng reign, government powers were nominally vested in a newly appointed committee composed of four "imperial assistants plenipotentiary" (*tsung-li shih-wu wang ta-ch'en,* literally princes and ministers taking charge of all state affairs). Two of the members of the committee were Yin-ssu and Yin-hsiang, both holding the rank of "prince of the first degree" (*ch'in-wang*); the other two were Maci (grand secretary) and Lungkodo (president of the Board of Civil Appointment).[1] The composition of this committee, which was representative of three important components of the Ch'ing government, deserves further comment: the two princes represented Manchu nobility and the grand secretary and the board president represented the Grand Secretariat and the central administration.

During the tenure of the committee, tensions between Yin-ssu and the emperor developed to an explosive degree; the emperor did not take any action because of the mourning period for the late emperor. When the tenure expired on March 27, 1725 (YC 3/2/14), the end of the mourning period, it was ordered that all members of the committee be discussed for reward except Yin-ssu.[2] He was put under house confinement in the middle of 1726 and died later in the same year.[3] Lungkodo was found guilty of factional alliance with Nien Keng-yao in the same year, shortly after the mourning period ended. He was first deprived of all titles and sent to a frontier region and then put under house confinement a year later. Maci, who did not receive any overt punishment, became almost a titular grand secretary. He had been blamed during his tenure as a member of the committee for having made an erroneous draft rescript[4] and was reprimanded for his irresponsibility.[5] In later years he seldom appeared for duty in the *Nei-ko*.[6]

After the committee was dissolved, the emperor continued the same practice by running the government through a small group of confidants. Yin-hsiang was almost a standing member of this group before he died in 1730. Shortly after his tenure as an imperial assistant plenipotentiary, he was appointed as superintendent of affairs of the Board of Revenue (*kuan-li Hu-pu shih-wu*), a position above all the presidents of that board.[7] In addition to affairs under his jurisdiction, he was continually asked to deliberate, in conjunction with two or so grand secretaries, on a variety of matters that were included in palace memorials from the provinces. These secretaries were called inner grand secretaries (*nei chung-t'ang*), as differentiated from other grand secretaries who remained in the original *Nei-ko* office, because they served the emperor in his palace. This tight group functioned as an inner deliberative body, as well as a secretarial organ to the emperor. Its functions eclipsed all the other deliberative organs in actual participation in decision-making.

Along with the structural changes, there were procedural changes within the central communication-decision network. One of the most significant of these was the introduction of a new kind of communication medium through which confidential imperial instructions could be dispatched directly to the provincial authorities. This medium, known as the "court letter," functioned as a counterpart of the palace memorial system. Because drafting court letters on behalf of the emperor was one of the inner grand secretaries' major functions, the court letter system must be studied as a prerequisite to detailed analysis of the formation and changing functions of the group of inner grand secretaries.

The Court Letter System. The court letter was one of the several ways whereby the emperor issued instructions to the provincial high officials. An instruction might be orally transmitted from one official to another when the first was summoned to the capital for special audience, although a message so transmitted usually concerned exhortations (*hsün-yü* or *sheng-hsün*) rather than formal decisions[8] and was usually called "imperial instruction orally transmitted" (*k'ou-ch'uan yü-chih*). There were two types of written instructions: vermilion endorsements (*chu-p'i*) that the emperor noted personally on palace memorials and vermilion instructions (*chu-pi yü-chih*) that he wrote on a separate sheet of paper. The court letter was a distinct kind of instruction, not written in the emperor's own hand. Its contents were first dictated to a certain type of court minister — originally various ministers could handle the task, but later it became almost the exclusive duty of an informal group (the inner grand secretaries, as a result of their functional expansion) — and this minister wrote up the instruction in the form of a letter and dispatched it to the provincial recipients.

Like the palace memorial, the prototype of the court letter originated in the K'ang-hsi period; but it evolved from its original uses to deal with administrative matters during the Yung-cheng reign. During the former period, instructions were first given orally or, sometimes, in written form to either a eunuch director or an official in the South Library. The latter then prepared a letter embodying the instructions.

The court letter at that time was used essentially to deal with nonadministrative affairs and concerned only the personal business of the emperor or that of the imperial household. For instance, one example shows its use for intra-imperial household communication: the letter, written in connection with the illness of the heir apparent Yin-jeng,[9] was transmitted from the eunuch director in the Summer Palace at Jehol to a eunuch in the capital. Sometimes court letters were used for communication between the K'ang-hsi Emperor and his staff members in the South Library; they concerned scholarly affairs pertaining to the functions of the library.[10] Occasionally, court letters were sent to provincial officials in order to urge them to send in palace memorials reporting on local weather conditions, harvests and so forth; the writers were usually eunuchs.[11] At other times, court letters were transmitted through staff members in the South Library or members of the Imperial Printing Establishment at the Wu-ying Hall to a provincial governor; these concerned recruiting scholars from the provinces to fill posts in inner court offices dealing with compilation works and scientific projects, and sometimes they concerned missionary affairs.[12]

On one occasion the K'ang-hsi Emperor issued a letter through the sub-chancellor of the *Nei-ko,* Chiang T'ing-hsi, who was concurrently serving in the South Library, to summon a local official by the name of Chu Wei-chün (a second-class subprefect in Chihli province). Two aspects of the document are significant: (1) Since Chiang T'ing-hsi later became one of the first inner grand secretaries in the Yung-cheng period, a certain kind of continuity between the South Library and that group can be firmly established. Chang T'ing-yü, the most important figure in the group, was also in the library from the last two decades of the K'ang-hsi reign through the first half of the Yung-cheng reign.[13] Chang and Chiang continued to draft court letters for the Yung-cheng Emperor from the early years of his reign until the system was institutionalized with the establishment of the Grand Council. (2) The practice of sending a court letter directly to a provincial official without going through the *Nei-ko* channel set a precedent of traditional justification for the Yung-cheng Emperor's use of court letters to deal with normal administrative matters, bypassing the "outer *Nei-ko.*"

In view of the fact that this valuable document — the emperor's letter itself — has not yet been published, perhaps it is worth translating; it was quoted in a palace memorial submitted from Chao Hung-hsieh in 1720.

> Your subject Chao Hung-hsieh, governor-general of Chihli and concurrently taking charge of the governor's affairs, and concurrently a junior vice-president of the Board of War and junior vice censor-general with additional meritorious ranks by ten degrees, reverently memorializes: This is to report that I had received a report on KH 59/2/2 [March 10, 1720], from Chu Wei-chün, subprefect of the Lin-ming Kuan, which states:
>
> > On 59/1/5 [February 16, 1720], I received an imperial order transmitted [*ch'uan-chih*] through the subchancellor of the *Nei-ko,* Chiang T'ing-hsi. It reads: "On KH 58/12/24 [February 2, 1720], I received a transmitted imperial order through Prince Ch'eng [Yin-chih] and the sixteenth son of the Emperor [Yin-lu], which reads: 'I [the emperor] heard that Chu Wei-chün, subprefect of the Lin-ming Kuan in Kuang-p'ing prefect, and his son[14] are both versed in music composition [*tz'u-p'u*]; let Chiang T'ing-hsi summon them to Peking and let them take an examination in the Office for Musical Science [*Tz'u-p'u kuan*].' I therefore have sent a messenger to summon you to the capital."
> >
> > In addition I [Chu] also received a personal letter from Subchancellor Chiang. Upon receiving this imperial order, I did not dare delay, and therefore set out on 59/1/24 [March 2, 1720]. To com-

ply with the administrative regulations, I hereby submit this report to you [the governor-general].[15]

The remaining portion of the memorial suggests that the governor-general considered this imperial order rather unusual and that he thought it warranted a palace memorial to report to the emperor secretly: "In view of the fact that Chu Wei-chün is a provincial official and now has been summoned to the capital by imperial order, and that no formal communication [document] was sent to me from the *Nei-ko* or the board, I therefore would like to report this matter in palace memorial since I have received the foregoing report [from Chu]." The vermilion endorsement reads: "Yes" (*shih*).

The court letter system in the Yung-cheng Period underwent important functional changes. In an edict issued in 1729, the Yung-cheng Emperor revealed why it was necessary for him to use court letters in the transmittal of imperial instructions to provincial officials:

> Occasionally, I ordered Prince [I] and/or ministers [*ta-ch'en*] to send court letters secretly to provincial governors-general and governors as well as others in order to deal with important and urgent matters [*chin-yao shih-chien*] or to apprehend important criminals; these matters happened frequently in the provinces. This practice was intended to handle such affairs carefully and to facilitate the [provincial officials'] carrying out their duties . . .[16]

About the functional expansion of the court letter system in the first half of the Yung-cheng reign, several points must be made immediately: (1) The "ministers" who transmitted court letters as mentioned in the above edict were not limited to grand secretaries, but included other court officials as well. (2) The reason these letters were transmitted through various officials was that the subject matter dealt with therein was quite comprehensive: thus, the subject bore upon the duties of the minister concerned in the transmittal. (3) Later, when the inner grand secretaries gradually expanded their functional jurisdiction to include areas that had been under various central administrative organs, they became the almost exclusive writers of court letters.

It has been discovered that the earliest court letter of the Yung-cheng period was written on February 2, 1724.[17] Its transmitters were A-erh-sung-a, chamberlain of the imperial bodyguard, and Nien Hsi, a censor and the son of General Nien Keng-yao. The letter's purpose was to ask

Huang Ping, governor of Shangtung, to present an explanation of why he had failed to impeach a local official named Lo Cheng-nien, a salt intendant whom the emperor had found guilty of corruption.[18]

The two most common types of court letters were signed by Prince I (Yin-hsiang) and/or one or more grand secretaries. After 1725, however, grand secretaries gradually became the main signatories. Meanwhile, a certain format was developed for them toward the end of the Yung-cheng reign.[19]

Although court letters could be sent out independently, in most cases they were written in response to incoming palace memorials that dealt with the arrest of major criminals and other "important and urgent matters" including (1) local finance and surtax problems,[20] (2) secret investigations,[21] (3) preliminary warnings to provincial officials who were secretly impeached by other memorialists,[22] (4) instructions as to local administrative policies,[23] and (5) much else.[24]

The Inner Grand Secretaries and the Origins of the Grand Council. As already mentioned, after the imperial assistants plenipotentiary committee was dissolved in 1725, the Yung-cheng Emperor continued the practice of appointing ad hoc committees (usually, but not always, three trusted men in the court) for carrying out specific missions and handling communications with provincial officials.[25] The origins of the *Chün-chi ch'u,* or Grand Council (a commonly used English translation which is indeed misleading when used for discussion of the origins of this organ in the Yung-cheng period), are closely related to the changing functions of this small group. In 1726, the emperor assigned Yin-hsiang and two grand secretaries, Chang T'ing-yü and Chiang T'ing-hsi, as a kind of committee to make necessary arrangements for the projected campaign against the Eleuths in the northwest. Their duties involved confidential communication with provincial officials in connection with the transport of military supplies to the front. Yin-hsiang was superintendent of affairs of the Board of Revenue; Chang and Chiang, who had both served as president of the board, continued to hold this title even after promotion to grand secretaryship; thus, their duties still accorded with the title.[26] Conferring concurrent titles was an important technique employed by the Yung-cheng Emperor to concentrate power in a small group of confidants over whom he could exercise effective control.

On July 5, 1729 (YC 7/6/10), the secret mission of this three-man committee was made public by the emperor:

> As to military affairs, I have made the necessary plans and prepara-
> tions for a long time. As to all matters concerning military supplies,
> I have entrusted Prince I, and the grand secretaries Chang T'ing-yü
> and Chiang T'ing-hsi, to manage them secretly. As to matters con-
> cerning the transfer of troops on the west front, I have entrusted the
> governor-general Yüeh Chung-ch'i to take full charge of it. They have
> carried out their responsibilities very carefully and secretly. Therefore,
> for over two years, people in the provinces have not known that we
> have been transferring troops and military rations to the front.[27]

Once the mission had been made public and two generalissimos had been formally commissioned to command the expeditionary troops, an office (according to Yeh Feng-mao[28]) was set up temporarily in the Military Manu-facturing Office just outside the Lung-tsung Gate to accommodate secre-tarial staff members called upon for service from the *Nei-ko* on what was apparently a shift basis. Inner Grand Secretary Chang T'ing-yü, how-ever, utilized the South Library to carry out his duties. It can be assumed that before 1729 no specific office had been erected for the committee in the palace. (Had such an office already existed, it would have been impos-sible for court officials and palace personnel not to take notice of it; it would have been ridiculous for the emperor to claim that the secret mission of this ad hoc committee had not been known even to the Manchu princes and court ministers.)

When war finally broke out on the front, the volume of palace memorials from the generals increased to such a point that a separate office was set up to handle them. The name of the office, after undergoing several changes, became the *Pan-li chün-chi ch'u,* or simply *Chün-chi ch'u.* The office was staffed by a group of selected court ministers, all of whom held positions such as vice-president of a central office (rank 2B).[29] Their function was described thus: "those who are on duty in the *Chün-chi ch'u*" (*tsai Chün-chi ch'u hsing-tsou*).[30] Since they were all *ta-ch'en* (a term used in the Yung-cheng period to mean "ministers with the rank 3B or higher"),[31] taking charge of *chün-chi* (military affairs) in the new office, they were referred to as *Chün-chi ta-ch'en* (generally rendered as "grand councillors" by Western historians).

Contrary to common notion,[32] however, the term *Chün-chi ta-ch'en* in the Yung-cheng period did not include the inner grand secretaries; the former were junior ministers in the *Chün-chi ch'u* under the direction of the latter. In all the Yung-cheng records I have examined, Chang T'ing-yü and Chiang T'ing-hsi were referred to as *ta-hsüeh-shih* (grand secretaries) instead of *Chün-chi ta-ch'en;* so they signed themselves in their memorials to the emperor.[33] This distinction explains the puzzling fact that in official records of the period, military affairs were deliberated in at least three ways: (a) by the inner grand secretaries alone,[34] (b) by the *Chün-chi ta-ch'en* alone,[35] or (c) by "the [inner] grand secretaries and the *Chün-chi ta-ch'en*."[36] Had the two types of ministers been the same, the conjunction "and" would be meaningless.[37]

Though semantically this distinction may seem only a quibble, historically it is not. In the power concentration process in the first half of the Yung-cheng reign, the inner grand secretaries played a key role for several years before the *Chün-chi ta-ch'en* appeared on the scene. Even after the *Chün-chi ch'u* was established, the *ta-ch'en* had only a limited function in this new council, handling only military affairs relating to the campaign, whereas the inner grand secretaries, though functioning as senior ministers in the council and also involving themselves with military affairs, performed a variety of additional functions in the central decision-making machinery. The common impression that the *Chün-chi ch'u* was the most powerful organ of the Yung-cheng period is the result not of the council's power per se, but of the comprehensive power of the inner grand secretaries who, after having become senior ministers of the council concurrently, began to utilize that office's secretarial staff to carry out aspects of their comprehensive functions in the central bureaucracy other than those connected with military affairs. To reveal changes in the Yung-cheng power structure, these distinctions must be kept in mind and the Yung-cheng Emperor's concentration of power in his own hands through the inner grand secretaries studied.

The exact date on which the *Chün-chi ch'u* was established is not given in any official account. Many conflicting dates have been suggested,[38] though sometimes the conflict is only apparent. In general, most contemporary historians seem to agree on three points: (1) If the appointment of the three-man committee can be considered the beginning of the *Chün-chi ch'u,* then the date should be somewhere late in 1726.[39] (2) If the date is to be set at the time when the seal *"Pan-li chün-chi yin-hsin"* was cast, then it should be 1732.[40] (3) If the exact date cannot be determined, it is probable that the *Chün-chi ch'u* was established somewhere between 1729 and 1732.[41]

This section is intended to clarify the problem by employing a different approach. First, from among the various documents that supply conflicting dates, that which is most probably correct must be determined. There can be only one correct date, given a common definition for the term *Chün-chi ch'u;* agreement on definition is a necessary prerequisite to meaningful discussion, since the original Chinese term for this organization underwent several changes. Second, in order to determine this most probable date, only the most authoritative documents must be relied upon. Finally, because establishment of the *Chün-chi ch'u* was such a crucial decision, it must have been based on a rationale. Taking the decision as a reference point, it should be possible to trace the various historical forces that explain why such a decision should be made at that particular time; in other words, if the date selected is assumed as based on the most authoritative source, this assumption should be logically supported by the circumstantial conditions.

To qualify as an independent organ in the Ch'ing administration, the *Chün-chi ch'u* should have possessed its own ministers *and* a permanent secretarial staff. Without the latter it could only be called a committee — a term used earlier in this discussion. It should also have had some offices (physical buildings) where secretarial work could be carried out. This is indeed the definition suggested in one of the highly reliable sources, written by Chao I, who served as a secretary in the *Chün-chi ch'u* in the eighteenth century and was a prominent historian in his own right:

> During the Yung-cheng years, military operations were going on in the northwest. Seeing that the *Nei-ko* was located outside the T'ai-ho Gate, and that on-duty staff members were many, the *Chün-hsü fang* [Office of Military Supplies] was established in a place just inside the Lung-tsung Gate so as to prevent divulgence of information. Some secretaries of the *Nei-ko* who were careful in handling things were selected to do the necessary copying. This office later changed its name to *Chün-chi ch'u* . . . offices [that were erected] consisted of only a few rooms built with wooden boards. It was only under the order of the present [Ch'ien-lung] Emperor that these wooden buildings were replaced by brick buildings . . .[42]

In his account, Chao I emphasizes both the physical establishment of the council and the acquisition of a permanent secretarial staff as necessary attributes for its becoming an independent organ; but he fails to suggest the exact time of establishment. If development of this organ could be traced to a year in which these two aspects occurred for the first time, that year could be regarded as the formal time of the *Chün-hsü fang's* establishment. Of course, the name of this office underwent several changes before it becomes *Chün-chi ch'u,* but such changes would not have affected the actual establishment of the office.

Another authoritative source, provided by Yeh Feng-Mao, helps narrow down the possible year in which the organ was established. It also sheds much light on the derivation of the various titles of the office, and on the relation between the court letter system and the palace memorial system on the one hand and the origin of this office on the other. Yeh became a "secretary of the *Nei-ko*" (*chung-shu she-jen* or *she-jen* or *chung-shu*) in spring 1730 and served in that office for ten years. Fellow secretaries of his were selected to serve in the newly erected offices of the *Chün-chi fang* — a term that court officials in the late years of the Yung-cheng reign frequently used to refer to either the original *Chün-hsü fang* or the later *Chü-chi ch'u* — and they became the permanent staff members of that new organ; it is inconceivable that he would not have known when this happened and who was involved. In his *Nei-ko hsiao-chih* (A brief account of the *Nei-ko*), he did indeed take note of these happenings.[43]

In this crucial document Yeh first defines the function of the *Chün-chi fang* in connection with the palace memorial system. "*Chün-chi fang:* This was the office where the inner grand secretaries were on duty. Some palace memorials submitted from capital and provincial high officials were not handed down to the boards for deliberation; they were deliberated on by the [inner] grand secretaries." He then describes the relations between the court letter system and the addition of a permanent secretarial staff to assist the inner grand secretaries — which meant formal separation of the council from the *Nei-ko:* "Originally, all copying work of court letters (*t'ing-chi yü-chi*) sent to the provinces [in response to palace memorials] were made by people [secretaries of the *Nei-ko*] who were on duty in the suburban villa. [Later] several secretaries, including the Manchus Shu-ho-te and Ya-erh-ha-shan and the Chinese Wu Yüan-an and Chiang Pin, showed their willingness to assist the inner grand secretaries permanently instead of being transferred alternately [between the Inner and Outer offices of the *Nei-ko.*]"

Then Yeh explains how this new office was named after it was formally separated from the *Nei-ko,* and how its title underwent several changes thereafter: "Meanwhile, campaigning forces were being sent out in two routes against Ts'e-wang [chief of the Eleuths], and the Board of Revenue had separately set up a suboffice entitled *Chün-hsü fang.* [The newly established office of the inner grand secretaries] was also given the name *Chün-hsü fang.* Gradually, this name was changed to *Chün-chi-fang;* still later this name was changed to *Chün-chi ch'u.*"

This valuable account provides much information about the origin of the *Chün-chi ch'u:* (1) Before the *Chün-hsü fang* was established as a formal body, the three-man group who later came to be called inner grand secretaries had long been functioning. (2) Deliberating on palace memorials and drafting court letters were the main duties of the inner grand secretaries. (3) The *Chün-hsü fang* was established only *after* military operations in the northwest had started. In view of the fact that the secretary Shu-ho-te was made a permanent secretary in this office only at the very end of the eighth year of the Yung-cheng reign (YC 8/12/?, January 1731),[44] the *Chün-hsü fang* would have been established at the same time. (4) Between 1731 and early 1732 (late eighth and early tenth year, the name of this office was changed several times.

On April 4, 1732 (YC 10/3/10), according to the *Ch'ing-shih-lu,* an official seal for this office was cast for the first time. The inscription reads: *Pan-li chün-chi yin-hsin* (Seal for the [Office] of Military Affairs).[45] The seal was intended to be affixed to court letters that dealt with "secret matters" (*mi-hsing shih-chien*). It must be pointed out that though the title *Pan-li chün-chi ch'u* appears for the first time in the *Ch'ing-shih-lu* only after the above date, it had already been in use before the seal was cast, as the context of the document above suggests. A contemporary source records, however, that this title did not become the final designation until the very end of the Yung-cheng reign and perhaps even later, in the early Ch'ien-lung period.[46]

Political and military developments also made it logical to professionalize this office around the same date. Despite the fact that the campaign nominally started in 1729, as symbolized by the designation of Yüeh Chung-ch'i and Fu-erh-tan as generalissimos of the forces of the western and northern routes respectively, fighting actually did not break out until the very end of the eighth year. It appears quite reasonable that the emperor would professionalize the secretarial staff of the *Chün-chi fang* at this time in order to deal with the increasing amount of paperwork resulting from the influx of military reports from the front.

Moreover, the death of Yin-hsiang (Prince I) on June 18, 1730 (YC 8/5/4) made it imperative for the emperor to seek more advisory help from the inner grand secretaries and thus professionalize their office. In an endorsement made on General Yüeh Chung-ch'i's palace memorial, the emperor revealed the confused condition of his mind at this juncture:

> Prince I has passed away. It is utterly impossible for me to describe my sorrows and bitterness in pen and ink. Now I have lost my mental bearing [*fang-ts'un i-luan*]. I am in need of someone who may assist me [as Prince I had done] in state policies and strategies [*shu-chi yün-ch'ou chih chu*]. Seeing that it is a grave matter to launch an attack [against the Eleuths] which will involve large numbers of troops, I therefore entrusted the grand secretaries to summon you secretly to the capital for personal consultations . . .[47]

Shortly after Yin-hsiang's death, the emperor revealed in an edict the multiple roles that this prince had played during his lifetime in assisting the emperor. Military planning, financial control, command of the imperial bodyguard divisions, work in irrigation projects and in matters great and small that were connected with the imperial family and the entire imperial household — "all these," the edict says, "had been handled and planned by Prince I himself [on my behalf]."[48] It was only a logical solution that the many functions performed by Yin-hsiang be distributed to others.

Meanwhile, the emperor became seriously ill, and it became imperative for him to rely more heavily on the inner grand secretaries in disposing of state affairs, including handling military reports from the northwest and transmitting his instructions in court letters. He did not fully recover for several months (sometime during September). In an edict issued on November 28, 1730, he said: "During the months between late summer and early autumn, I was temporarily ill. [The grand secretaries] Ma-erh-sai, Chang T'ing-yü, and Chiang T'ing-hsi, assisted me in handling state affairs [*chi-wu*]; they did this always with great impartiality, carefulness, and propriety . . . Therefore, for several months, I was enabled to rest quietly and achieved recovery — all due to their assistance . . ."[49]

Secretarial professionalization of the *Chün-chi fang* must have been catalyzed, however, by the war that actually started at the very end of the eighth year. After Yüeh Chung-ch'i had been summoned to the capital, the Eleuths made some surprise raids against Chinese military posts; reports first reached the emperor on January 28, 1731 (YC 8/12/21).[50] Subsequent military reports must have multiplied. This, then, would seem to be a logical time for the emperor to have assigned a permanent secretarial staff to the *Chün-chi fang* in order to meet the urgent demands of communications — an assumption supported by the fact that Shu-ho-te became the first "secretary of the *Chün-chi fang*" (*chün-chi chang-ching*) exactly at this juncture. Procedural evidence also supports this conclusion. For instance, in the archives of the National Palace Museum, there is an unpublished palace memorial submitted by Yüeh Chung-ch'i in early 1730 dealing with military supplies (*chün-hsü*) on the front. Replying to this, the emperor's vermilion endorsement reads: "You have handled this matter very properly. Let this memorial be handed down to the Board [of Revenue] so that a duplicate may be made and filed in the said board (*chiao pu ch'ao-lu ts'un-an*)."[51]

From 1731, however, palace memorials dealing with reports on the same matter were no longer handed down to the board; their duplicates were for the first time made and filed in a special office that was called *Pan-li chün-hsü ch'u.*[52] In the same year it is recorded that similar matters were handed down to the *Pan-li chün-hsü ta-ch'en* ("grand councillors") in order to keep them informed.[53] These procedural changes suggest that though the new office had existed for perhaps a couple of years, it did not become an independent entity until the early months of 1731. The earliest reference in published official records to a rather descriptive term *Pan-li-chün-chi shih-wu ta-ch'en* (also referring to the grand councillors) is found in the same year.[54]

In sum, if establishment of the *Chün-chi ch'u* is treated as a reference point in a dynamic process of historical developments, the sources drawn upon here all support the conclusion that this establishment should have occurred in early 1731. After the campaign in the northwest had been concluded, at the end of the Yung-cheng period, the inner grand secretaries continued their service in the *Chün-chi ch'u,* assisting the emperor in deliberation of both civil and military affairs. In other words, the *Chün-chi ch'u* or, more accurately, the inner grand secretaries, now continued, rather than began, the nonmilitary functions that had already been theirs in the precampaign period. The difference lay in the fact that the group was now an official organ, totally separated from the *Nei-ko* after 1731. Its institutional status was sanctioned by the professionalization of its personnel and the seal cast for its office.

Functions of the Inner Grand Secretaries. Contemporary studies have left the Yung-cheng period nearly a blank in their descriptions of the functions of the inner grand secretaries — a fact that is due mainly to the extreme scantiness of relevant sources. So far, no documents have been published that would provide historians with enough raw material to study the problem. Therefore, in dealing with *Chün-chi ch'u* functions, which became nearly synonymous with those of the inner grand secretaries after 1731, administrative historians have relied almost entirely on documents of the post-Yung-cheng reigns, sometimes dating as late as the end of the Ch'ing dynasty.[55]

The following discussion is of the comprehensive functions of the ad hoc committee of inner grand secretaries (and sometimes Prince I), who greatly assisted the Yung-cheng Emperor to concentrate power in his own hands during the first half of his reign. It is based essentially on some unpublished documents discovered only recently in the National Palace Museum archives, "the only surviving original documents of the Yung-cheng period" with direct bearing on our subject.[56] The documents are kept in a wooden box wrapped with yellow damask and labeled thus: "*Tsou-p'ien* [short memorials] containing secret deliberations of the Prince and ministers are kept in this box" (*Wang ta-jen mi-i tsou-p'ien tsai-nei*). The "Prince" (*Wang*) refers to Yin-hsiang and "ministers" (*ta-jen*) to the three inner grand secretaries, Chang T'ing-yü, Chiang T'ing-hsi, and Ma-erh-sai. Although no dates are affixed to these *tsou-p'ien,* nor to their "attachments" (*fu-chien*), I have identified them by cross-references and internal evidence as written during the years 1729–1731. Occasionally, other sources may be used to supplement this group of documents.

In general, the inner grand secretaries performed in three basic kinds of capacities in the Yung-cheng bureaucracy: advisory, secretarial, and coordinating. Their advisory function concerned mostly deliberations on various suggestions or petitions contained in palace memorials presented by provincial authorities; their secretarial function concerned primarily the drafting of imperial instructions (mainly court letters); and their coordinating function concerned predecisional consultations between the emperor and his high-ranking officials both in the capital and in the provinces. Of course, in the actual governmental process, the three functions overlapped; for instance, in performing either the advisory or coordinating functions, the grand secretaries would inevitably involve themselves with secretarial work as well. Moreover, all three functions entailed intragovernmental communications involving prescribed procedures. Due to the unique structure of Ch'ing documents, such procedures were often shown right in the documents themselves, for which reason it is desirable here to translate them or major parts of them.

Two cases may be cited to illustrate the function of the inner grand secretaries in military affairs related to the campaign in the northwest: (1) The committee deliberated on some palace memorials of Ch'a-pi-na, the acting governor-general of Shensi, probably in 1729. These memorials were handed down to the ad hoc committee made up of Chang T'ing-yü and other inner grand secretaries; Chang, as noted earlier, was concurrently president of the Board of Revenue, hence he referred in his memorial to that board as "my board" (*ch'en pu*). After the deliberation, the committee prepared a *tsou-p'ien* that reported to the emperor two actions taken regarding the memorials: first, "we have made a duplicate copy of Ch'a's memorial for records." (Ch'a's memorial reads: "As to the military rations that are under the management of the Kansu area, I [Ch'a] have issued strict orders to the various routes to make them ready so that these rations may be transported for sure beyond the Pass [*ch'u-k'ou*].") The second action was a recommendation: "Ch'a-pi-na and others have impeached Wang Tzu-chung, magistrate of the Chuang-lang district, for the latter's illegal uses of the military rations wagons for carrying smuggled rice and beans. We have made a copy of the said palace memorial and sent the copy to the Board [of Personnel] for deliberating a severe punishment [*yen-ch'a i-tsou*]."

After the Board of Personnel's deliberation, a *tsou-p'ien* was presumably presented to the emperor for final decision. This kind of *tsou-p'ien* usually contains a closing phrase reading: "We reverently present this memorial for your decision [*chin-tsou ch'ing-chih*]." [57]

(2) When Hsü Jung, governor of Lan-chou, presented a palace memorial requesting imperial permission to leave Lan-chou for Su-chou in order

to better execute his duties, the inner grand secretaries made the following suggestions: "We find that the distance between Lan-chou and Su-chou is one thousand and five hundred *li;* and that Su-chou still falls within the jurisdiction of the governor, hence [Hsü Jung] can still take care of his duties as a governor [even after having moved to Su-chou]. Therefore, if Hsü Jung's request be permitted that he move to Su-chou temporarily in order to assist the management of military affairs, we feel this measure would be a beneficial one." [58] Presumably a court letter was sent to Hsü Jung to inform him of the emperor's permission.

Palace memorials dealing with the noncampaign military affairs of the Miao tribes of Kweichow and Yunnan (*Miao-wu* or *Miao-chiang shih-wu*) were not deliberated by the grand councillors, but by the inner grand secretaries (later, princes and other court ministers were also assigned to manage the Miao affairs). The communications exchanged in 1729 between the latter and O-erh-t'ai, governor-general of Yunnan, Kweichow, and Kwangsi, serve as an excellent illustration.[59]

Earlier in 1729, O-erh-t'ai sent the emperor a palace memorial in which he suggested that additional guard-stations (*hsün*) be set up in the Miao area. The emperor endorsed the memorial, instructing O-erh-t'ai to present a *t'i-pen* through the *Nei-ko* channel so that a formal decision could be made. When the *t'i-pen* had reached the emperor, in the seventh month of the same year, he felt that there were still some doubts as to the feasibility of the suggestion; hence he ordered the inner grand secretaries Chang T'ing-yü and Chiang T'ing-hsi to return the *t'i-pen* secretly to O-erh-t'ai with a covering court letter embodying the emperor's instruction that O-erh-t'ai reconsider the matter. Upon receiving the court letter, O-erh-t'ai replied in a letter (*ch'i-chien*) that was sent directly to the inner grand secretaries:

> O-erh-t'ai, governor-general of Yunnan, Kweichow and Kwangsi, hereby sincerely replies: On YC 7/7/29, a joint court letter from you two grand secretaries reached me through the express delivery service of the Board of War [literally, the express warrant of the Board of War (*Ping-pu huo-p'ai*) has delivered to me a joint letter], which reads:
> "We received an imperial instruction [*feng shang-yü*] on YC 7/7/2, which says: 'With regard to the establishment of new guard-stations in the Miao region as O-erh-t'ai had memorialized earlier, I have given him detailed instructions in my endorsement . . . You may

send back his *t'i-pen* to him secretly and make out a court letter transmitting my instruction that he carefully reconsider the matter. If he still thinks that guard-stations should definitely be established in those palaces [Pai-ting, Tsung-ti, and other places], he may go ahead and do this while returning this *t'i-pen* secretly to me. I will approve his request accordingly. If, however, he thinks there are additional places where guard-stations should also be established, he may rewrite his *t'i-pen* and return it to me while at the same time he may go ahead and establish them right away lest the matter should be delayed by the long journey of communications.' We, therefore, reverently send you this court letter according to the imperial order [*chin-tz'u tsun-chih chi-hsin ch'ien-lai*]. You, governor-general, may carefully consider these matters and carry them out according to your best judgement."

In the remaining part of this letter, O-erh-t'ai, having reiterated his original view and given the reasons for it, concluded:

According to Erh-t'ai's opinion, it would still seem necessary to establish guard-stations in these several places. While I am going right ahead with this work according to the imperial instruction, I would like to return to you the original *t'i-pen* through the post express so that you may present it to the emperor. I sincerely send this letter of reply.

After receiving this letter, the inner grand secretaries made up a draft rescript for the *t'i-pen;* in addition, the following undated *tsou-p'ien* was written:

Concerning the *t'i-pen* presented by Governor-general O-erh-t'ai in which he requested that in several places, such as Pai-ting and Tsung-ti of the Kweichow province, guard-stations be established, we received the imperial instructions to send a court letter to him . . . Now according to his letter in reply, he still claims that guard-stations should be set up in those places just mentioned. He has also returned the original *t'i-pen*. We have made up a draft rescript slip reading "let this be carried out according to the request of the said governor-general" [*chao kai-tu so-ch'ing hsing*]. Now we reverently present this *t'i-pen* with the draft rescript slip inserted therein together with the letter that O-erh-t'ai has sent us.

Two cases illustrate the inner grand secretaries' deliberation of general military affairs: (1) On YC 8/7/14 (Aug. 27, 1730), the amount of silver taels to be allotted to Chinese troops (*lü-ying*) as reward was deliberated.[60]

The emperor approved the secretaries' deliberation accordingly. (2) Sometimes, once an imperial decision had been made on the basis of the inner grand secretaries' deliberation, local officials would memorialize again, making different suggestions. The case of Ch'en Wang-chang serves as a good example. Based on an earlier deliberation made jointly by Yin-hsiang and the inner grand secretaries, an imperial order was given to the effect that some able-bodied male militia be selected to serve as personal bodyguards (*ch'ang-sui*) to local officials below the level of governor, such as financial and judicial commissioners, taotai and prefects. Upon receiving this imperial order through the Board of War, Ch'en Wang-chang, commander-in-chief of Nan-ch'ang, memorialized the emperor, suggesting that able-bodied men not be selected from the common people:

> I think since financial and judicial commissioners as well as circuit intendants were stationed in the same city with the governors-general and/or governor in the provincial capital, then soldiers from the various units [*piao*] under the latter's command may be used to protect the former when the former hold official conferences with the latter or when they leave the capital for other locales. Even those circuit intendants and prefects who are not stationed in the capital may also reply on the soldiers under the command of the commanders-in-chief or brigade generals for protection.[61]

The emperor referred this memorial to the original deliberators headed by Yin-hsiang. The prince and the grand secretaries replied to the emperor's request in a palace memorial that stated the inconveniences involved in Ch'en's suggestions, expressed their views by concluding that "it would seem still better to retain our original deliberation," and requested that the emperor finalize the decision.

Yin-hsiang and Grand Secretaries Chang T'ing-yü and Chiang T'ing-hsi all held posts concurrently in the Board of Revenue in the positions of superintendent or president; it was quite logical, therefore, that palace memorials dealing with financial matters were handed down to them for deliberation. Financial reports submitted to render annual expenditures of the provincial governments (*tsou-hsiao*), among many other items, were strictly checked and deliberated by the ad hoc supreme deliberative committee.[62]

Yang K'un, acting governor-general of Chihli (YC 7/1/? to YC 7/6/?) submitted a *t'i-pen* in 1729 in which he reported to the emperor the annual expenditures during the fiscal year of 1728 in the province of Chihli, together with the Yellow Book in which the expenditures were itemized.[63] Upon examining the Yellow Book, the committee found that some items were funded properly but some were not; thus, in their *tsou-p'ien* they stated: "As to the public funds that the said governor-general [Yang's predecessor] spent on his attending joint sessions of trying provincial criminals, we wonder how this could be justified since he had already been given additional supplementary salaries [*yang-lien yin-liang*] [64] to meet such expenses." [65] In addition, the committee found three more items for which public funds were illegally spent. They therefore suggested that "these four items ought to be denied approval" (*ying pu-chun k'ai-hsiao*). Such a draft rescript was inserted in the Yellow Book and presented to the emperor. The committee also suggested that the total sum involved in unapproved items be paid back by the former governor-general I Chao-hsung and the associate governor-general Liu Shih-shu.

The case of Chang Kuang-ssu illustrates the committee's deliberative powers on civil appointment. Chang, governor of Kweichow (YC 6/6/? to 10/2/?), memorialized the emperor and requested permission to have a number of new *chin-shih* and some expectants of local offices sent to his province for appointments. The committee saw the feasibility of this request and recommended that it be granted.

Regarding judicial matters:[66] in 1730, the inner grand secretaries deliberated the case of Ts'ao Liu, who had been exiled to servitude in frontier regions under an imperial order (YC 8/3/30)[67] but later found guilty on still another count. The grand secretaries suggested that he be brought back for retrial. Cases like this usually involved serious crimes.

Matters involving river conservancy were under the jurisdiction of the director-general of river conservancy (*ho-tao tsung-tu*) and the Board of Works. For instance, when K'ung Yü-hsün, director-general for conservation of the South River (*Nan-ho tsung-tu*) (YC 7/3/? to 8/4/?), memorialized the emperor on some financial problems in connection with the river work, the inner grand secretaries suggested that "the said director-general should provide an honest report" on some details which required clarification before the grand secretaries would make concrete proposals.[68]

An important feature in the Yung-cheng Emperor's control policy was literary inquisition. Suspicious writings presented by provincial authorities to the throne were usually examined and evaluated by the inner grand secretaries in order to determine the real nature of the contents. For instance, a *tsou-p'ien* submitted by the inner grand secretaries in 1730 reveals their role in this process. The *tsou-p'ien* contains their deliberation on two Chinese scholars: Hsü Chün and Chang Ching-heng, both suspected for writing treasonable innuendos in their poems. The Hsü Chün case is seldom mentioned in Ch'ing sources or by contemporary writers,[69] and is therefore worth translating:

> Your subjects, Grand Secretaries Chang T'ing-yü and Chiang T'ing-hsi memorialize: We have read Hsü Chün's books entitled *Chien-chiao shih-kao* (two volumes), *Wu-hsü wen-kao* (one volume), and *Tsa-lu* (one volume), and one sheet of paper containing some random verses. Yin-chi-shan [governor-general of Liang-kuang] has marked out all the sneering phrases therein. Other poems and essays in his writings contain not a single grateful word. His *Tsa-lu* even contains language implying his strong resentment of Master Chu Hsi's being elevated to one of the Ten Great Philosophers; a pair of parallel verses, for instance, in the *Tsa-lu* reads:
>
> > How sad for the Confucianists:
> > To bend their knees to such degeneracy!
>
> Being rebellious and arrogant, he deserves a punishment more severe than death.
>
> We would like to mention that Hsü Chün is the son of Hsü Ch'ien-hsüeh, formerly president of the Board of Punishments. His father and uncles all achieved the highest official positions in the court and all his brothers were awarded the advanced degrees, and he himself is a member of the Hanlin Academy, yet it is indeed a hateful thing that he should dare to behave lawlessly, maliciously defaming [the late emperor]. We earnestly request your instruction to order Yin-chi-shan to arrest Hsü Chün and put him in chains. He ought to be delivered to the capital so that the Board of Punishments may conduct a severe trial in order to arrive at a proposal for his punishment. We have placed all his writings in securely sealed envelopes and we will turn them over to the said board for detailed examinations when he arrives.
>
> As to the *K'ung-ming-tzu chi* by Chang Ching-heng, though Yin-chi-shan has said that no rebellious words were found in it, we will nevertheless report our findings separately because this book contains many volumes and it thus requires a longer time to complete our reading carefully.[70]

Hsü Chün was later found guilty, sentenced to "immediate decapitation," and executed accordingly.[71] This affair again illustrates how skillfully the early Manchu emperors used Chinese to control Chinese. Chinese played a major role, not only in discovering crucial cases,[72] but also in reviewing them before they were referred to the judiciary departments for trial. The fact that Chang Ching-heng was apparently found not guilty indicates that the Yung-cheng Emperor could be discriminating in such decisions.

In their deliberation on a palace memorial of Yin-chi-shan, director-general of grain transport, the grand secretaries considered that Yin's suggestions were excellent regarding the charge of transport fees, hence they recommended that his suggestions "be made a permanent rule" (*yung-wei ting-li*).[73]

Though ceremonial matters had originally fallen under the jurisdiction of the Board of Ceremonials, they were now also referred to the inner grand secretaries for deliberation. For example,[74] the secretaries were asked to deliberate on the proper formalities to be maintained between the new special censors (*kuan-feng cheng-su shih*) on the one hand and the local provincial commissioners and circuit intendants on the other, as well as on the proper documents to be used in their communications.

Imperial decisions in the Yung-cheng period were not always arrived at solely by the deliberations of inner grand secretaries. Following the example of his father,[75] the Yung-cheng Emperor often referred some memorials to provincial authorities for their opinions. Such intragovernmental coordination involving predecisional communications, a few examples of which will serve to illustrate, were carried out through the inner grand secretaries.

(1) Predecisional consultations were sought with provincial authorities before appointments were actually made. The following case concerning the qualifications of Ch'en Lun-chiung, who was being considered for the post of commander-in-chief, is a good illustration.[76] The *tsou-p'ien* presented by the inner grand secretaries also sheds light on the actual procedure of the "draft rescript" system in the *Nei-ko*:

> Following an imperial order we have asked Governor-general Kao Ch'i-cho about the feasibility of considering Ch'en Lun-chiung's qualifications for the post of commander-in-chief. Kao Ch'i-chao's memorial in response to this inquiry says, "Ch'en Lun-chiung, as far as talent goes, is a mediocre person, hence is not suited to the post. However, in view of the fact that he is young and sturdy, and is acquainted with naval affairs, he would make a good candidate for a post of colonel or lower and so forth." Therefore, on the draft

rescript slip concerning Ch'en Lun-chiung's demotion or transfer we have added another phrase, "Let [Ch'en] come to the capital for an interview with the emperor" [*lai-ching yin-chien*]. We will expect the imperial instruction as to his actual appointment after the interview. Obeying the imperial order Kao Ch'i-cho also has recommended that Ts'ai T'ien-lüeh and others be considered in order of descending priority for the said post. We also have entered these candidates in the draft rescript pending your final decisions [*kung-hou ch'in-ting*]. The original list of candidates presented by Kao Ch'i-chao is also herewith enclosed [with this *tsou-p'ien*].[77]

The post was assigned to Chang Ch'i-yün, not to Ts'ai T'ien-lüeh, who ranked number one on the list. Why was Chang chosen? Before his elevation to this new post as acting commander-in-chief he had been the brigade general of Nan-ao.[78] In less than three years he had risen from the post of major (rank 3B) to this highest military position (rank 1A). A series of palace memorials he had submitted, and the emperor's responses to them, suggest that no personal relationship existed between them; the documents reveal, however, that Chang was extraordinarily conscientious and hard-working and, most important, highly competent. The emperor thought very highly of him.[79] According to the Fukien gazetteer,[80] he died in 1732 of overwork, only a year after his new appointment; the gazetteer included his biography under the heading "distinguished officials." This case suggests, then, that in making crucial appointments, the Yung-cheng Emperor carefully and meticulously sought officials whose diligence and competence matched his own.

(2) Predecisional consultations were sought from provincial authorities before new regulations were made, as illustrated by the following *tsou-p'ien:* "Concerning the suggestion that robbery cases in the provinces ought to be tried jointly by both the civil and military officials, we have asked Li Wei [in a court letter] for his opinion. Now Li Wei has replied to our request, saying that 'this matter ought to be carried out but the regulations governing this practice [*li-fa*] ought to be perfect.' We have copied this item separately to request the imperial permission that it be handed down to the board concerned for deliberation." [81]

(3) Predecisional consultations were sought through the original memorialist before his *t'i-pen* was formally acted upon by the emperor. The aforementioned case relating to O-erh-t'ai's suggestions that guard-stations be established in the Miao region serves as a good illustration of this procedure.

The emperor sometimes even asked the grand secretaries to send a court letter to a certain memorialist in order to instruct the latter how to write his *t'i-pen* before he presented it; a palace memorial submitted by T'ien Wen-ching illustrates:

> T'ien Wen-ching, governor of Honan, reverently memorializes . . . On YC 4/12/17 [January 8, 1727] I received a court letter from the grand secretaries of the *Nei-ko* Fu-ning-an, Chu Shih, and Chang T'ing-yü. It reads: "We have been ordered by the emperor to give you the following instruction: 'As to censor Hsieh Chi-shih's impeachment of T'ien Wen-ching, governor of Honan, I have issued an edict to announce my decision based on impartiality and justice. T'ien Wen-ching, after having seen this edict, naturally ought to express his thanks to me by submitting a *t'i-pen*. You three people may send a court letter secretly [*mi-chi-hsin*] instructing him to present his thanks-giving *t'i-pen* secretly, together with his palace memorial. After I have read it, I shall return it to him. Then he may submit his *t'i-pen* [publicly through the *Nei-ko*]' . . ." [82]

This court letter was sent to T'ien in connection with a factional struggle in the bureaucracy. T'ien was then one of the most trusted provincials of the emperor; Hsieh impeached him at the instigation of other interests who were jealous of T'ien's position of imperial favor. The emperor suspected this and punished Hsieh instead of T'ien. The emperor instructed T'ien to send his *t'i-pen* draft secretly to him first, so that T'ien could make necessary corrections to fit his intention and thus win public opinion in the court — at the time, antagonistic forces were still strong and constantly critical of the emperor's decisions. [83]

(4) Predecisional consultations were sought from provincial authorities in order to determine the feasibility of changing military systems (*ying-chih*). The case embodied in Hao Yü-lin's palace memorial of 1730 provides a good illustration. [84]

The whole process began with a suggestion made by Wang Shao-hsü, commander-in-chief of Kwangtung, who, in four palace memorials, suggested that the military systems in that province be reorganized. The matter was first referred to Yin-hsiang and the inner grand secretaries and subsequently to K'ung Yü-hsün, director-general of river conservancy, for their respective opinions. After all this, however, the emperor still could not arrive at a decision; he therefore ordered the grand secretaries to dispatch a court letter to Hao Yü-lin, governor-general of Kwangtung, and

Fu-t'ai, acting governor of the same province, requesting that they deliberate on the matter. Along with the letter were sent copies of Wang Shao-hsü's palace memorials, the original memorial of Prince I and the inner grand secretaries, and the palace memorial of K'ung Yü-hsün, all embodying their respective deliberations on the matter. Subsequently, Hao and Fu submitted a palace memorial (dated YC 8/3/26) enclosing the records of their deliberations. The emperor, in his vermilion endorsement, praised the conscientious attitude in their deliberations; but he felt that the matter was so weighty that he must ask court ministers (the grand secretaries) for further deliberation before announcing his final decision.

From the above, it becomes clear that the role played by the inner grand secretaries in the communication-decision process of the Yung-cheng bureaucracy was indeed a comprehensive one. In addition to drafting the imperial rescripts, which was originally their chief function, they were asked to deliberate on matters that had been within the jurisdiction of the central boards and other deliberative bodies. It was through a process of concentrating advisory, secretarial, and coordinating functions all in one informal committee that the Yung-cheng Emperor achieved a high degree of concentration of power in his government.

The secretarial function of the inner grand secretaries was essentially connected with the drafting procedures of two types of imperial instructions (*shang-yü*): one was issued publicly through the *Nei-ko* and hence was called "public imperial instruction" (*ming-fa shang-yü* or, in abbreviation, *ming-fa*);[85] the other was issued through the inner grand secretaries on duty in the inner court and was thus called "court dispatch" (*t'ing-chi*) or "court letter" (*tzu-chi* or *tzu*). When inner grand secretaries were called upon to draft imperial instructions, the procedures were essentially the same, so that brief analysis of the drafting procedure of court letters clarifies the secretarial role of the inner grand secretaries in the imperial decision-making process.

When the Yung-cheng Emperor wanted a court letter drafted by the inner grand secretaries, he would call in one of them, usually the chief grand secretary, for a personal audience. The secretary would "receive an oral instruction from the emperor" (*ch'eng-chih* or *mien-ch'eng*),[86] which he had to "commit to memory" (*ch'iang-chi*).[87] The inner grand secretaries then "made up a draft in the form of a *che-p'ien* or *tsou-p'ien*, according to the emperor's oral instruction" (*tsuan-ni* or *ni-chih*); the draft was then presented to the emperor again so that he could check the accuracy of the written instruction (technically, *shu-chih* or *shu*).[88] One example suffices to illustrate this step: the following *che-p'ien* suggests that the court letter concerned was issued on the emperor's own initiative without asking for deliberation:

> We received the following imperial order [orally]: "Chang Yuan-tso hired six hundred extra porters beyond the authorized number. This he did in order to show his cautiousness in transporting military supplies. All the wages and rations, as well as those oxen and donkeys that died as a result of this mission, are permitted to be paid from public funds instead of charging him to repay it personally." We have now made a duplicate copy of his original palace memorial and have reverently written up the imperial order in a dispatch [*hsing-wen*] [that is, a court letter].[89]

Sometimes the draft was made on a separate piece of paper and sent with a separate *tsou-p'ien* that contained only one simple phrase, such as: "We would like to present this imperial instruction for your review that we have reverently drafted under the imperial order" (*ch'en-ten tsun-chih kung-ni shang-yü ch'eng-lan*).[90] Once the emperor had approved the draft, it was "returned to the grand secretaries" (*fa-ch'u*).[91] Finally, a formal court letter, based on the approved draft, would be prepared and delivered to the courier office for dispatch.

Court letters were transmitted by the horse express service of the postal system. They were first sealed securely in a paper envelope in the *Chün-chi ch'u*, and the seam of the envelope was stamped with the official seal of the council. It was then sent to the Couriers Office (*Chieh-pao ch'u*),[92] a sub-office under the remount department of the Board of War.[93]

The required speed of transmission of a court letter was noted on the outside of the envelope by the secretaries of the *Chün-chi ch'u*. If the notation read "by horse express rate" (*ma-shang fei-ti*), it meant that the document was to be transmitted at the rate of 300 *li* per day. If the court letter dealt with not only important but also urgent matters, the rate would be specified: "400 *li* or 500 *li* per day" or "600 *li* per day." [94] The court letter and this rapid transmission system were the ingenious innovation of the Manchu rulers. The following comment by Chao I (1727–1814), an eminent historian of the eighteenth century, may well reflect how effective his contemporaries thought it was:

> This is something which never happened in previous dynasties. When the emperor's decision on some important state affair had to be made public [through the *Nei-ko* channel] and then followed by a communication [*tzu*] of the board concerned, the content of the decision would have been known to every one. Furthermore, the ordinary postal service was too slow. People who were sent from the provinces to the capital in order to learn the imperial decision on a certain matter [concerning the province] might hire an express horse rider to outrun the [ordinary] postal courier [so that people in the province with whom the decision was concerned] might take measures in advance. Ever since the court letter system was invented [the communication system] became not only secret but also swift. This new institution began in the Yung-cheng period. The format of the court letters was designed by Chang T'ing-yü and approved [by the Yung-cheng Emperor].[95]

The Transformed Structure. The official establishment of the *Chün-chi ch'u* and the use of court letters to transmit major imperial decisions in the Yung-cheng bureaucracy signaled the final step in institutionalization of the palace memorial system. Within the new communications network, imperial response to incoming palace memorials could take various forms. There were at least three possible outgoing channels now associated with the palace memorial system.

First, if a palace memorial simply contained secret reports, the Yung-cheng Emperor would return it with his vermilion endorsement to the sender via the same route;[96] no official decision would result. The great majority of palace memorials in the *Chu-p'i yü-chih* fall into this category, which constituted the secret channel of communication handed down from the K'ang-hsi Emperor. Second, incoming palace memorials could result in the issuing of court letters, either to the original sender or to other provincial officials; this was the semisecret channel of communication in the Yung-cheng reign. Third, incoming palace memorials could also result in the issuing of edicts or rescripts publicly through the *Nei-ko*. Under such circumstances, memorials and imperial decisions would be made public in the same procedure used for *pen-chang*.[97]

Four types of political usage, each represented by one of the four channels of communication, can be perceived: secret, semisecret, semiopen, and open politics. The first three were outgrowths of the use of palace memorials, whereas the other — the *pen-chang* channel — had existed before the new system originated. From the Yung-cheng reign on, all imperial decisions on important state affairs were made through one of the three new channels, whereas the *pen-chang* channel was used only for routine affairs which could be settled according to precedent or administrative regulations.

Judging from the scope of deliberative power of the inner grand secretaries, it is clear that the Yung-cheng Emperor practically transferred major deliberative powers from all the deliberative bodies to a small group of trusted ministers. In this sense, the expanded use of palace memorials not only resulted in basic alteration of the communication-decision network, it also affected the functions of the deliberative bodies and institutionalized the *Chün-chi ch'u* into an all-inclusive organization in the central administration. These changes, commented on by several influential observers in the eighteenth century, were summarized by Prince Chao-lien (1780–1833) in his *Hsiao-t'ing tsa-lu*: "According to the established institutions at the beginning of our dynasty, deliberative princes and ministers had always been appointed from among the Manchus [banner officials]. All weighty military and state affairs which, according to the early Ch'ing practice, were not entrusted to the *Nei-ko* to make draft rescripts were handed down to them for deliberation . . ." Chao-lien then noted the fundamental change which had occurred: "During the middle of the Yung-cheng reign, the *Chün-chi ch'u* was established which gradually absorbed the power of the deliberative princes, leaving merely the name of the latter which became no more than honorable concurrent titles for Manchu ministers." He also noted the termination of the assembly, remarking that: "Eventually, in 1790, even these empty titles were abolished forever by the Ch'ien-lung Emperor." [98]

That edict of 1790 relates the changes in somewhat more detail:

> From the beginning of our dynasty, deliberative princes and ministers had been appointed. This was because, during that time, there existed a Deliberative Council [*I-cheng-ch'u*]. Princes and ministers were appointed to staff this office to take care of the affairs concerned. But, ever since the *Chün-chi ch'u* was established in the Yung-cheng period, the grand councillors were called in daily for audiences and to receive imperial instructions. Thereafter, however, Manchu grand secretaries and presidents of the Six Boards were still given the empty title of

"deliberative princes or ministers"; yet they were not given anything to do. This is indeed an institution which bears only a name without any reality . . . Therefore, let these empty titles be abolished forever.[99]

As mentioned, the organizational breakup of the *Nei-ko* into two parts was the natural result of the expanded use of palace memorials at the expense of the functions of the *pen-chang* system. Therefore, after separation of the *Chün-chi ch'u* from the outer *Nei-ko*, the latter lost much of its importance as the supreme secretarial organ of the emperor. As Chao I observed: "Since the Yung-cheng period only *pen-chang* were entrusted to the *Nei-ko,* and it became the duty of the grand councillors to receive the emperor's [oral] instructions concerning major decisions on important civil state affairs and weighty military affairs." [100]

The Assembly of Nine Ministers was equally affected by the appearance of the *Chün-chi ch'u.* As has been discussed, this deliberative body never functioned properly up to the end of the K'ang-hsi period [101] — a situation perpetuated during the early years of Yung-cheng.[102] One of the major functions of the assembly, to nominate candidates for high-ranking official posts, was practically superseded by the secret nomination practice (*mi-pao*) that used palace memorials.[103] After the *Chün-chi ch'u* had come into being, the assembly gradually became an unimportant body from which the emperor occasionally sought information about conditions in various areas of the empire. The Yung-cheng Emperor explained its value in the following terms: "The reason why I have handed those cases [memorials] to the Assembly of Nine Ministers for deliberation was because I did not know [their] details and was not familiar with the local conditions [with which the memorials were concerned]." [104] In other words, memorials were generally handed down to the assembly primarily to seek factual information in connection with their contents, not to seek proposals concerning decisions.

In conclusion, I shall try to draw the various strands of this study together, treating the K'ang-hsi and Yung-cheng reigns in sequence. The different value systems of the two emperors meant that their control policies were directed toward different ends; their personal motivations dictated the forms that structural changes to the communication system would take. For the K'ang-hsi Emperor, the main problem was that of imperial succession and the curbing of factionalism; the Yung-cheng Emperor used the palace memorial system to increase the effectiveness of his control over the bureaucracy in general. This survey of the transformed communication-decision structure — its rationale, working principles, and prerequisites — will, it is hoped, shed some light on the monarchical decay that came later in the Ch'ing dynasty. Once the role played by human motivation in the lives of these two emperors and the impact of that motivation on their social milieu has been perceived, it is possible to look at their successors with new eyes.

The K'ang-hsi Reign. By the middle of the K'ang-hsi reign, the communication-decision structure of the central government had three main components: the emperor himself was at the apex; there were the central administrative organs, such as the Six Boards and the various departments; and there were the deliberative bodies, made up of princes and ministers or of the nine ministers and censors or of representatives from all these groups. The main function of the central bureaucracy was to assist the emperor in governing the provinces. Though each province had its own administrative hierarchy, important matters were always referred to Peking. Judicious decisions by the emperor were essential to the efficiency of provincial administration and to the political stability of China; accordingly, efficient communications and reliable information-gathering techniques were essential to the imperial decision-maker.

The K'ang-hsi Emperor received the bulk of his information from the provinces through memorials conveyed by the Transmission Office, sorted in the *Nei-ko,* and referred to one of the boards or to one of the deliberative bodies for comment. He could also get information from the censors, from provincial officials summoned to an audience, from special commissioners dispatched to the provinces to investigate specific problems, or by his own observations during imperial tours. Each source had operational limitations. The traditional memorial system was limited by rigid formalities, and the open clearing process meant that members of the bureaucracy knew the memorials' contents long before the emperor did. The censors often proved unreliable: they might themselves be involved in a particular faction, they could be timorous, or they might rely on hearsay. The audience system was inevitably limited by the time and expense of travel. Similar problems made it impossible to organize an imperial tour, or even to appoint special commissioners, whenever a local crisis occurred.

These limitations would not have been serious if the various components of the central government had operated efficiently and impartially. But all the deliberative bodies suffered from tensions and inequalities between Manchus and Chinese, and their proceedings were often dominated by strong factional leaders. Also, the size of these bodies — often fifty men or more would meet at a time — made careful debate impossible. Proceedings were marred by selfishness, personal connections, and nepotism and by rigid formalities. As might be expected, the emperor found that the recommendations made by the deliberative bodies were frequently distorted or even erroneous.

By the middle of his reign, the K'ang-hsi Emperor was clearly aware that the existing communication-decision structure had inherent flaws. It can be said that the presence of these flaws increased the potentialities for constructive change; but there was, of course, nothing predetermined about the form this change would take or when it would occur. The origins of the 1693 system lie outside an institutional context; the motivational factors that led the emperor to make certain decisions must be specially sought before his behavior can be explained in human terms. And, since modern behavioral science suggests that human behavior results from the interaction of human motivation with "precipitating factors" in the social milieu, the latter must be investigated as well.

Before beginning the present analysis, "ideology" and "values" must be distinguished. Ideology is taken here to mean a set of political ideas (a myth) with the function of preserving the political order; in a given society these ideas will be absolute standards, hence "noncontroversial." Values, on the other hand, as discussed below, are not absolute standards and vary widely from person to person.[1]

Central to Confucian ideology was the idea of "mutual response between Heaven and man (ruler)." This the K'ang-hsi Emperor accepted. According to this ideology, each ruler must heed the warnings of Heaven, expressed in the form of bad weather and poor harvests, lest he be deprived of the mandate to rule. The emperor would often be unaware of these warnings unless he had a reliable information-gathering service because, as observed earlier, the regular provincial officials often concealed news of adverse portents which could be taken as judgments on their own administrative shortcomings. If the emperor was sincere in his desire for full information, he would have to look outside the ordinary bureaucratic channels to find it. One means, hitherto neglected, lay at hand: the *ch'ing-an che* (greetings memorial) which, by old Manchu tradition, had been used by bannermen to offer ritual greetings to their overlord. A slight twisting of current usage was all that was needed to convert this system into a secret and reliable means of acquiring vital information. Here, in acculturation terms, was a reciprocal contribution made by the Manchus that profoundly altered the techniques of imperial control in China.

The geographic origin of the new system was in the South, an area politically unstable but also culturally and economically vital, the training ground of many of the best officials and the source of an annual quarter-million tons of tribute-rice. Yet, in this area of grave issues, the embryonic form of the system resulted from the interplay of human motives, when in 1693 Li Hsü decided to enclose a little information on local prices and weather in his *ch'ing-an che*. His action was without precedent, but he was willing to act "unduly" in order to please his emperor. He could do this because of his special relationship with the emperor as an Imperial Household bondservant and Soochow textile commissioner: he was both inside and outside the bureaucracy, a link between the Chinese and Manchu worlds. Though the K'ang-hsi Emperor approved of Li Hsü's action, he did not immediately exploit the possibilities it opened; but, neither was he blind to them. A few years later another bondservant, Ts'ao Yin, textile commissioner at Nanking, was commissioned similarly to Li Hsü. And still later, the type of information to be transmitted was expanded to include local economic and political matters. This only took place after the bondservants' nominal role had been changed: Ts'ao Yin was made salt censor in 1704, and Li Hsü was given the same post the following year; later, they were given concurrent titles in the Transmission Office and the Board of Revenue, respectively. The titles were not just honorary; their holders were formally entitled to report on political matters.

Around 1700 the K'ang-hsi Emperor began to draw regular provincial officials into the new system. First a few bannermen officials, then senior Chinese bureaucrats, were given the privilege of sending secret information enclosed in their *ch'ing-an che*. The system was spread to Peking when Wang Hung-hsü, long a personal adviser to the emperor on scholarly matters in the South Library and president of the Board of Works, was given the same privilege. In his new dual role, Wang became a channel of communication between the central bureaucracy and the emperor's personal staff in the inner court. As a minister, he had representational power through participation in the deliberative assemblies; any irregularities that he noticed there would, through his advisory role, be passed on to the emperor. On the 1705 southern tour this advisory role became of great importance: a southerner with excellent local contacts, Wang was able to bring vital information to the emperor's attention — like Li Hsü, he had built-in qualifications for the job. The emperor's use of these men was not accidental and arbitrary, but based on sound rationale.

In 1712 all senior court ministers with the third rank or above were ordered to present palace memorials. Thus in just under twenty years an extrabureaucratic, informal communication device had been developed into a full-fledged channel for secret communication, and it became an integral part of the formal bureaucracy. The functional changes were a response to personal motivation and political challenges.

At this point, three observations should be made concerning the distinctive patterns of development of the palace memorial system in the K'ang-hsi reign. First, though it is a political process in terms of interpersonal relationships that has been under discussion, there is clearly a paradox here: the documents show that not only Wang Hung-hsü and Ts'ao Yin, but also the emperor himself, were prey to mysterious fears and passionately concerned with maintaining absolute secrecy in their communications. If the emperor feared for his own life and the lives of his informants, then an analysis that implies the emperor as a free agent must be modified. Second, though the K'ang-hsi Emperor developed the palace memorial system, he used it only for limited purposes; the same system in the hands of his successor underwent enormous functional expansion. And third, though the K'ang-hsi Emperor used the new system side by side with the existing communication-decision structure, which he did not think needed change, the Yung-cheng Emperor drastically transformed the same structure. There are difficult historical problems here, and the field of values must be entered in search of an answer.

There is plenty of evidence that both the K'ang-hsi and Yung-cheng Emperors accepted the same Neo-Confucian ideology. Their contrasting policies reflect their different value systems. By "values" are meant those ideas that the actor holds to be desirable; if the actor is in a position of power he will make demands for his values and his value system can be reconstructed by studying his conscious motive statements. I follow modern political theory in distinguishing between "principal values" and values of lower priority that may be called "secondary" or "derivative." If the actor has effective control over the principal values of a given group, then he can influence its motivations. If its principal value demands are met, it will follow that the group is willing to subordinate its secondary values to the demands and expectations of the actor.

The principal value demand of the K'ang-hsi Emperor was for harmony (*ho*)[2] The main derivatives of this value were threefold: first, caution — respect for the status quo — which led him to make ad hoc adjustments but avoid drastic changes.[3] Second, tolerance (*k'uan*), which entailed appeasement, compromise, and a middle-of-the-road position on difficult issues; this meant that factions would be tolerated as long as they did not resort to extremism.[4] Third, moral suasion (*chiao-hui*) to deal with bureaucratic irregularities; this entailed the exploitation of moral exemplars who, it was hoped, would shame their colleagues into correct behavior.[5]

These value demands explain the K'ang-hsi Emperor's dilemma and the fear that obsessed him and his palace memorialists. The emperor wanted prior information on factional activities so that he could take precautionary action, but he refused to take direct steps to rout the challengers. The Yin-jeng clique had different values: extremism rather than caution, revenge rather than tolerance. After Songgotu's death in 1703, the emperor feared for his own life. Wang Hung-hsü feared for himself and his family. All non-partisan court officials were in a quandary: ideology demanded absolute loyalty to the emperor, and his value demand was for harmony; compromise with factional leaders was disloyal, but without compromise there could not be harmony — and if a new harmony was sought through attacking a faction, the emperor's support was nevertheless uncertain. No wonder many court officials lamented that they might die, whichever side they took. The Manchu establishment, too, was fragmented and fearful.

Enormous pressure was required to goad the emperor to action. Only when his own life was definitely threatened did he depose the heir-apparent, once the heir-apparent's sexual aberrations had become common knowledge, disgracing the imperial image and seeming to threaten withdrawal of Heaven's mandate. The issue now involved the most fundamental value of all — dynastic and self preservation. Even so, the emperor restored Yin-jeng, on the grounds that Yin-t'i had been casting spells which had led to the heir-apparent's insanity. This restoration in the face of all the evidence pointing to Yin-jeng's unsuitability was dramatic proof of the emperor's value demands. There was always the chance that things could be smoothed over, and even if they could not, there might be certain advantages: another prince might show his hand (as Yin-ssu did) and the factional forces be dissipated. This was simple expediency, not a long-term solution.

The final and irrevocable deposition of Yin-jeng three years later in 1712 had a two-fold significance. It marked the bankruptcy of the emperor's previous control policy, and it motivated him to make functional changes to the palace memorial system. The bankruptcy had to be proved beyond all shadow of doubt before the emperor would make the functional changes. He tried dismissing T'o-ho-ch'i (the factional leader of the Yin-jeng clique, general commandant of Peking) on the euphemistic grounds of "sickness." He tried the moral exemplar strategy, ordering the court to recommend officials renowned for filial piety, recalling Yin-jeng and his adherents to their sense of duty. He tried a scapegoat strategy of killing one to scare the other hundred (*sha-i ching-pai*). Only after all these had failed did he strike at Yin-jeng personally. In that major edict of March 5, 1712, he first explained his expansion of the palace memorial system into the provincial administration in order to get accurate information on local affairs. Court ministers were now to do the same, he added, though he emphasized the motivational difference: this information was to help him deal with "seditious and treacherous ministers." Thus was the information-gathering device converted into a mechanism for self-defense. When Yin-jeng launched a final coup after this edict, all options were gone and he had to be removed.

All this shows clearly how directly the K'ang-hsi Emperor's initial control policy, and his development and use of the new communication system, reflected his personal value system. He was not interested in pushing the new system to its limits; the heir-apparent and his faction represented a specific problem, and the palace memorials might help him to solve it. This was the rationale for extension of the system. Its impact was meant to be psychological. If princes and officials knew they were being reported on in secret, it was hoped that they would become "watchful and fearful" and be led to "examine themselves." Drastic action was taken by the emperor only when palace memorials revealed that factional leaders were planning to take human lives. As he repeatedly declared, "killing" was the ultimate form of extremism, and must be avoided at all costs.[6] This is why he intervened personally in the three cases examined previously, involving Chang Po-hsing, Ch'en P'eng-nien, and Ch'en Ju-pi — not so much to uphold justice, but rather to prevent blood being spilled. Indeed, these cases clearly show how the emperor played the role of mediator rather than of final judicial arbiter.[7]

With very few exceptions, and despite the gradual expansion of the system, the K'ang-hsi Emperor seems to have been content to keep it at the ideological level — in the sense that Li Hsü's original 1693 palace memorial can be defined as ideological. A large proportion of the substantive (that is, excluding the formal *ch'ing-an che*) palace memorials stored in the National Palace Museum archives deal with weather reports, food prices, and signs of local unrest. These were the warning signs for any general disruption of political equilibrium. The emperor reacted swiftly to information concerning these matters: relief rice was ordered distributed, local robberies were given immediate attention. News of the death of Hsiung Tz'u-li, a prominent Confucian scholar from the South and formerly a trusted grand secretary and personal adviser in the South Library, led the emperor to see to his funeral expenses and the needs of his family. And when the emperor received news of the "caving in of the Ming imperial tomb ground," he reacted equally thoroughly, ordering his secret informant Ts'ao Yin to make a careful investigation lest wild rumors begin to spread. All such matters were ideological in that they might disrupt the status quo of the political machinery. They were not directly relevant to the improvement of administrative efficiency.

This lack of interest in using the palace memorial system to improve the efficiency of bureaucratic administration again sprang from the K'ang-hsi Emperor's particular value demands. A brief analysis of his response to incoming information from palace memorialists makes this clear. For example: in the thirty secret palace memorials that he sent to the emperor, Wang Hung-hsü included a great deal of information on irregularities in the local and central bureaucracy, yet fourteen memorials received the cool and ambiguous endorsement "noted" or "I see" (*chih-tao-le, ming-pai-le*); four received no comment; three had the briefest possible endorsement, "yes" (*shih*); three had some brief interlinear comments of a phrase or two — this left only six memorials that received anything approaching an encouraging endorsement. In two of the six the emperor praised Wang Hung-hsü's memorial in general terms; in the remaining four he made terse but significant comments on such vital matters as the secrecy of the system or the importance of the heir-apparent case.

Certain patterns can be detected in these imperial endorsements. As a general rule, the K'ang-hsi Emperor never showed the memorialist his true thoughts about a given issue, nor did he even hint about the action he intended to take on the basis of information submitted. Almost all memorials that reported administrative abuses were simply endorsed "noted" or had no comment whatsoever. Sometimes, indeed, the emperor responded negatively to such information. For instance, after transfer from the Board of Works to the Board of Revenue, Wang submitted a secret palace memorial giving details of serious financial abuses in the Board of Revenue; far from delighted at Wang's loyalty and conscientiousness, the emperor wrote: "You should not be too harsh in handling board matters" (*pu-chung chih shih pu-k'o k'o-ch'iu*).[8] Another memorial, in which Wang pointed out that his predecessor as president of the Board of Revenue had connived with board officials, clerks, and merchants to steal over 100,000 taels, received the endorsement: "This is only a trivial matter; I've completed the important task" (*tz'u pu-kuo hsiao-shih; chin ta-shih i-ch'eng*).[9] (The important task was proving the heir-apparent's evil conduct in the South; in such a context even thefts of 100,000 taels by board officials was trivial to the K'ang-hsi Emperor.) The emperor was consistent in his adherence to the status quo value. Intervention came only when human lives were at stake; he was not concerned with mere administrative efficiency.

This consistency in the K'ang-hsi Emperor's value demands explains why he did not use the palace memorial system to effect more radical changes within the existing communication-decision structure. He did not want drastic change; he wanted to strengthen the existing structure, not undermine it.

The Yung-cheng Reign. The Yung-cheng reign presents a complete contrast. During it, the palace memorial system underwent both structural and functional changes that caused a complete reorientation of the existing communication-decision structure. The principal value demand of the Yung-cheng Emperor was for efficiency. As Kent Smith has correctly pointed out: "The central theme which runs through the Yung-cheng Emperor's administrative policies is his effort to push the machinery of the imperial state to its utmost efficiency." [10] The main derivatives of this value were, first, the favoring of radical reforms (as opposed to the caution or status quo policies of the emperor's predecessor). Second, instead of an indiscriminate "tolerance," he advocated tolerance accompanied by severity according to the particular circumstances (*k'uan yen hsiang chi*),[11] warning his officials not to expect from him only that tolerance and benevolence (*k'uan-jen*) which they had grown accustomed to in his father's reign.[12] Third, in cases of administrative laxity or dishonesty he valued punishment (*hsing*), as well as moral suasion.[13]

Immediately upon his accession to the throne, the Yung-cheng Emperor found himself in a dangerous situation. There were few friends he could trust, the bureaucracy was riddled with inefficiency, and his reckless brothers had switched their hatred from dead father to new emperor. To bring efficiency back into the bureaucracy, new men had to be found; and while the search was on, the present incumbents had to be reformed and re-educated. Instead of trusting his officials to come to their moral senses, he felt it wiser "to place the officialdom under surveillance." His brothers also had to be closely watched and information obtained on their illicit activities. All these pressures motivated the emperor to develop the palace memorial system, a system that also promised to satisfy his value demands. He moved immediately toward expansion and reinforcement. As outlined earlier, provincial officials below the rank of governor, mainly financial and judicial commissioners, were told to send in palace memorials, as were many more members of the central bureaucracy — though here the emperor remained flexible as circumstances demanded: for example, censors were initially given the right to present palace memorials, but the privilege was withdrawn when the emperor decided it was being abused. The special palace memorial boxes to ensure absolute secrecy in transmission, each with only two keys, one for the memorialist and one for the emperor, were distributed to the eligible provincial officials. The memorialists were prompted to keep up a constant flow of information, which the emperor read as soon as it had been received and of which he made full use.

Palace memorials containing secret information that did not call for immediate administrative action were returned via the same route to the sender, and no overt action was taken. However, if the incoming palace memorial dealt with some urgent military or civil problem, the emperor responded swiftly, using the contents of the memorial as the basis for his decision. This process of response was even further speeded after the ad hoc committee had been formed to help the emperor handle the memorials. Unlike his father, the Yung-cheng Emperor diligently utilized the new channel to improve administrative efficiency. Even Jesuit missionaries serving at the Yung-cheng court, though naturally critical of the emperor's attitude toward their religion and his punitive action against his own brothers, were profoundly impressed by his conscientiousness in operating the new system:

> As little a Favorer of Religion as this Prince appear'd, it is impossible not to praise his unwearied Application to Business, for he applied his Thoughts night and day to the reforming of errors in the Government, and to procure Happiness to his subjects: You cannot do him a greater Pleasure than to present him a Plan [memorial] which tends to promote the publick Welfare, and the Ease of the People; he immediately enters therein, and puts it in Execution without any regard to Expence: He hath settled a great many excellent Rules to dignify Merit, and reward Virtue, to cause a worthy Emulation among Artificers, and to assist his subjects in Years of Famine. These Qualities have gained him in a short time the Respect and Love of all his Subjects.[14]

The structural expansion of the palace memorial system in the early years of the Yung-cheng reign brought to the emperor a tremendous amount of raw information. In the interests of both secrecy and efficiency, he chose not to pass this information on to his existing deliberative bodies for discussion; instead, he turned for both advisory and secretarial assistance to a small ad hoc committee of inner grand secretaries — men personally selected by himself. Development of this committee, which later evolved into the *Chün-chi ch'u* and was so famous in the history of later Ch'ing administration, and of the concomitant palace memorial system, are central to historians' arguments that the Yung-cheng Emperor was one of the most despotic in Chinese history. Though the degrees of that despotism can be debated, there is no doubt at all that the transformed communication-decision structure contributed greatly to the emperor's effective control of his bureaucracy, and that it became a key part of Ch'ing government until the middle of the nineteenth century.

It has been noted that the Yung-cheng Emperor's principal value demand was efficiency. Inevitably, this demand involves the problem of control; in the Ch'ing imperial government, the key facet of political control was control over the high-ranking bureaucrats. In studying the Yung-cheng Emperor's control policies, concern here is not with their "ruthless," "tyrannical," or "arbitrary" aspects, as it has been for many scholars. Such adjectives suggest a control based on coercion or sheer force, which would have been inherently unstable. Instead, this study's focus is on a rational imperial control, which was based on the effective regulation of interpersonal relations, eased some of the tensions that had always existed between ruler and bureaucrat, and, indeed, met the Chinese people's own value demand that the government fulfill its responsibilities.[15]

Karl Deutsch has compared the role of communication systems in the political machinery to that of nerves in the human body and shown how political control depends on the effectiveness of those systems.[16] In what ways did the new communication system enable the Yung-cheng Emperor to control his bureaucracy and attain his principal value of efficiency? Analysis will be conducted along three lines. (1) What were the structural advantages of the new communication system in comparison with the old one? (2) What role did the emperor play in the actual operation of the transformed system? (3) What were the prerequisites for effective functioning of the new machinery?

In regard to information-gathering, there were many structural advantages. The emperor received information from the provinces firsthand, not through hearsay. Because the system was effectively secret, the informants did not have to fear reprisals from fellow officials or court factions. The information was likely to be accurate, since each informant knew that the emperor was constantly cross-checking through other informants; accordingly, the extremely expensive forms of information-gathering, such as summoning officials to audience, dispatching imperial commissioners, and embarking on personal imperial tours of inspection, could be curtailed. The emperor could draw easily on the reserve of bureaucratic expertise for both objective and subjective judgments on administrative and personnel problems. The K'ang-hsi Emperor, of course, could have done the same, as the example of Wang Hung-hsü shows, but he chose not to. An examination of the Yung-cheng reign palace memorials in the *Chu-p'i yü-chih* shows how completely "internal" the Yung-cheng control system had become.

The palace memorialists were not "secret agents" or "spies." They were completely different from the "parasites" in the spy systems of Stuart Britain, who were salaried agents reporting through the major-generals to the secretaries of state, and were "hated by all decent people." [17] The Chinese palace memorialists were a privileged group of high-ranking officials who reported directly to the emperor; they drew honor and prestige from this function and received no extra remuneration for it. Nor can they be compared with the secret police or "agencies" of modern times, which are separate groups, outside the regular bureaucracy, whose identity is often concealed and who are controlled by their own chief, not directly by the head of state. The palace memorialists were readily identifiable senior bureaucrats, controlled directly by the emperor within the regular control system. Their special qualifications, the type of information they gathered, and the way they gathered it — all suggest that this Chinese-Manchu system was a unique one. If a parallel must be sought, it should probably be among the intendants of Louis XIV; but even there so many differences exist that the exercise is unlikely to be fruitful.

If there were structural advantages in the new system as far as information-gathering went, the same thing was true from the point of view of transmission. Each memorial was transmitted secretly and directly to the emperor, but some were more urgent than others. Government postal facilities were available for express delivery; less urgent memorials were brought to Peking by the memorialists' own messengers, who frequently gathered extra information en route.

Second, the role of the emperor in the operation of the new system was now fundamentally altered. The traditional memorial system had brought information to the emperor through channels both open and indirect; decisions concerning matters contained in a *t'i-pen* had been first proposed by the grand secretaries and subsequently discussed in the various deliberative assemblies. This had inevitably given the emperor a somewhat passive role in the decision-making process. In the developed form of the system, all that was changed: now the emperor took the initiative as both the "nerve center" and the "switchboard" in the new communication machinery. The raw data came directly to his attention, and it was now he who could withhold information from the bureaucracy, rather than vice versa. The emperor had become the controller of the outflow of information: at his discretion a given matter could be dealt with in the sphere of secret, semisecret, semiopen, or open politics. In this sense he had become a bona fide autocrat — a "self-ruler."

The greatly increased operational role of the emperor leads into the third point, concerning the prerequisites for effective functioning of the new system. As an increasing volume of secret palace memorials flooded in to the emperor, how was he to avoid the problem of "decision overload" at the switchboard? Evidence suggests that the Yung-cheng Emperor developed a relatively sound operating procedure. Governmental affairs were classified broadly as special or routine. Routine matters continued to be reported in the traditional *t'i-pen* form, governed by prescribed administrative regulations under board supervision; in this category fell such matters as the rendering of annual accounts, recommendations to the more junior official posts, judicial reports on cases that presented no unusual difficulties, and so on. The palace memorials were devoted to "special" matters that required the emperor's personal attention because they were outside the scope of normative administrative routine and precedent. The Yung-cheng Emperor insisted that this important distinction be maintained. Provincial officials who used a palace memorial to report on routine matters — perhaps hoping that in so doing they would get the emperor to notice their dedication to duty — had the memorials returned to them with the blunt endorsement: "memorialize this matter in a *t'i-pen*" (*chü-t'i,* or *kai chü-t'i*). The new channel was to be a complement to the old, in the interests of more efficient administration; it was not intended to supplant it.

The inflow of extra information in the new palace memorial system was not quite so formidable as it might first appear to be. About three thousand memorials are extant from the K'ang-hsi period, suggesting the sparing use of the system by that emperor. The Yung-cheng Emperor probably received about fifty thousand palace memorials during his reign; in normal circumstances, this meant that he had to deal with about ten a day, by no means an impossible load — though of course he had the extra work of endorsing each one, often at great length, in his own hand. In special circumstances, however, the number received in one day could rise to fifty or even sixty, as the Yung-cheng Emperor testified.[18] At such times his conscientiousness must have been put sternly to the test.

As a shrewd and efficient administrator, the Yung-cheng Emperor was of course aware of the dangers of "jamming" at the center of the communication-decision structure. Insisting on the rigid routine/special distinction was a help but not a complete solution. Accordingly, he moved to develop alternative outgoing channels, to speed the processing of the information received. A palace memorial containing secret information that the emperor wanted to keep to himself was returned to the sender via its incoming route (as before), thus its secret character was retained. But if a memorial dealt with some urgent civil, military, or judicial case that would require a lot of time and paperwork, the emperor referred it first to an ad hoc committee (or, later, to the *Chün-chi ch'u*) for predecisional deliberation: this was the semisecret channel. Other palace memorials might be referred to the *Nei-ko* or a central organ of the bureaucracy for deliberation, becoming semiopen in that they were seen by a large number of officials. In all these cases, since the Yung-cheng Emperor began to base his major decisions extensively on information contained in the palace memorials, the outgoing channels became increasingly important.

The final prerequisite for efficient functioning of the new system was inevitably the emperor's own value system. With his demand for efficiency, the Yung-cheng Emperor naturally made the most of his dual role as operator and switchboard. He read all incoming information in person and carefully, "applied his thoughts throughout night and day" to the problems of government raised in the palace memorials, and diligently sought to establish priorities for the reception, screening, and handling of these valuable messages. The system would not necessarily be so effective for the differently motivated emperors who succeeded him; the information, after all, was only valuable if used intelligently. But as far as the Yung-cheng Emperor was concerned, his values not only ensured the success of the system, but they contributed greatly to his success in winning other values such as loyalty and conscientiousness from his officialdom.

From the realm of efficiency it is a short step into the more nebulous —

but no less important— realm of the sociopsychological functions of the palace memorial system in strengthening imperial control. The system undoubtedly had what can be called a depersonalization effect on official-dom. Mutual surveillance made the formation of large-scale bureaucratic factions almost impossible. Secrecy discouraged group interests and at the same time, conversely, encouraged a new individualism in the two-way emperor-official relationship. As George Simmel argues, by strongly emphasizing the "exclusion of all outsiders," secrecy "makes for a correspondingly strong feeling of possession . . . Moreover . . . since the others are excluded from the possession — particularly when it is very valuable — the converse suggests itself psychologically, namely, that what is denied to many must have special value." [19] There is little doubt that the officials who were allowed to present palace memorials to the emperor felt appreciation for the privilege and that this strengthened the vertical bonds of the emperor-official relationship.

As intrabureaucratic relations were depersonalized, so was the emperor-official relationship personalized. In his regular palace memorials each official revealed his ability and his values, giving the emperor a good knowledge of his personality. When the emperor was impressed by the personality revealed, he could rocket a given official to the highest posts in the empire: three of the Yung-cheng Emperor's most trusted officials (Li Wei, T'ien Wen-ching, and O-erh-t'ai) owed their prominence to the confidence in their sincerity and ability that the emperor had gained by reading their palace memorials. Other officials, not surprisingly, fell from favor after consistently evoking negative responses from the emperor.

When the personalization effect was positive, strong emotional ties developed between emperor and official. There seems no reason for doubting that both the Yung-cheng Emperor and O-erh-t'ai were sincere when each wrote that he had been moved to tears by the other. The tears were of gratitude and admiration, proof of the strong affinity between the two men. Such involvements had a practical aspect also: officials emotionally tied to the emperor would be not only most receptive to his values and attitudes, but also secured in their loyalty and less likely than ever to form horizontal attachments within the bureaucracy.[20] The result, as the Yung-cheng reign progressed, might be called an umbrella structure: the emperor was the central shaft and the officials the spokes. Each spoke was firmly attached to the center, yet separated from every other spoke.

It is true that this relationship between emperor and provincial officials was an essential component of the new communications system; but an inadequate picture results without a glance at the most important institutional byproduct of the new system, the emergence, first, of the ad hoc committee, then of the *Chün-chi ch'u* — symbolizing the completion of the power concentration process in early Ch'ing times.

In the K'ang-hsi reign, as noted in the introduction, the bureaucrats had gained strong representational power. The K'ang-hsi Emperor insisted on upholding this type of power throughout his reign, despite the fact that bureaucrats had persistently attempted to encroach on the imperial power through their factional intrigues. The Yung-cheng Emperor met this challenge by streamlining the communication system and gaining the initiative in information control and also by successfully converting representational power into advisory power, thus greatly facilitating imperial control.

Though the techniques employed by the Yung-cheng Emperor are familiar, it is clear that he acted with great subtlety. What he did was to employ a "multiple-role" technique in order to concentrate bureaucratic power in a small ad hoc committee; once this was achieved, he increasingly stressed the committee's advisory role in order to concentrate all power in himself. The officials called, first into the committee and later to the *Chün-chi ch'u,* held ministerial positions and were thus nominally vested with representational power. Palace memorials dealing with major government affairs were all sent to them for deliberation. But there were no administrative precedents or even customs to guide their deliberations, and all they could do was report back to the emperor in an advisory role. The channel of communication was vertical, back up to the emperor, not horizontal, out to the boards and departments. The emperor called directly on the expertise of his officials but granted no new powers in compensation. He thus held almost total power.

The *Chün-chi ch'u,* developed in the interests of efficiency, was a necessary corollary to the extended palace memorial system. Information passed on to it became semisecret, never more. The council's doings were shrouded in secrecy and its members forbidden to have unnecessary contacts with outside bureaucrats.[21] Even imperial instructions couched in the form of court letters were dispatched directly to the provincial recipient, and members of the council were held responsible if any leakage occurred. There was a tight personal link between the emperor, who sent the court letter, and his provincial addressee. Moreover, predecisional consultations with the provincial officials concerned on some particular matter gave the latter an intimate sense of participation that had often been lacking hitherto and won the emperor increased support.

It was a well thought-out system, and it could be expected to provide stability for as long as the emperor was fairly shrewd and fairly conscientious and as long as no strong pressures from outside were brought against the system or the ideology that sustained the entire structure of government. Through the eighteenth century, and well into the nineteenth, these conditions were met. Then the pressures became unbearable: weakness at the center, internal rebellions, Western military and economic forces, and the arguments of "modern nationalism." Even so, it was a long time before the spokes were finally torn from the shaft and the umbrella shredded in the wind.

Appendix	127
Abbreviations	151
Notes	153
Bibiography	181
Glossary	189
Index	197

Case A

Account of Governor Ch'en Pin's Special Audience with the K'ang-hsi Emperor

The following account by Ch'en Pin, governor of Hunan before he went to Peking for this audience and subsequently was transferred to the post of governor of Fukien, describes his special audiences with the K'ang-hsi Emperor, the first of which was held on December 26, 1715. He was summoned for audiences again in the days that followed until he bid the emperor farewell on January 7, 1716. An edict was issued on December 30, 1715, to the effect that he should be transferred to the new post at Fukien. This lively account forms part of a palace memorial that he presented, following arrival at his new post, in order to show his gratitude to the emperor. The fact that such thanks-giving palace memorials (*hsieh-en che*) sometimes contain valuable information on the actual operation of the Ch'ing bureaucracy and are not merely routine expressions of gratitude can readily be seen.

The practice of including a lengthy account not only of a particular audience, but also of the oral imperial instructions given in it, was probably based on the same rule governing the *shu-chih* procedure when court letters were drafted in the *Chün-chi ch'u* (see Chapter VIII). Its purpose was to assure the emperor, who might make corrections in the account if he found it inaccurate, that the imperial oral instructions had been correctly understood by the recipient. This type of quotation of imperial instructions occurs frequently in the beginning of a palace memorial.[1]

Judging from the fact that the *Ch'ing-shih-lu* recorded in almost exactly the same wording the K'ang-hsi Emperor's compliment to Ch'en's honesty and hard-working spirit on January 3, 1716, at the morning audience, this memorial appears to be quite a faithful account. A reading of it suggests that: (1) officials tended not to criticize other officials in the context of an imperial audience; (2) the K'ang-hsi Emperor used the audience to evoke fear on the part of officials that any attempt to hide the truth from him would be uncovered by the information forwarded by other officials.

Document

While I still held office as the governor of Hunan, I memorialized Your Majesty requesting the privilege of having a special audience [*pi-chien*]. My memorial received Your Majesty's endorsement, which read: "Let Ch'en Pin come to Peking for a special audience, and let the Board [of Personnel] be notified of this decision." Then I received a communication [*tzu*] from the board to the same effect. I therefore set out from Ch'ang-sha on November 16, 1715, and I arrived at the Ch'ang-ch'un yüan [imperial suburban villa] [where I reported my arrival]. On December 26, I went to the palace gate to enquire after Your Majesty's well-being and asked the audience officer to transmit my greeting. Your Majesty ordered that I be brought in by an imperial guard and stand waiting until the grand secretaries had finished their briefing. After I had performed the three kneelings and nine kowtows ceremony, I moved further toward the throne. Then Your Majesty began to ask me questions:

[Emperor]: "Where are you from?"

[Ch'en]: "I am a Cantonese."

[Emperor]: "Which prefecture of Kwangtung?"

[Ch'en]: "The prefecture of Lei-chou; my native place is Ch'ung-chou."

[Emperor]: "How old are you?"

[Ch'en]: "I am sixty years (*sui*) old."

[Emperor]: "Is this your real age?" [2]

[Ch'en]: "Yes, my real age; I was born in the year *ping-shen* [1656]."

[Emperor]: "Where did you hold official posts from the very beginning?"

[Ch'en]: "My first post was as magistrate of the Ku-t'ien district (*hsien*) of Fukien."

[Emperor]: "What was the next?"

[Ch'en]: "I was first transferred to be the magistrate of Taiwan district; then I was called back to serve in the Board of War as a department director (*lang-chung*); I was appointed the educational commissioner (*hsüeh-cheng*) of Szechwan province; then I was transferred to the post of taotai of the circuit of Taiwan and Amoy; last, I was appointed governor of Hunan due to Your Majesty's heavenly grace, which was so great that I can not show my gratitude even by sacrificing my own life."

[Emperor]: "How long did you stay in your post as taotai of Taiwan and Amoy?"

[Ch'en]: "Over five years."

[Emperor]: "How was the situation in Taiwan?"

[Ch'en]: "Taiwan today is different from the Taiwan in the early days [when it had just become part of the empire]. The population has grown and there is a great deal of commercial activity. It is almost as prosperous as Chang-chou and Ch'üan-chou [Zayton] on the mainland."

[Emperor]: "If the population of Taiwan continues to grow, what will be the possible consequence?"

[Ch'en]: "Although the population is growing, when people eventually settle down and raise their own families, the situation will be even better. After all, it is all due to Your Majesty's reputation and spirit which exert great influence on distant places that the common people and the soldiers are peacefully living together."

[Emperor]: "What are the main products of Taiwan?"

[Ch'en]: "Rice, cereals, sugar, and so forth."

[Emperor]: "Do they harvest sufficient rice and cereals every year?"

[Ch'en]: "Yes, but the weather of Taiwan is different from that of the mainland. Farmers sow seeds in early summer between the fifth month and the sixth month of the year. They can expect a good harvest for the year if they get enough rainfall at that time."

[Emperor]: "Is the weather cold there?"

[Ch'en]: "It is not too cold or too hot. During the winter months, wearing some wadded garments is sufficient; fur clothing is not needed."

[Emperor]: "How do you compare the weather there with that of the Lei-chou prefecture [Ch'en's native prefecture] in Kwangtung?"

[Ch'en]: "In Lei-chou fur clothing is needed during winter months."

[Emperor]: "But it was not until recently that people in Kwangtung began to wear furs; they didn't wear them before."

[Ch'en]: "Yes."

[Emperor]: "Why does Taiwan often suffer earthquakes?"

[Ch'en]: "Taiwan is a piece of floating land in the sea, with a width of 50 *li* from east to west and a length of 2,000 odd *li* from south to north. It is surrounded by water on all sides; therefore it is only natural that earthquakes occur. There is nothing extraordinary about it."

[Emperor]: "What is the situation concerning uncultivated land in Taiwan?"

[Ch'en]: "There is no uncultivated farmland in Taiwan. Although there is much uncultivated land along the south and north routes, that is all deer-hunting land for the native barbarians; they pay taxes and support their families from these lands, so that if the lands were opened up for cultivation, they would lose their hunting lands and in turn they would have no way to support themselves. This is why the governor of Fukien has repeatedly issued notices strictly forbidding any local villains from annoying them along these routes under the pretext of opening uncultivated lands. This is why these barbarians have been able to live peacefully together with the common people without any disturbances." (Your Majesty nodded assent.)

[Emperor]: "In what year did you get your *chin-shih* degree?"

[Ch'en]: "The year *chia-su* [1694]."

[Emperor]: "Who was the *chuang-yüan* [the one who ranked first among the *chin-shih* in that year]?" [3]

[Ch'en]: "It was Hu Jen-yu."

[Emperor]: "Who were the *pang-yen* and *t'an-hua* respectively [those who ranked second and third respectively among the *chin-shih* in that year]?"

[Ch'en]: "Ku T'u-ho got the *pang-yen* and Ku Yüeh-li the *t'an-hua*."

[Emperor]: "How did you rank yourself in the provincial examination?"

[Ch'en]: "I ranked thirty-fourth in order in the provincial examination."

[Emperor]: "How is your writing?"

[Ch'en]: "My writing is just average. Nevertheless it is not too bad; I can write a little. For instance, in the year 1708 I took the examination for the candidacy for the prospective provincial examiners. Yü Cheng-chien, who is currently the educational commissioner of Chiang-nan, ranked first and I second through Your Majesty's personal judgment."

[Emperor]: "What was the subject for that examination?"

[Ch'en]: "It was on the passage in the *Mencius* starting from 'Let mulberry trees be planted about the homesteads with their five *mou* [Chinese acre]." [4]

[Emperor]: "Any theme for poem composition?"

[Ch'en]: "No, there was none."

[Emperor]: "What books have you been studying?"

[Ch'en]: "I used to study the Four Books — that was all. But since Your Majesty recently issued copies of the books on human nature and heavenly principle to the scholars of the entire nation for them to learn, I therefore also have roughly studied them."

[Emperor]: "Can you recite any of them?"

[Ch'en]: "I still can recite the *T'ai-chi*[-*t'u shuo*] [An Explanation of the Diagram of Great Ultimate] and the *Hsi-ming* [Western Inscription]." [5]

Then the Emperor asked me to recite the *Hsi-ming*. I successfully recited it except on one occasion when I came to the sentence "[Yin] Po-ch'i vigorously obeyed his father's command." I suddenly forgot what was next, and on another occasion I made one mistake in the sentence " . . . while poverty, humble station, care, and sorrow will be my helpmates to fulfillment";[6] and on both occasions Your Majesty corrected me word by word. I also told Your Majesty that the *Hsi-ming* consists of 153 characters; but Your Majesty said, "the number of characters is not important." Then Your Majesty asked me to recite the *T'ai-chi-t'u shuo*. But when I came to the sentence "The five agents constitute one system of *yin* and *yang*," Your Majesty stopped me and asked a question: "Why is it said here that the five agents are merely *yin* and *yang*? Which of the five agents are *yin* and which of them are *yang*?" I answered: "When we speak of the order of producing each other among the five agents in terms of substance [*chih*], we would say Water first, then Fire, Wood, Metal, and Earth; in this case, Water and Wood constitute the *yang*, and Fire and Metal the *yin*. But when we speak of their operation [motion, action] in terms of material force [*ch'i*], we would mention Wood first, and then Fire, Earth, Metal and Water; in this case, the Wood and Fire constitute the *yang* and Metal and Water the *yin*." Your Majesty nodded assent and asked me again: "How do you explain the sentence, 'Heaven, which is one, produces Water; Earth, which is six, makes it complete?' " I could not answer this question. Your Majesty then explained to me: "Five plus one is six, isn't it? Five plus two is seven, isn't it?" I said: "Your Majesty knows this because you understand the *Book of Changes* very thoroughly." [Then the emperor asked him questions on the *Book of History*. He answered most of them, except on one point, which he failed to answer. He explained to the emperor: "I have not been keeping up with my studies on the Classics because I have been serving in the provincial government for a long time." The emperor said: "You have indeed failed to keep up your studies!" Then the emperor changed the subject].

[Emperor]: "Did any of your ancestors become an official?"

[Ch'en]: "My ancestors were all farmers for many generations; none of them ever became an official."

[Emperor]: "How many sons do you have?"

[Ch'en]: "I have two sons. One of them got the *chü-jen* degree in 1711, the other is a *sheng-yüan* in my own district."

[Emperor]: "In your memorial of yesterday, you suggested that illegal increase in surtax should be prohibited. When did this start? I remember the former governor of Hunan, Chao Shen-ch'iao [governor of Hunan 1703–1710] forbade such a practice before, didn't he?"

[Ch'en]: "After I took over the office, people swarmed to my office to file their complaints, saying that the surtax had gradually been increased again after Chao left office; this is why I again ventured to memorialize for a reiteration of the former order. This is perhaps a stupid suggestion."

[Emperor]: "Didn't the governor-general forbid such practices?"

[Ch'en]: "Although the governor-general forbade it, yet I am afraid that some of the subordinate officials pretended to obey the order while actually violating it."

[Emperor]: "Is the governor-general a good official?"

[Ch'en]: "Very good."

[Emperor]: "Who succeeded Chao Shen-ch'iao as the governor of Hunan? Was it P'an Tsung-lo?"

[Ch'en]: "Yes."

[Emperor]: "Who else?"

[Ch'en]: "Li Hsi, now governor of Honan, also served as governor of Hunan for a few months, but soon he was transferred to Honan."

[Emperor]: "When you passed through Honan, did you hear whether he is a good governor?

[Ch'en]: "Yes, I heard he is a very good official."

[Emperor]: "How was the harvest result in Hunan this year?"

[Ch'en]: "The overall average was seventy to eighty percent [of the normal yield]."

[Emperor]: "How about the rice price?"

[Ch'en]: "It ranges from seven-tenths or eight-tenths *ch'ien* to one and one-tenth or one and two-tenths *ch'ien* per picul."

[Emperor]: "What type of *tou* [peck] are you talking about?"

[Ch'en]: "Even the figures I just mentioned are merely rough estimations, because the prices in the morning and those in the evening are not at all the same."

Your Majesty doubted how one could decide the two prices in the morning and the evening. [So he dropped this subject.]

[Emperor]: "You are from Lei-chou; do you speak some kind of dialect too?"

[Ch'en]: "Yes, I do. Not only the Lei-chou prefecture, but practically all the prefectures in Kwangtung have their own dialects."

[Emperor]: "This is just like those prefectures in Fukien; but do you understand all those dialects in Kwangtung?"

[Ch'en]: "I cannot speak them, but I can understand them a little."

[Emperor]: "Your Mandarin sounds quite good; you don't have any accent."

[Ch'en]: "Thank you, Your Majesty, I really don't know how to speak."

[Emperor]: "Why does your face look so pale?"

[Ch'en]: "I have always been physically weak."

[Emperor]: "Did you encounter any danger when you crossed the sea?"

[Ch'en]: "When I was summoned to the capital in 1704, the boat lost its rudder as soon as we were beyond the harbor Lu-erh-men. Our boat drifted in the sea [Taiwan Strait] for a whole night; then suddenly at dawn a gale blew upon the boat and pushed it back to the harbor, thus the lives of all those on the boat were saved. After we sailed out the second time, our boat encountered a violent gale and we were nearly swallowed up by the roaring billows. This was the first time I ran into danger on the sea. This year during the fourth month when I crossed the sea, it was entirely due to Your Majesty's blessing that I only spent one day and two nights on the sea and made the crossing successfully [to the mainland from Taiwan] with the aid of a favorable wind."

While I was speaking, Your Majesty looked very pleased with my answers. Finally, I performed the kowtow and retreated from Your Majesty's presence.

The Second Audience. On December 29, 1715, I followed the grand secretaries and the presidents of the boards to attend the morning audience. While I was standing there, Your Majesty called me to come to your presence, and then asked me more questions:

[Emperor]: "Do you have anything to say to me?"

[Ch'en]: "On account of Your Majesty's immense grace, I, incompetent as I was, received the appointment as governor of Hunan. Since the province is vast and the responsibility is heavy, I am afraid I have failed in my duty and the people have suffered because of me."

[Emperor]: "How do you compare Hunan with Fukien?"

[Ch'en]: "The people of Hunan rely entirely on their farmland for living. Several districts are close to the Tung-t'ing Lake, and every year in late summer and early autumn, the Yangtze River pours its waters into the lake and the lands in these districts suffer from flood. Fortunately the people have managed to live because of Your Majesty's special favor in granting tax exemptions and relief measures. After all, the life of the people of Hunan is very difficult. Fukien province is very mountainous and its land is not sufficient for growing rice. People rely on fishing for their living. Neither province is easily governed." [The emperor asked again about the rice of Hunan, then changed the subject.]

[Emperor]: "Who is the financial commissioner of Hunan?"

[Ch'en]: "A-lin."

[Emperor]: "How is his performance as an official?"

[Ch'en]: "He is very competent."

[Emperor]: "He is competent all right, but I am not sure about his heart [morality]."

Then Your Majesty continued your questioning, asking: "Who is the judicial commissioner?"

[Ch'en]: "Wang Ch'ao-en, but he has just been promoted to be the financial commissioner of Kwangtung."

[Emperor]: "Is he a good official?"

[Ch'en]: "Yes, he is very good; the people all loved him."

[Emperor]: "How would you compare him with the financial commissioner?"

[Ch'en]: "He is even better than the financial commissioner."

[Emperor]: "How about the governor-general of Hu-Kwang O-lun-t'e? Is he a good official?"

[Ch'en]: "He is good."

[Emperor]: "How good is he?"

[Ch'en]: "I saw him this time when I passed by Wu-ch'ang; he was very kind and affable."

[Emperor]: "How do you compare him with the governor-general of Fukien, Man-pao?"

[Ch'en]: "Both are extremely good."

[Emperor]: "Who is the financial commissioner of Fukien?"

[Ch'en]: "Sha-mu-ha."

[Emperor]: "And the judicial commissioner?"

[Ch'en]: "Tung Yung-chi."

[Emperor]: "Are they good officials?"

[Ch'en]: "Yes, both are good."

[Emperor]: "Of the last two naval commanders-in-chief, which one is better?"

[Ch'en]: "Both are good; the former is more mature and experienced."

[Emperor]: "How is the brigade general of Taiwan?"

[Ch'en]: "Oh, he governed his forces very strictly. Originally the troops in Taiwan were very arrogant; now they have been brought under control."

[Emperor]: "Do you know any good military officers in Taiwan?"

[Ch'en]: "Yes, I know one naval colonel in An-p'ing by the name of Chang Kuo. He conducted naval training and patrolled the sea, but he has been promoted to be the brigade general of Ting-hai."

[Emperor]: "Do you know anything about Wu Sheng?"

[Ch'en]: "Since I was an official abroad [that is, in Taiwan], I didn't get to know him; but I heard that he was a good official."

[Emperor]: "Wu Sheng is a most honest official; he has only seven or eight house servants and never steals any military rations. This is known to everyone. But you say that you don't know him too well; this makes me feel suspicious."

[Ch'en]: "Your Majesty's vision searches into the truth of everything; you have no reason to feel doubtful."

[Emperor]: "When you passed through the province of Honan, did you hear whether the governor was a good official?"

[Ch'en]: "I heard all the way that he was a good official."

[Emperor]: "He is a sincere man; did you meet him?"

[Ch'en]: "I didn't meet him because I didn't pass through K'ai-feng [the capital of Honan]."

[Emperor]: "Those suggestions you mentioned in the memorial you presented a few days ago appear quite honest; but today you have told me that you didn't know this or that too well — this attitude is very different from that of your suggestions! For instance, the former naval commander-in-chief about whom I just inquired is under the indictment of the board, which has proposed that he be dismissed from his office because it was reported that the sea bandits disturbed the peace on the sea several score times while he was in office, but you told me that he was very good. Aren't you rather dishonest about this?" Your Majesty proceeded to ask me more questions: "What is the difference between a plague of caterpillars in Hunan and a plague of locusts?"

[Ch'en]: "Destructive caterpillars eat right into the very hearts of the young rice plants. They are different from the locusts in the North and cannot be destroyed by human efforts. This is why I didn't impeach local officials when I sent a *t'i-pen* to report on such a plague. After I had received the *Peking Gazette* and learned that an imperial decree had been issued to the effect that all local officials concerned be discussed for proper punishment because they hadn't tried to destroy the locusts [caterpillars] nor had they investigated the matter and impeached the responsible officials, I hurriedly sent in another *t'i-pen* impeaching all the local officials and confessed that I was guilty of negligence. As a matter of fact, such destructive caterpillars were a plague sent down from heaven because the local officials had neglected their official duties and thus disturbed the harmony of the universe; surely I should have impeached them earlier on this account."

Your Majesty nodded assent; then I performed the kowtow and retreated from the imperial presence.

The Third Audience. [Ch'en received an imperial instruction that he be transferred to the post of the governor of Fukien on December 30, 1715.] Therefore, the next day, I went to the palace gate requesting the audience officer to transmit my hope that I might show my personal gratitude to the emperor and receive his advice on general policy regarding my new post. Around 10 A.M. I was called in and brought to the emperor by an imperial guard. I knelt down before Your Majesty.

[Emperor]: "Do you have anything to say to me?"

[Ch'en]: "On account of Your Majesty's immense grace I was appointed governor of Hunan. During my office, I didn't carry out my duty properly, and I made many mistakes. Your Majesty didn't dismiss me immediately; rather, you have shown me your special benevolence by transferring me to be the governor of Fukien. I feel extremely grateful. However, in view of the fact that Fukien is a crucial province as regards both land and sea, I, being so lacking in knowledge, would like to receive your kind instructions."

[Emperor]: "Was there any unauthorized surtax increase in Fukien?"

[Ch'en]: "There is no surtax at all besides the land-poll tax levied in the three districts of Taiwan."

[Emperor]: "But what about those districts on the mainland?"

[Ch'en]: "The surtax charges in the prefectures and districts on the mainland part [of Fukien] are less than one percent."

[Emperor]: "Exacting surtax charges certainly is not a good thing. But if such exactions are forbidden, I am afraid the district governments will practice other abuses under different names, which is unavoidable. Formerly, the district governments were allowed to retain a certain amount of the annual tax reserve in their treasuries to meet official expenditures. Later, the Board of Revenue memorialized that this tax reserve be turned in to the board treasury in Peking. As a result the district governments did not have any financial resources to meet official expenditures.[7] According to what you suggested in your memorial, the surtax charge should be forbidden. I am afraid that may be impractical."

[Ch'en]: "Your Majesty's comment is quite right. But may I say that the district magistrates should be forbidden to exact surtax charges amounting to more than prescribed by the law. For instance, although one percent is allowed by the law, yet many places exact more than that ratio."

[Emperor]: "It is indeed good to be an honest official, this has been valuable ever since very ancient times; but being honest alone is not sufficient. One should do something for the court. Otherwise what is the good of being honest? Being a governor-general or a governor, one should maintain the necessary dignity. For example, it is indispensable that a certain amount of money should be given to one's subordinates as rewards every year. It is not practical only to claim that one is an absolutely honest official. Being a governor is quite different from being a taotai, or a prefect or a magistrate."

Your Majesty then asked: "What do you predict about the future of Taiwan in the long run?"

[Ch'en]: "In Taiwan, only those native barbarians along the southern and northern routes are very stupid; they don't know anything about farming, and they make their living by hunting deer. All the rest of the inhabitants are from the prefectures of Chang-chou and Ch'üan-chou of Fukien or from Ch'ao-chou of Kwangtung. They plow their land for a living. In future times they will all have their own families and property; then there will be nothing to worry about. The only necessity is that good officials be appointed to Taiwan and that the military and civil officials cooperate with each other. I am sure no trouble will arise for several centuries."

[Emperor]: "What is the population now in Taiwan?"

[Ch'en]: "Roughly several hundred thousand households. Since Taiwan produces rice and other grains, it is not hard to make a living, except that the price of foodstuffs is rather high."

[Emperor]: "Why is it so high?"

[Ch'en]: "Because of the population growth."

[The emperor asked about the fresh water problem and then moved to the next question.]

[Emperor]: "What do you think of Yao T'ang, the brigade general of Taiwan?"

[Ch'en]: "Very good, he disciplines his soldiers most strictly."

[Emperor]: "Indeed, he has a very sturdy figure and is skilled in archery and horseback-riding. I have known him ever since he was the major of the Ku-pei Pass. His term of office should have been terminated from yesterday and he should be promoted to a new office. But since you are now in Peking, I have kept him there for the time being to take care of local peace and order."

[Ch'en]: "Yes, he indeed has a sturdy figure and is skilled in archery and horseback-riding. I worked with him for three years; I know him very well."

[Emperor]: "Who is the taotai of Taiwan and Amoy?"

[Ch'en]: "Liang Wen-k'o."

[Emperor]: "Where is he from?"

[Ch'en]: "He is a bannerman."

[Emperor]: "Is he a good official?"

[Ch'en): "Very good. He was originally the grain intendant of Fukien and has been promoted to this office by Your Majesty's special order."

[Emperor]: "How is the prefect?"

[Ch'en]: "The former prefect Feng Hsieh-i was a good official, and was gifted in administrative ability. He has retired because of some ear ailment. The new prefect hasn't arrived yet."

[Emperor]: "Now I want to tell you that the so-called pirates in the Fukien area are merely those fishermen who went out to sea and were later unable to return. You know that all the inhabitants of the Fukien, Kwangtung, Chekiang, Chiang-nan, and Shantung coasts rely on fishing for their living. If no fishing boats are allowed to go out, they all lose their means of making a living. As long as they possess the required permits, the inspecting military officers at the ports should let them out; by the same token, when they return, they should not be forced to offer money. This way, they can support themselves. But the actual situation is that the inspecting officers often will not let them in or out unless they offer money to them; if they fail to catch enough fish and are unable to come back, they take the risk of having to rob commercial vessels and thus become professional pirates. Furthermore, even if real pirates do exist, as long as the coastal guards are serious in patrolling the sea and strictly inspecting every fishing boat before it is let in or out, the pirates will not dare to engage in any activities on the sea. For instance, Nan-ao-chen is a most important port as far as Fukien is concerned. As long as every boat is strictly inspected and searched, pirates from Kwangtung will not be able to move to the north; by the same token, as long as all boats passing through the port of Hai-t'an-chen [are inspected], pirates from Shantung, Chekiang, and Chiang-nan will not be able to cross over to the south. If, for example, the military garrisons in Ting-hai and Chenkiang of Chekiang province, and Chin-shen and Hua-niao of Chiang-nan province are always vigilant, pirates will automatically disappear when they find no chance to engage in activity."

[Ch'en]: "Yes, Your Majesty's view is indeed right. The most important thing is that the military ships should patrol the sea constantly."

[Emperor]: "Patrolling is of course the most important thing; this is the unavoidable duty of the military officers. But in addition, you must have able pilots and crew members who are good swimmers; you also need sturdy boats to carry out the mission. You know how dangerous the sea is when one encounters strong winds and roaring billows; without sturdy boats and good sailors, I am afraid you cannot carry out your mission satisfactorily. All the military boats are built under the supervision of you governors-general or governors; you should build good ships. You ought to tell governor-general Man-pao about this. I have ruled the country for over fifty years. Although I remain distant from the common people, their welfare is my constant concern. I am afraid they don't know about this and think that probably I don't care about them at all. Now I tell you this so that they may also know my feelings toward them through you. Whenever bandits are discovered in your province, you should seize the earliest opportunity to put them down; don't tolerate them, lest they grow and plague the localities. As soon as you discover them, you should report to me immediately in a palace memorial.[8] I will know how to deal with such situations. But if you governors-general and governors should cover up the situation and not report to me, you will be subject to the death penalty if I come to know of it through other channels."

[Ch'en]: "I reverently beg the immense grace of being allowed to report to Your Majesty by using palace memorials."

Your Majesty nodded your assent to my request; I, therefore, performed the kowtow to express my gratitude for such a privilege.

[Emperor]: "The qualifications of the district magistrates [in Fukien] are quite different. Some of the Chinese were appointed to the magistracy with academic degrees, some of them were bannermen, and some purchased their offices. You should not discriminate between them because of their qualifications. They are all new officials without too much experience; you should therefore first teach them and give them guidance. If you should find that they prove themselves utterly unteachable and very bad in their official performance, you may impeach one or two in order to warn the rest to show respect to the law, but you should not overdo it; by all means try to avoid extremes and hold to the mean. Each year, you should report honestly as to the percentage of harvest and the rice prices; otherwise I will ask officials from other provinces; if they tell me the truth, wouldn't your untrue report be found out? For instance, I just asked you about the rice prices in Honan and Hupeh provinces so that I may check them against their own reports; how can one hide the truth from me?"

[Ch'en]: "I will obey Your Majesty's instructions."

[Emperor]: "When you set out to P'u-ch'eng on your way to Fukien, you should go there by land, not by sea; the sea route in the Chien-ning vicinity is very dangerous. Do remember this!"

[Ch'en]: "I will remember this. I am very grateful for Your Majesty's concern."

Then Your Majesty told me to retreat to the courtyard to perform the ceremony of three kneelings and nine bowings. After that, I left the palace.

The same afternoon, the emperor bestowed on me some Neo-Confucian books; they were the *Yüan-chien lei-han, P'ei-wen yün-fu, Chou-i che-chung,* and *Chu-tzu ch'uan-shu.*

The Fourth Audience. On January 2, 1716, early in the morning, I waited at the palace gate for a farewell audience with Your Majesty. I was summoned to the inner palace of the Ch'ang-ch'un yüan and knelt down in front of the imperial throne.

[Emperor]: "Concerning all the instruction you requested from me, I have nothing more to add besides what I told you yesterday. It would be satisfactory if you just followed those instructions. [But there are a few things of which I want to remind you.] First of all, it is indeed a wonderful thing that you are an honest official. But besides being honest, one should be able to have good relationship with his colleagues. [For instance,] officials [in your province] have all kinds of different qualifications: some are *chü-jen* or *chin-shih,* some have gotten their posts through purchase, some are bannermen and some Chinese. Even among those who have entered the government service through purchase some make good officials; on the other hand, among those who possess *chü-jen* or *chin-shih* degrees, I have found many corrupt officials.

Furthermore, since those local officials in your province have all just entered government service without much experience, you should try to teach them first. Who can avoid mistakes? As long as one can correct his mistakes, he is considered to be a good man. If he is unwilling to correct his wrongs then you may impeach him according to law; he'll have no grounds for complaint.

Secondly, officials should maintain dignity. There is a great difference between being a governor and being a lower-ranking official, such as a prefect or taotai, or a district magistrate. You should not try to avoid spending money in making rewards and gifts as well as engaging in other activities. I am afraid you will run into difficulties if you claim that you do not give one penny to anyone because you don't receive one penny from anyone either. If one can't accomplish anything constructive, what is the use of merely being honest? For instance, while Chang Po-hsing was the governor of Fukien, he had a very good reputation. During the first year after being transferred to Soochow [as the governor of Kiangsu] he was still quite good. But his reputation gradually deteriorated during the second and third years. People began to criticize him because, although he was not greatly gifted, he thought too highly of himself. He always said: 'I am an honest official'; therefore, he had no concern about others. As a result, he could not get along with his colleagues, the governor-general, the commander-in-chief, and the brigade general. He not only failed to accomplish anything, but he also caused a great deal of trouble. This is the shortcoming of a mere 'honest official.' By the same token, everyone knows that you, Ch'en Pin, are an honest official; but I am worried that you may become too austere with others just because of your own honesty."

[Ch'en]: "Being honest is merely one's official duty, and doesn't concern others. Indeed, if one fails to accomplish anything constructive, what is the use of his being honest? I entirely concur with Your Majesty's most enlightened point of view. I was originally among the low-ranking officials; I knew their difficulties. I will not dare to treat them too strictly. Especially since Your Majesty has given me this special instruction, I'll be even more careful to obey your injunction." [The Emperor asked him again what official posts he had held.]

[Emperor]: "Do you know any good official who doesn't take money?"

[Ch'en]: "Well, speaking of talent and ability, many officials possess such qualities. But offhand I don't dare mention anyone who doesn't take money. I will report to you in a palace memorial as soon as I discover any."

[Emperor]: "All right, you report to me in palace memorials on good ones as well as bad ones. I'll not believe only what you have to say, but after I have made further inquiries I'll find out the truth."

[Ch'en]: "While I was a magistrate in Fukien, I learned that Yang Lin, then commander-in-chief, was very fair and honest. Now he has been promoted to be the governor of Kwangtung. Ever since he became commander-in-chief, the bandits in the mountains all disappeared. The soldiers and the common people lived together peacefully under his administration."

[Emperor]: "Yes, he is really good. I know him very well. He always writes [his palace memorials] with his own hand. He has a clear mind, never takes money, and doesn't steal rations."

Then the emperor asked: "Do you know anyone else?"

[Ch'en]: "I know one Pai Huang, a judicial commissioner of Kweichow, formerly grain intendant of Fukien under whom I was an official. He is both gifted and honest: he never became too fussy with his subordinates."

[Emperor]: "Where is he from? Is he a bannerman?"

[Ch'en]: "Yes, he is a bannerman."

Then I recalled another person and said to the emperor: "I know another official by the name of Yü Cheng-chien. He is the current educational commissioner of Chiang-nan, very learned and with a high standard of morality. Your Majesty knows him very well; there is no need for me to recommend him."

[Emperor]: "Yes, he has a very good reputation in his current office."

Your Majesty then asked: "How is the present naval commander-in-chief in comparison with his predecessor Wu Ying?"

[Ch'en]: "Wu Ying is an honest and experienced official. The present commander-in-chief is willing to take time in drilling his naval forces and fleet, which I think is a good thing."

[Emperor]: "How many men did you take along with you from home to your last office?"

[Ch'en]: "Only one or two servants; my wife stayed home because I couldn't move my family."

[Emperor]: "Do you have any sons?"

[Ch'en]: "I have not been able to see my sons in well over ten years. We couldn't see each other because we didn't have money to travel. Only my second son went to Szechwan to see me once; this was several years ago. This year when I left Taiwan for Fukien, I didn't have any money to meet my travel expenses, but the governor of Fukien helped me out. When I arrived at Ch'u-chou to see the governor-general [of Hu-kwang], he said to me: 'When you arrive at your post, you should request a special audience; the emperor will definitely want to see you. But if you don't have any money, how will you travel?' The governor-general kindly gave me some money, and I was enabled to come to Peking."

Your Majesty, after sighing for quite a while, said: "You are like an old monk who wants to obtain enlightenment through enduring sufferings and mortifying all his desires!" You then asked: "Why didn't you impeach A-lin, the financial commissioner of Hunan?"

[Ch'en]: "Because I was in office as governor of Hunan only for a short time. While I was still in the midst of making inquiries about local officials, I was summoned for this special audience."

That day, because I had been kneeling for a long time while the audience was held, Your Majesty granted me the special favor of allowing that I hold on to the imperial throne to get off my knees. I then retired from the imperial presence.

On the same day, I was called to the palace gate to receive the emperor's gift, which was the *Yü-chih wen-chi* [Collected works of the K'ang-hsi Emperor].

On January 3, 1716, early in the morning, after the presidents of the boards went in and had presented their memorials, Your Majesty turned to your grand secretaries and said: "Ch'en Pin is from Lei-chou of Kwangtung — a distant and insignificant place, but one from which a good man like this can come all the same. He doesn't flatter others, nor does he associate with influential figures. I think he stands as an auspicious sign of a really peaceful country like ours!" [9]

When the grand secretaries came out, they told all the court officials Your

Majesty's comment about me. As I was kneeling outside, I was greatly moved upon hearing this. I felt that I was unworthy of a single word of Your Majesty's compliment.

Then Your Majesty called me in and said: "You have always been a very honest official, taking no money from others. Today the weather is really cold because of the heavy snowfall. I observe that you don't have enough warm clothes. I want to grant you a sable jacket of mine. In addition, I want to bestow a farewell poem in my own handwriting. Do you wish to have it?"

[Ch'en]: "It was all due to Your Majesty's immense grace that I was promoted from a taotai to be the governor of Hunan. For half a year in that office, I committed many wrongs without having any merits. But this time Your Majesty again has kindly transferred me to be the governor of Fukien. I really don't know how to show my gratitude. Today Your Majesty has cherished me like a father does his son by granting me your own sable jacket so that I might be protected from this severe cold weather. Surely I wish very much to have a farewell poem in Your Majesty's own handwriting. I will reverently take it home and cherish it as the most precious treasure of my family."

Your Majesty was greatly pleased by my answer. Your Majesty then composed a farewell poem for me.[10] I knelt down to receive it and expressed my thanks to Your Majesty.

On January 7, 1716, early in the morning, an imperial order was transmitted that I be called in for an audience. [But since Your Majesty was leaving the Ch'ang-ch'un yüan that day for T'ang-shan] I therefore had gone to Ch'ing-ho beforehand, waiting there to see you off. When the imperial chariot arrived at Ch'ing-ho, Your Majesty summoned me to Your presence and said: "I knew of your coming here; you may proceed from here to your new office in Fukien." Your Majesty also inquired how long it would take me to get to Fukien. I said that it would take me about forty days. Unfortunately, after I had got up from my knees and walked backward a few steps, I stumbled because the snowfall was so deep. Your Majesty kindly told the audience officer to help me to my feet. At this moment, I was so deeply moved that I could not help but shed grateful tears. Your Majesty then asked me: "Governor, how many times have you encountered such heavy snowfall? Have you ever lived in Peking?" "I lived in Peking for five years, and I saw heavy snowfalls three or four times." "What office did you hold them?" "I was an official in the Board of Personnel." "When was that?" "From the forty-third year of K'ang-hsi [1704] to the forty-seventh year [1709]. Then I was sent out to Szechwan as the educational commissioner." "Did you see any snow out there?" "I never saw such heavy snowfall out there." [11]

Case B

Li Hsü and Ts'ao Yin's Secret Reports on the Examination Hall Scandal of 1711 and the Gali-Chang Mutual Impeachment Trials

The following five documents have been selected to illustrate some of the important aspects of the palace memorial system as a secret channel of communication in the K'ang-hsi period. They are all concerned with the famous Examination Hall scandal of 1711 and the mutual impeachment case between Gali, the Manchu governor-general of Chiang-nan and Kiangsi, and Chang Po-hsing, the governor of Kiangsu (Chiang-nan). Since these cases have been described elsewhere,[1] a brief introductory note will suffice to give the context in which these palace memorials appeared.

The protest demonstrations which followed the posted results of the 1711 Chiang-nan provincial examination — coupled with the open memorials submitted from the chief examiner, Tso Pi-fan, and the governor, Chang Po-hsing — forced the K'ang-hsi Emperor to appoint an imperial commission headed by Chang P'eng-ko to try suspects in the examination scandal, which had thus been brought to light. During the trial, two members of the imperial commission, Gali and Chang Po-hsing, impeached each other. As a result, both were dismissed from the commission, as well as from their official positions, and tried by a second imperial commission also headed by Chang P'eng-ko. The fact-finding reports of the two commissions were rejected by the K'ang-hsi Emperor because, as he explained, "both commissions had been strongly manipulated by Gali."[2] The final solution to both cases, the scandal and the impeachment, was only reached after the emperor had permanently deposed the heir apparent Yin-jeng — the real power behind the Gali faction, as mentioned in Chapter VI.

While the trials were being conducted, by three successive imperial commissions, the emperor received palace memorials from his secret agents concerning the actual facts involved in the two cases and thus was able to critically judge the reports of the imperial commissions. The following documents illustrate the contents and comprehensiveness of palace memorials as a means of giving secret information to the emperor. The reports were presented by Li Hsü and Ts'ao Yin before the first imperial commission had submitted its fact-finding memorial and were therefore concerned only with the first stage of the story. The K'ang-hsi Emperor's final decision to take a stand against Gali after he had publicly deposed the heir apparent was not the sole work of Li and Ts'ao's palace memorials, but was perhaps influenced more by a secret palace memorial submitted by his most trusted grand secretary and scholar-adviser, Li Kuang-ti.[3]

The first document is a ch'ing-an che (*greetings palace memorial*) *from Ts'ao Yin, which illustrates how a secret report could be conveyed to the emperor in this type of ceremonial document. The secret report deals with the demonstration held by the* hsiu-ts'ai (*or* sheng-yüan) *after the examination scandal had become known. It was written on November 11, 1711 (KH 50/20/2).*

Document I

Ts'ao Yin, the superintendent of the Imperial Manufactory and commissioner of the Transmission Office, reverently inquires after Your Majesty's well-being. Both Chiang-nan and Chekiang provinces have enjoyed a plentiful harvest this year. The price of the autumn harvest rice ranges from 6 to 7 *ch'ien*. Because of this year's plentiful harvest, the people feel at ease about the prospects for the next year. They all praise the great peace and are enjoying a peaceful life. Unfortunately, however, all the *hsiu-ts'ai* in Yangchow have complained very strongly about the result of this year's examination in Chiang-nan. They all declare that "this year's *chü-jen* quota has been enlarged on account of the emperor's immense kindness. By doing this the emperor meant to encourage and select the impecunious ones. But the new *chü-jen* winners have been chosen on an extremely unfair basis; it is quite obvious that abuses have occurred." Therefore, the *hsiu-ts'ai* in the Yangchow area congregated in a noisy crowd. They tore down the shrine which had been erected in honor of the chief examiner, Tso Pi-fan. The violent demonstration temporarily subsided after they had heard that the deputy examiner Chao Chin was actually responsible for the scandal. Both the governor-general and the governor have prepared their impeaching memorials. At the present time, two persons, Wu Pi and Ch'eng Kuang-k'uei, have been put under arrest. Both of them are sons of wealthy merchants. Rumor says that there are a great many more people on the list who are not versed in literature at all. All these local conditions and the weather record are herewith enclosed to keep Your Majesty informed.[4]

This palace memorial, written by Li Hsü on February 22, 1712 (KH 51/1/16), describes the manner in which the first imperial commission conducted the scandal trial, the reaction of the local populace in the South, and the conflicting opinions of the two commissioners, Gali and Chang Po-hsing, which eventually led to mutual impeachment.

Document II

Li Hsü reverently memorializes: I have heard that the imperial commissioner, after the cross-examinations, has obtained the following confession: *Chü-jen* Ch'eng Kuang-k'uei is an old friend of the deputy examiner Chao Chin and the magistrate of Shan-yang district Fang Ming. This is why he succeeded in winning the degree. Concerning the details of the bribery case of the *chü-jen* Wu Pi, the arrangement was contracted with Yü Shih-ch'eng [Yü Shih-ch'en], who in turn asked a certain Yüan Hsing-jo to handle the transactions. According to the deposition of Yüan, Yeh [Chiu-ssu], the former governor of Anhwei, received 5,000 taels, while the assistant prefect of river defenses, Yeh, received 3,000 silver taels. But Yüan subsequently changed his deposition, saying, "because governor Yeh did not want to see me, I therefore asked Li Ch'i, the clerk [in the office of the financial commissioner of Anhwei Ma I-tzu], to do it." Li Ch'i was then immediately cross-examined. He confessed that he had transferred fifteen ingots of gold to Hsien San, the house servant of Ma. Then Hsien San was tortured, but he disclosed nothing more.

However, according to the report of Su Hsün, magistrate of Nanking district, a certain Yao Chen-tsung secretly reported that the gold was actually concealed in Li Ch'i's own house. He falsely implied that Hsien San had done it. That magistrate then went to Li's home and questioned his wife. He discovered that the fifteen ingots of gold were hidden in his house. The gold, together with Yao Chen-tsung, was delivered to the imperial commissioners for cross-examination. The hearing has not yet been concluded.

But at the present time there are all sorts of criticism. People all say that there are differences of opinion among the commissioners, that Chang Po-hsing has an extremely suspicious mind, that he insisted on forcing Hsien San to confess that he had taken the gold. Governor-general Gali and Governor Liang Shih-hsün, however, argued: "Formerly, Li Ch'i confessed that he had delivered the gold to Hsien San, yet now the gold has been found in his own house through questioning his wife. Thus, his deposition seems merely a false accusation." Both sides insisted on maintaining their own views and disputes arose between them.

As for Chang P'eng-ko, he does not have any definite view of his own. Furthermore, Gali will leave Yangchow for Huai-an on the seventeenth of this month in order to hold a conference with Ho-shou, the director-general of grain transport on another official matter. He, therefore, will not be in Yangchow [for a while] to participate in the trial.

I hereby reverently memorialize on what I have learned.

[The vermilion endorsement reads:] The governor-general and the governor are not on good terms. This fact is known to every one. The governor is an absolutely honest official who has never been corrupted by a penny of bribery, whereas the governor-general is also a bright and diligent person. Their mutual impeachment memorials have just arrived. How is the public opinion in the South? Continue to inquire, finding out the facts and reporting to me quickly! [5]

After the mutual impeachments by Gali and Chang Po-hsing, Li Hsü wrote this palace memorial on March 25, 1712 (KH 51/2/19), reporting on public reaction to the second imperial commission's conduct of the two cases. In addi-

tion, Li mentioned the popular demonstration and petitions made on behalf of Gali.

Document III

Li Hsü reverently memorializes: My servant brought back my secret palace memorial on 2/15. After I opened it, I read Your Majesty's vermilion endorsement [the endorsement in Document II is then repeated]. Public opinion in the South holds that the governor-general never sold any *chü-jen* degrees, but because the governor was too suspicious and hated the governor-general, he went so far as to impeach him. Now both of them have been discharged. Although the governor is an honest official, he often failed to make clearcut decisions. Therefore too many people were arrested when he handled disputes. The governor-general never took any money. He is also very able and quick-witted. All of the people love him in their hearts, and the localities [under his jurisdiction] have all benefited [from his good administration]. This is the nature of public comment on this issue. I therefore report to Your Majesty according to your secret instructions.

Furthermore, the people in Nanking, Chenkiang and Yangchow prefectures all closed their shops [*pa-shih*] and swarmed to my office urging that I send a memorial to request imperial permission to retain the governor-general in his office. I did not dare do so without your authorization; I therefore wish to mention this matter along with my report on public opinions.

[The vermilion endorsement reads:] Continue your secret inquiries; and report your findings swiftly.[6]

In this memorial, written on March 30, 1712 (KH 51/2/24), Li Hsü gives a detailed description of popular support for Gali in the impeachment case. (As Document V will show, the demonstrations and petitions did not necessarily imply genuine popular support for Gali.) The vermilion endorsement reveals the fact that the imperial commissioner was also under the surveillance of a secret agent of the emperor.

Document IV

Li Hsü memorializes: The people of Chiang-ning [Nanking], Chen-chiang, and Yangchow prefectures, upon hearing the news of Gali's dismissal, voluntarily closed their shops and halted all business transactions for two consecutive days, on the eighteenth and nineteenth days of the second month. They first came to my office petitioning that I submit a *t'i-pen* to the throne to request Your Majesty's permission to keep Gali in office. On the twenty-second day of the same month, the governor-general sent an official to transfer his official seal to the yamen of the governor of Kiangsi. Unexpectedly, however, soldiers and common people closed the gate of the city to prevent the official from doing this; they grabbed the seal and sent it to the official residence of Liang Shih-hsün [the governor of Anhwei]. The governor could not come out to meet the crowd because of his foot ailment. Then the crowd fetched the seal to my office and requested that I temporarily take care of it and that I send a memorial swiftly to ask Your Majesty's permission to keep the governor-general in his present office. I told the crowd: "The emperor loves you soldiers and common people as dearly as he does his own beloved sons. This is why he speedily appointed [Gali] governor-general of Chiang-nan. At the present time, he has been discharged from his office because of the mutual impeachments between the governor-general and the governor and is awaiting trial. After the trial is over, the emperor will make his own illustrious final decision. Therefore, you should not behave like this." It was only after I had repeatedly exhorted them that the crowd began to disperse.

The next day, the crowd allowed the official to send the seal to Kiangsi, but the soldiers and common people blocked the front gate of the governor-general's official residence with wood blocks and stones to prevent him from leaving.

The situation here caused by the soldiers and common people is extremely explosive. As to the seal of the governor, it was sent to Chekiang on the twenty-fourth day of the second month. I hereby reverently memorialize.

[The vermilion endorsement reads:] I understand. When Chang Po-hsing saw this situation, did he say anything? How is Chang P'eng-ko doing [with the trial] at present? [7]

Before receiving Li Hsü's reply to his vermilion endorsement, the K'ang-hsi Emperor received this report from Ts'ao Yin (dated KH 51/3/26 — May 1, 1712) concerning the following matters: the imperial commissioners' conduct of the trial, the true nature of the demonstrations on behalf of Gali, the reason why Chang Po-hsing had impeached Gali, public reaction to the two cases being tried, and Ts'ao Yin's personal dissatisfaction with the procrastinating tactics of the chief imperial commissioner.

Document V

[Ts'ao Yin] Reverently memorializes: I have been in Yangchow for a whole month since I arrived here on the twenty-sixth day of the second month. I carefully inquired about how Chang P'eng-ko and Ho-shou conducted the trial on the examination scandal. In connection with Wu Pi's purchasing the degree, they only pressed Li Ch'i and his wife concerning the source of the gold. By doing so, they meant to close up Wu's case by sacrificing Li Ch'i as the scapegoat. In connection with Ch'eng Kuang-k'uei, they intend to close his case based on his confession that he had brought reference materials to the examination hall. As for Tso Pi-fan, and Chao Chin as well as the other associate examiners, they did not cross-examine them very carefully.

According to public opinion, Chang P'eng-ko intended, on the one hand, to mediate a compromise between the governor-general and the governor so that he might close their case. On the other hand, he did not want to penalize the chief examiner, deputy examiner, and the associate examiners, in the hope that the opportunistic channel in the examination system [that is, to accept bribes] might be preserved. Ho-shou was also maintaining a middle-of-the-road policy, waiting to see which side would win.

The governor-general actually did not make a contractual deal to sell the degrees, but it is possible that he exerted his influence in protecting Yeh Chiu-ssu [the former governor of Anhwei, who had been accused of accepting bribes]. After Gali was released from his office, a crowd presented petitions to retain him in office; however, all these were prearranged gestures by his subordinate officials and underclerks just for the sake of whitewashing, and they do not mean that the people sincerely love him.

The reason that Chang Po-hsing impeached Gali actually was because he intended to get revenge for Gali's impeaching him on the problem of transporting tribute grain to Peking. After his discharge, people also filed petitions to various yamen to help him retain office. *Hsiu-ts'ai* constituted the majority of the crowd. This was also prearranged by his subordinate officials and not because the people love him.

All public opinion on this case is in agreement that "the people of Chiang-nan have received repeated exemptions from taxes because of the emperor's kindness. The people also have been comforted by the emperor's relief measures. It is really a shame that the governor-general and governor have failed to show their appreciation for the emperor's kindness. Instead of trying to protect the people, they formed their own factions from selfish motives and for their own vanity. They indeed have failed to behave properly, as should the emperor's high officials." As for Chang P'eng-ko, he, being the imperial commissioner, should have upheld justice and tried the case in fairness and determination; but he acted on the contrary. He only wanted to protect the accused examiners and has been following a procrastinating policy — there must have existed some particularism and selfishness in it.

It has been four months already since he began to try the cases. Every day, the imperial commissioners question the accused suspects individually; he [Chang] has never let both sides defend themselves face to face. He has suspended hearings on Ch'eng Kuang-k'uei's case, trying only the case of Wu Pi. Moreover, he has never questioned the chief examiner and the associate examiners so as to determine what cheating techniqeus they used. For instance, he has not asked which words in the examination papers were used so that the associate examiners could identify Wu Pi's paper.

At the present time, it is said that the gangster Li Ch'i uttered many rude and reckless words during the trial. He said that people had collaborated to betray him by putting gold in his own house so that the financial commissioner of Anhwei [Ma I-tzu] might be proven innocent.

[The imperial commissioner] has never made any final judgment. Officials of the Chiang-nan and Kiangsi areas have all been called to attend hearings in

Yangchow. Since this case has been on trial for several months and has involved officials from a vast region, it may well cause severe damage to local administrations . . . If it continues in this manner, the trial will not be able to close until the fall or even the winter.

These are the public opinions given by impartial people. As for those who are for Gali or for Chang Po-hsing, they have all tried to justify their own views. Therefore, I do not dare believe them. I have sincerely reported to Your Majesty on local conditions which I have critically collected.

[The vermilion endorsement reads:] Make further inquiries; then report again.[8]

Case C

The Yung-cheng Emperor's Vermilion Endorsements on the Palace Memorials Submitted by General Nien Keng-yao

The following vermilion endorsements reflect the emotional temperament of the Yung-cheng Emperor; they also demonstrate how he partially reduced the palace memorial system to a medium of petty personal communication in order to further the relationship between himself and the memorialist. Often the endorsement was totally unrelated to the subject matter discussed in the palace memorial itself. These endorsements should be read together with Chapter VII in connection with the third social function of the palace memorial system in the Yung-cheng period.

The following lengthy vermilion endorsement was written on a palace memorial submitted by Nien Keng-yao on August 3, 1724 (YC 2/6/18), in order to express his gratitude for having received two fans on which the emperor had written some poems with his own hand.[1] The endorsement was emotional in nature and was totally unrelated to the memorial.

Document I

I have instructed Uncle Lungkodo to adopt [your son] Nien Hsi as his own child. Nien Hsi became very sick this spring — sometimes he was better, sometimes worse. Although he has been receiving all kinds of medical treatments, they have not proven too effective. I therefore devoted some thought to this matter. I thought this son [of yours] should not just die like that.

Recently I asked a fortune-teller to determine his fate. I was told that Nien Hsi was encountering his unlucky cycle at the present time. Furthermore, in the next few decades, he should be able to enjoy his luckiest period. But [the fortune-teller said]: At the present time, you are now undergoing a period of "being destined to destroy" [k'o] your own first-born [Nien Hsi]. This is why I was motivated to issue the instructions on a selected auspicious date. I did not even discuss this matter with your father. Thus this son of yours will have nothing to do with you [and therefore he will not be destroyed because of your unlucky period]. Uncle [Lungkodo] has changed Nien Hsi's name; he will naturally become healthy and strong hereafter.

I should have told you about this earlier when Nien Hsi became sick. But since you are thousands of *li* away from the capital, it would have just increased your own worry and anxieties if I had done so. I did not cheat you, however, on this matter. [You should remember that when] I endorsed your palace memorials last year, I always told you that all your family members, old and young, were in good health. But since this late spring and early summer time, I merely told you that your father was healthy and did not mention how your son was — this proves that [my conscience] would not permit me to cheat you even by one single word . . .

[The latter half of the endorsement describes how happy Uncle Lungkodo and Nien's father felt when they had been informed of the arrangement made by the emperor.] [2]

On August 20, 1724 (YC 2/7/2), Nien Keng-yao sent a palace memorial expressing thanks for several gifts the emperor had granted him. The gifts included two snuff bottles newly made of enamel, four boxes of new tea of various kinds, and "four fresh lichees." Only one of the four lichees survived the "long journey [several thousands of li] under the summer heat"; it took nine days and nine nights for the super-express horse post to transmit them from Peking to Sian. Interestingly enough, the vermilion endorsement noted on this palace memorial is twice the length of the memorial. In the first half, not given here, the emperor, among other irrelevant chatter, inquires about the general's foot ailment. The second half is even more unrelated to the original subject; it is merely a joke, though it reflects the Yung-cheng Emperor's religious concepts.

Document II

I still have a joke to tell you. We have in the capital a Taoist priest with the surname Liu. He has been very famous for a long time. Maybe he is already several hundred years old, nobody can tell for sure. The last time that Prince I [Yin-hsiang] saw him, the priest told the prince that he could tell people what they had been in the previous life. He said that Prince I had been a Taoist priest. [When Prince I told me this] I burst into raucous laughter and said: "This was the close relationship between you and the Taoist priest — this was true!" Then I kidded with him [and asked]: "Why did you decide to be born into this world to serve me, a Buddhist monk?" [3] The prince could not answer my question. Then I said: "It is not that one wants to be the real Buddha, or the real immortal, or the real sage; rather, one [ought to] cultivate his own field of blessing for the interest of the common millions. It is by no means our goal to labor solely for the pleasure of this world. If anyone is less capable, he still has to [abandon this officialdom and] become a Buddhist monk, or a Taoist priest, so that he might set up his own sect — there is no choice other than this!" After I had said this we all burst into loud laughter.

I have told you this joke simply because I am not busy at the moment, and because I want to make you laugh, too.[4]

On January 27, 1724 (YC 2/1/2), Nien Keng-yao, the governor-general of Szechwan and Shensi, sent a palace memorial solely to express thanks to the emperor because the latter had granted him some gifts including a sable jacket and hat, a pair of New Year scrolls upon which a pair of parallel verses were written with the emperor's own hand, an attractive snuff bottle, and some other items. In response to this palace memorial, a completely independent vermilion endorsement was attached, of which the following is only a portion.

Document III

Now I want to give you a precious pearl which I ordered during the first year of Yung-cheng and which has now arrived. Also, I want to grant this pair of earrings to your wife [literally, your woman] as a sign to predict that you will be successful in carrying out your duty, and that both you and your wife will be happy and blessed by Heaven, and that we will have a happy reunion in the future. [Then the emperor informed Nien of his father's condition,[5] and added:] My physical condition is excellent. Your father is very healthy. Everything in the capital is peaceful and tranquil — I tell you this in order to make you happy.[6]

CKTP	*Chang-ku ts'ung-pien*
CPYC	*Chu-p'i yü-chih*
CSL	*Ta-Ch'ing li-ch'ao shih-lu*
HT	*Ta-Ch'ing hui-tien*
HTK	*Ch'ing-ch'ao hsü wen-hsien t'ung-k'aɔ*
KH	K'ang-hsi reign
SC	Shun-chih reign
SH:KH	*Sheng-tsu Jen huang-ti sheng-hsün*
SL	*Ta-Ch'ing hui-tien shih-li*
SYNK	*Shang-yü Nei-ko*
THL	*Tung-hua lu*
WHTP	*Wen-hsien ts'ung-pien*
YC	Yung-cheng reign

In the notes, and occasionally in the text as well, Chinese dates have been used primarily for the purpose of identifying documents. Dates of memorials signify, whenever possible, the date of preparation, not the date of arrival. As an example of Chinese notation, the 28th day of the 6th month of the 32nd year of the K'ang-hsi reign would read: KH 32/6/28 (that is, the order is from year to month to day). A question mark is used whenever the particular day does not appear in the document. The Gregorian calendar date (either in full or merely the year) is given next to the Chinese date only when it is deemed relevant to the discussion of historical development.

Chapter I. Concept, Method, Scope
1. Richard C. Snyder, "A Decision-Making Approach to the Study of Political Phenomena," in Roland Young, ed., *Approaches to the Study of Politics* (Evanston, 1958), p. 28.
2. See the discussion by William Skinner, "What the Study of China Can Do for Social Science," *Journal of Asian Studies,* 23, no. 4 (August 1964), 520.
3. Compare Karl A. Wittfogel, *Oriental Despotism: A Comparative Study of Total Power* (New Haven, 1957); F. W. Mote, "The Growth of Chinese Despotism: A Critique of Wittfogel's Theory of Oriental Despotism as Applied to China," *Oriens Extremus,* 8, no. 1 (August 1961), 1–41.
4. An influential work in this category is Ch'ien Mu's *Chung-kuo li-tai cheng-chih te-shih* (A critical review of the political institutions in Imperial China) (Taipei, 1952).
5. Three such works are worth noting: Charles O. Hucker, *The Censorial System in Ming China* (Stanford, 1966); Kung-ch'uan Hsiao, *Rural China: Imperial Control in Nineteenth Century China* (Seattle, 1960); and T'ung-tsu Ch'ü, *Local Government in China under the Ch'ing* (Cambridge, Mass., 1962).
6. Pao-chao Hsieh, *Government of China, 1644–1911* (Baltimore, 1925). In addition, there are two earlier manuals on governmental organizations of the Ch'ing dynasty: W. F. Mayers, *The Chinese Government* (Shanghai, 1897), and H. S. Brunnert and V. V. Hagelstrom, *Present Day Political Organization of China* (Shanghai, 1912).
7. The earliest studies on Ch'ing communication-decision procedure include the two pioneering articles by John K. Fairbank and S. Y. Teng entitled "On

the Transmission of Ch'ing Documents," *Harvard Journal of Asiatic Studies,* 4 (1939), 12–46, and "On the Types and Uses of Ch'ing Documents," *Harvard Journal of Asiatic Studies,* 5 (1940), 1–71; both have been reprinted in *Ch'ing Administration: Three Studies* (Cambridge, Mass., 1960), the work to which I refer in these notes. These studies concern, essentially, the nineteenth-century process. Some modifications of the definitions in the latter article can be found in my article entitled "The Memorial Systems of the Ch'ing Dynasty, 1644–1911," *Harvard Journal of Asiatic Studies,* 27 (1967), 7–75. Jonathan Spence, in his *Ts'ao Yin and the K'ang-hsi Emperor* (New Haven, 1966), has devoted one chapter to a description of the role of bondservants in the palace memorial system. For the Yung-cheng period, a pioneering study is Miyazaki Ichisada's *"Shuhi yushi kaidai"* (Notes on *The Vermilion Endorsements of the Yung-cheng Emperor*), *Tōyōshi kenkyū,* 15 (March 1957), 1–32. Huang P'ei has published a supplement to Miyazaki's article entitled "Yung-cheng shih-tai ti mi-tsou chih-tu" (The secret-report system during the Yung-cheng period), *Tsing-hua hsüeh-pao,* NS 3 (May 1962), 17–52.

8. H. D. Lasswell and A. Kaplan, *Power and Society* (New Haven, 1961), p. 75.

9. Snyder, p. 27.

10. For a discussion of the communications systems in Communist China as a "closed" one, see Franz Schurmann, *Ideology and Organization in Communist China* (Berkeley, 1966), pp. 58–68. The degree of "closedness" in the imperial bureaucracy was far greater than in its contemporary counterpart, as far as I can see.

11. For example, in his "T'an Chün-chi ch'u" (On the Grand Council), *Shih-hsüeh nien-pao* (Historical annual), 2, no. 4 (1937), p. 195, Teng Wen-ju misinterpreted the term *shu-chih* as "transmitting an imperial instruction to someone." But the term is a crucial one for an understanding of the decision-making procedures in the council; for its actual connotation, see section on drafting procedures of court letters in Chapter VIII.

12. For recent studies of this sort, see E-tu Sun Zen, *Ch'ing Administrative Terms* (Cambridge, Mass., 1961), which deals with terminology concerning the administrative details of the Six Boards. Jerome Cohen, of the Harvard Law School, and his associates are now working on the legal terms of the Ch'ing dynasty as a part of their Chinese Legal history project.

13. *CSL*:KH 275.20.

14. For discussion of this concept as it applies to political behavior in Japanese history, see Yoshio Sakata and John W. Hall's article, "Motivation of Political Leadership in the Meiji Restoration," *Journal of Asian Studies,* 15, no. 1 (November 1956), 31–50.

15. Gordon W. Allport, *Personality and Social Encounter* (Boston, 1966), p. 95.

16. *Ibid.,* p. 101.

17. For more discussion of this concept, see Snyder, p. 30.

18. Ch'ien Mu, p. 123. Like Ch'ien Mu, when Li Tsung-huang, in his *Chung-kuo li-tai hsing-cheng t'ung-lun* (A historical treatise of the administrative systems in China) (Taipei, 1961), p. 135, comments on the Manchu control policy, he makes special reference to the Yung-cheng Emperor's "secret-police organization" (*t'e-wu tsu-chih*) that "spread its agents all over the empire" in order "to keep him well informed" (*ch'ing-pao ling-t'ung*).

Unless otherwise noted, all translations are my own.

19. Ch'ien Mu, pp. 121, 123.

20. For instance, the Grand Council was by no means an organ symbolizing mere military control (see Chapter VIII). Also, the decision-making procedure during Ming times was not operated in exactly the way Ch'ien described; see my article, "Transmission of Ming Memorials," in *T'oung Pao*, 54, nos. 4–5 (1968), 275–287.

21. Hamil Grant, *Spies and Secret Services* (London, 1915), p. 36; Charles H. Carter, *The Secret Diplomacy of the Habsburgs, 1598–1625* (New York, 1964); James Walker, "The Secret Service under Charles II and James II," *Royal Historical Society Transactions*, 4th ser., 15 (1932), 211–242.

22. Franz Michael, *The Origin of Manchu Rule in China* (Baltimore, 1942), p. 118.

Chapter II. The Early Ch'ing Deliberative Structure

1. For discussion of the functions of this judicial deliberative body, see S. van der Sprenkel, *Legal Institutions in Manchu China* (London, 1962), pp. 67–68; and Derk Bodde and Clarence Morris, *Law in Imperial China* (Cambridge, Mass., 1967), pp. 132–134. This body was composed of the Board of Punishments, the Censorate (*Tu-ch'a yüan*) and the Court of Revision (*Ta-li ssu*).

2. See Kanda Nobuo, "Shinsho no gisei daijin ni tsuite" (On the deliberative ministers in the early Ch'ing dynasty), in *Wada hakushi kanreki kinen Tōyōshi ronso* (Essays on Asian history in commemoration of Dr. Wada's sixty-first birthday; Tokyo), pp. 171–189. According to Kanda, *pei-le* was used both generically to denote "deliberative kings [princes]" (*i-cheng pei-le*) and specifically as an official title. For detailed discussion on *pei-le*, see Kanda's "Shinsho no bairoku ni tsuite" (On the *pei-le* in the early Ch'ing dynasty), in *Tōyō gakushō* (Reports of the Oriental Society), 43, no. 4 (March 1958), 1–23.

3. *Man-chou shih-lu* (Peking, 1927), pp. 293–294.

4. Fu Tsung-mao, *Ch'ing-tai Chün-chi ch'u tsu-chih chi chih-chang chih yen-chiu* (A study of the organization of the Grand Council and its functions under the Ch'ing) (Taipei, 1967), p. 54.

5. Michael, p. 67: "In 1616, the offices of five High Government Secretaries [*ta-ch'en*] and ten Executive Secretaries [*cha-erh ku-ch'i*] were created." Also, p. 86: "They [the five *ta-ch'en* and the ten *cha-erh ku-ch'i*] were his technical advisers. In political questions, however, he had to rely, before his descendants grew up, on the help and advice of a few older companions in arms."

6. Fu Tsung-mao, p. 54.

7. In 1660, this title was converted to *tu-t'ung* in Chinese. See *Ch'ing-ch'ao wen-hsien t'ung-k'ao* (1882), 6393.

8. *T'ai-tsung shih-lu* (Tokyo, 1937), 1.11b.

9. The nine categories of nobility are: (1) *ho-shuo ch'in-wang* (prince of the blood of the first degree), (2) *to-lo chün-wang* (prince of the blood of the second degree), (3) *to-lo pei-le* (prince of the blood of the third degree), (4) *ku-shan pei-tzu* (prince of the blood of the fourth degree), (5) *chen-kuo kung* (prince of the blood of the fifth degree), (6) *fu-kuo kung* (prince of the blood of the sixth degree), (7) *chen-kuo chiang-chün* (noble of the imperial lineage of the ninth rank), (8) *fu-kuo chiang-chün* (noble of the imperial lineage of the tenth rank), (9) *feng-kuo chiang-chün* (noble of the imperial lineage of the eleventh rank); see *HT*:KH 1.1b; see Brunnert and Hagelstrom, 22, 23, where princes of the blood of the seventh and eighth degrees are also listed. With this new peerage, seven of the ten surviving *ho-shuo pei-le* were given the title *ho-shuo ch'in-wang* and three were given the title *to-lo chün-wang* or *to-lo pei-le*.

10. *CSL*:SC 103. 30.

11. *CSL*:KH 144.17.

12. *Hsiao-t'ing tsa-lu* (1880) 2.13.

13. *Ibid.*

14. See Fu Tsung-mao, pp. 58–65, and Kanda Nobuo, "gisei daijin," p. 184.

15. Kanda Nobuo, "gisei daijin," p. 185.

16. *HT* 69.1b; Juan K'uei-sheng, *Ch'a-yü k'o-hua* (Peking, 1959), p. 170.

17. *CSL*:KH 88.246; 89.12.

18. When this practice was first instituted in 1649, it applied only to governor-generalships and governorships (*SL* 23.6–6b); in 1665, it also came to be applied to the functional heads of the Six Boards and the Censorate (*SL* 28.13b).

19. *CSL*:SC 2.1b–2, 44.11.

20. For the subjects dealt with in the joint sessions, see Fu Tsung-mao, pp. 70–91.

21. During the meetings, the grand secretaries also acted as transcribers and were responsible for writing up the final memorials reporting the outcome of deliberations to the emperor. During the Shun-chih reign they were not allowed to participate in such deliberative meetings; but they were again allowed to do so during the K'ang-hsi reign

In 1656, the Shun-chih Emperor decreed: "I think since the grand secretaries are serving me in the Grand Secretariat (*Nei-yüan*), it is not feasible for them to serve in the capacity of deliberative ministers. Hereafter let them be exempted from participating in such deliberations." *CSL*:SC 103.30). In doing so, he probably hoped to avoid being criticized for using the grand secretaries to influence the ministers to abide by the imperial will.

22. For an excellent discussion of this subject, see Miyasaki Ichisada, "Shincho ni okeru kokugo mondai no ichimen" (One aspect of the Manchu language problem in the early Ch'ing period), in his *Ajiashi kenkyū* (Studies in Oriental history), 3 (Kyoto, 1963), pp. 336–365. For the origin of the *Nei-ko* in the Ming dynasty, see Tilemann Grimm, "Das Neiko der Ming-Zeit von den Anfangen bis 1506," *Oriens Extremus,* 1, no. 2 (1954), 139–177.

23. *THL*:T'ien-ming 1.11; also see Arthur W. Hummel, ed. *Eminent Chinese of the Ch'ing Period.* (Washington: U.S. Government Printing Office, 1943–1944), pp. 225–226.

24. For a concise treatment of the banner system, see Spence, pp. 2–18.

25. *THL*:T'ien-ts'ung 4.2.

26. *THL*:Ch'ung-te 1.4b–5.

27. *THL*:Ch'ung-te 1.5.

28. These included suggestions on political affairs, reports on foreign affairs, or proposals for special plans and strategies.

29. *THL*:SC 20.1b.

30. Their presence was obviously due to the fact that the nature of the subject under discussion had reference to their functions.

31. *THL*:SC 20.2b.

32. *THL*:SC 20.6b. It is interesting to note that the Shun-chih Emperor was, at this stage, following the Ming founder's practice of endorsing all memorials by himself. Compare Sun Ch'eng-tse, *Ch'un-ming meng-yü lu* (1883), 49.2b–3.

33. *THL*:SC 20.8.

34. *THL*:SC 21.5.

35. *SL* 13.3b.

36. *CSL*:KH 3.9.

37. *HT*:KH 2.7.

38. Brunnert and Hagelstrom, 732A.

39. *CSL*:KH 149.18b–120b.

40. *CSL*:KH 148.19.

41. See Fu Tsung-mao, pp. 65–68. Fu's assertion that the deliberative council might also convene without an imperial request seems rather unlikely.

42. *Hsiao-t'ing tsa-lu* (Miscellaneous notes on Ch'ing history), by Chao Lien (1880), 2.13.

43. *SH:KH* 44.2b, 4b.

44. *Ibid.*

45. *Ibid.; CSL*:KH 164. 3b–4b.

46. *CSL*:KH 200.8b–9b.

47. *CSL*:KH 83.10; 209.2b.

48. See their roles in the Ch'en Ju-pi case in *WHTP* 79–80.

49. *CSL*:KH 133.28.

50. *SH:KH* 44.4.

51. Cf. *Ch'ing-shih* (Taipei, 1961), p. 4022, biography of Wang Shan.

Chapter III. Audience, Censors, Imperial Commissioners, and Tours

1. Snyder, p. 24.

2. *CSL*:KH 161.11.

3. For more details on this practice, see Wu Chen-yü, *Yang-chi-chai ts'ung-lu* (Miscellaneous notes from the Yang-chi study) (1896), 5.5b; *SL* 14.26b.

4. *Hsiao-t'ing tsa-lu,* 2.44: "When an official was summoned for a personal interview with the emperor at the morning audience hours, his name was always written on a wooden tablet and was presented to the emperor beforehand . . . The tablet head was dyed in green color. On it, in addition to the name of the official, were written his native place, data of initial appointment, military merits, and so forth, so that the emperor could become better acquainted with his background."

5. Quoted in *Wu Chen-yü,* 5.6.

6. *CSL*:KH 169.15; also Wu Chen-yü, 5.5b.

7. Chao I, *Kai-yü ts'ung-k'ao* (A collection of miscellaneous notes), in *Ou-pei chüan-chi* (The complete works of Ou-pei [Chao I]) (1877 reprint), 18.21b–15.

8. *CSL*:KH 109.2.

9. E-tu Sun Zen, *Ch-ing Administrative Terms* (Cambridge, 1961), no. 92.

10. *CSL*:KH 107.5b–6.

11. *CSL*:KH 167.16.

12. *CSL*:KH 191.16b.

13. For an example, cf. *CSL*:KH 104.3; cf. also appendix to this book, Case A.

14. Each of the six sections was charged with issuing the endorsed "red memorials" to one of the Six Boards. For example, the particular section dealing with the Board of Personnel was called the Section of Personnel (*Li-k'o*). This was, of course, in addition to the more important function of supplying political information to the throne. The role of the supervising censors in the memorial system will be further discussed in Chapter III.

15. For example, a censor might "itemize his suggestions" (*t'iao-ch'en*) in a memorial on political achievements and maladministration, and the people's livelihood (*SL* 113.1b).

16. T'ang Chi-ho, "Ch'ing-tai k'o-tao chih kung-wu kuan-hsi" (The censorial functions in the Ch'ing administration), in *Hsin she-hui k'o-hsüeh chi-k'an* (The new social sciences quarterly) 1, no. 2 (1949), 209–211. (This is a rather sketchy article.)

17. *CSL*:KH 201.4b.

18. Inspecting censors were seldom sent to the provinces after 1653; see SL 1025 (edict of 1653) and 5 (edict of 1660).

19. *CSL*:KH 197.5b.

20. Cf. *CSL*:KH 116.3–6b for an example.

21. *CSL*:KH 197.5b.

22. The six tours were made in the years 1684, 1689, 1699, 1703, 1705, and 1707. For an account of them see Spence. pp. 124–151.

23. See *CSL*:KH 139.14b.

24. Hsiao I-shan, *Ch'ing-tai t'ung-shih* (A general history of the Ch'ing dynasty) (Taipei, 1951–1953), I, 643.

25. See *CSL*:KH 234.18.

26. *CSL*:KH 166.4.

27. *CSL*:KH 112.14b.

28. *CSL*:KH 211.16, 214.18–18b.

29. *CSL*:KH 235.12b–13.

Chapter IV. The Traditional Memorial System

1. Cf. *HT*:YC 67.20; *HT*:KH 50.29b; also Wu Chen-yü 23.2.

2. Cf. *HT*:YC 225.1b, 2b–3; Wu Chen-yü, 23.2.

3. For a more detailed treatment of the transmission of memorials in Ch'ing times, see Fairbank and Teng, pp. 1–26, which, though mainly concerned with the nineteenth-century situation, serves as a good summary of the entire Ch'ing period.

4. For other types of stations which varied in name because of their differences in function and location, see Fairbank and Teng, pp. 4–5.

5. *HT*:YC 142.6, quoted in Fairbank and Teng, p. 4.

6. For example, since Fukien, Kwangtung, and Kwangsi were "water post" (*shui-i*) provinces, boats were used. Most provinces used horses or donkeys, some also used oxen, camels, or carts; horses and boats were the major types of transportation. Cf. *HT*:KH 100.1; *HT*:YC 143.6–6b; see also Fairbank and Teng, p. 6, n. 15.

7. *HT*:KH 118.19–2.

8. *SL* 1042.11b–12 (edict of 1685); *SL* 684.1–3b.

9. *SL* 1042.1.

10. *SL* 1042.7b.

11. *SL* 1042.3.

12. *SL* 1042.7b.

13. *Ibid.*

14. *HT*:YC 225.2; SL 1042.12. For the prescribed time limits for the transmission of memorials between the capital and the provinces, see *SL* 1042.8b–11b. The horses were pushed so hard to assure punctuality of transmission of Ch'ing documents that the stations were allowed to report a 30–40 percent death toll of horses annually. See edict of 1707 in *HT*:YC 143.6–6b.

15. See SL 13.4 (edict of 1724). The only exception was for memorials dealing with provincial financial and judicial reports, which could exceed this maximum number.

16. See *HT*:KH 2.7.

17. The procedure in the *Nei-ko* after consolidation of the palace memorial system became amplified and more complex, but it is advantageous for the

time being to ignore these changes and consider only the procedures related to the traditional memorials.

18. Alternate proposals were written on two draft slips so that the emperor could choose between the two; see *Nei-ko hsiao-chih* (A brief sketch of the Grand Secretariat) by Yeh Feng-mao (Shanghai, 1940), p. 4. For this study, the single draft will suffice. For the procedure after the Grand Council was established, see Wu Chen-yü, 23.2b.

19. Cf. *Nei-ko hsiao-chih,* p. 7; *Nei-ko chih* (An account of the Grand Secretariat) by Hsi Wu-ao (Shanghai, 1937), p. 4; and *Hsiao-t'ing tsa-tu,* 1.34b.

20. Cf. *Nei-ko chih,* p. 5, and *Nei-ko hsiao-chih,* p. 2b.

21. *HT*:YC 18b–19; *SL* 14.33b. For the organization of the Six Sections, see *HT*:YC 245.1–17b.

22. *SL* 14.33.

23. *SL* 14.33b.

24. Cf. *Nei-ko chih,* p. 4; Fairbank and Teng, p. 54.

25. *SL* 703.13.

26. *HT*:YC 245.1; *SL* 1014.2. The *mi-pen* should not be confused with the palace memorials; they were often memorials in connection with the appointment of examiners of the provincial and metropolitan civil examinations or criminal cases involving death penalties; see *Nei-ko chih,* p. 4.

27. *SL* 703.14.

28. *SL* 703.13–14.

29. Cf. *SL* 14.14.

30. *SL* 14.17.

31. By the time of the Yung-cheng Emperor, the Grand Secretariat had developed a set of phraseology for the draft rescripts. For some examples, cf. *SL* 14.14–17; also Fairbank and Teng, p. 49 n. 24 for such phraseology used throughout the entire Ch'ing period.

32. The board or department with which the matter was chiefly concerned would draft the memorial for the assembly, which then needed only to endorse the draft; cf. *SL* 1014.1.

33. Cf. *HT*:YC, "Explanatory Note" pp. 1b–2, for these terms.

34. *Nei-ko chih,* p. 4.

Chapter V. Origins of the Palace Memorial
System in the K'ang-hsi Reign

1. Edict of 1689, in *SH:KH* 4.3b–4.

2. *Ta-Ming hui-tien* (Collected statutes of the Ming dynasty; 1585), 76.2–b.

3. For further discussion on this point, see E. T. Backhouse and J. O. P. Bland, *Annals and Memoirs of the Court of Peking* (Boston and New York, 1914) pp. 185–212; Mo Tung-yin, *Man-tsu shih lung-ts'ung* (Essays on the history of the Manchus; Peking, 1958), p. 113.

4. Of 4,088 *chin-shih* degree holders of the entire K'ang-hsi period, 666 were from Chiang-nan and 567 from Chekiang, amounting to one-third of the

total number; and Chiang-nan ranked first among all the provinces of China. Cf. Ho Ping-ti, *The Ladder of Success in Imperial China* (New York, 1962), p. 288.

5. Brunnert and Hagelstrom, 834.

6. Li Hsü's memorial, dated KH 51/5/26, *WHTP* 869; J. K. Fairbank, E. O. Reischauer, and A. M. Craig, *East Asia: Modern Transformation* (Boston, 1965), pp. 111–112.

7. A. L. Kroeber, *Anthropology* (New York, 1958), p. 367.

8. The term *ch'ing-an* means "greetings" and *che* "memorial" (literally, "to fold" as a verb or "a folder" as a noun). Just as its name suggests, the *ch'ing-an che* (sometimes simply *che-tzu* or *che*) in the Manchu tradition was used by the bannerman to greet the imperial princes, who headed the banners, or the emperor himself. It was called *che* because it was always in the form of a long sheet of paper "folded over in concertina fashion" so that it could "either be opened out flat or folded back into a thin booklet" (Spence, p. 220). The English translation of *tsou-che* into "palace memorial" was originally suggested by me, to show where it was submitted at the capital. Traditional memorials from the provinces were submitted at the *T'ung-cheng ssu* (Transmission Office), hence they were called *t'ung-pen* (*t'ung* stands for *T'ung-cheng-ssu* and *pen* for *pen-chang*). The present translation follows the same principle because such *tsou-che* were submitted directly at the palace gate (*Ch'ien-ch'ing-men*).

9. This was in answer to a previous *ch'ing-an che* in which he inquired about the emperor's well-being.

10. This suggests that the emperor had received information through people who came to the capital from the South, not through any secret agent who, by that time, might have presented a similar palace memorial. Cf. *CSL*:KH 159.15 for an imperial edict issued in the sixth month of the same year, in which the emperor made the same statement.

11. *WHTP* 854.

12. *WHTP* 303–305.

13. Ts'ao Fu Archives, no. 2855, dated KH 55/5/19.

14. See Spence, p. 86.

15. *Yung-hsien lu* (Historical records of the Yung-cheng period; Shanghai, 1959), p. 390.

16. Chou Ju-ch'ang, *Hung-lou meng hsin-cheng* (New studies on the *Dream of the Red Chamber*; Shanghai, 1953), p. 215.

17. Li Hsü's cousin was married to Ts'ao Yin. See Chou Ju-ch'ang, p. 101.

18. Spence, p. 67.

19. *Ibid.,* p. 65.

20. Li Hsü's memorial, dated 52/12/9, *WHTP* 878.

21. Li Hsü's memorial, dated 32/12/?, *WHTP* 854; Spence, pp. 116–117.

22. *CSL*:KH, 159.14–15b (edict dated KH 32/6/28).

23. Endorsement to Li Hsü's memorial (dated KH 32/7/?), *WHTP* 856.

24. Ts'ao Yin Archives, no. 2736, dated KH 36/5/3. The memorial was sent to congratulate the emperor on his victory over the Galdan.

25. Ts'ao Yin's memorial, dated KH 36/10/12, *WHTP* 293.

26. *Ibid.,* dated KH 38/5/26, *WHTP* 293.

27. *Ibid.,* dated KH 39/4/?, 40/3/?, 40/6/?, 40/10/?, *WHTP* 856–857.

28. For more discussion on their roles, see Spence, pp. 173–212.

29. See rescript to Li Hsü's memorial, dated KH 47/3/?, *WHTP* 863.

30. See Li Hsü, Ts'ao Yin, Ts'ao Yung, and Ts'ao Fu's memorials, in *WHTP, passim,* submitted in the post-1700 period.

31. Chao Hung-hsieh Archives.

32. Li Lin-sheng Archives, no. 1818, dated KH 40/10/24.

33. Li had affixed his official seal at several places on the envelope containing his palace memorial.

34. See note 32.

35. Li Lin-sheng Archives, no. 1817, dated KH 41/6/6.

36. *WHTP* 858.

37. Sung Lao Archives, no. 2419, dated KH 42/6/?.

38. Sung was one of the few memorialists who queried the well-being of the heir apparent. This probably suggests both his intimate relationship with the heir apparent and the latter's prestige.

39. Sung Lao Archives, no. 2421, dated KH 42/7/?.

40. Only one of Sung's memorials, dated KH 51/3/? (no. 2410), could be definitely regarded as "secret" according to our standards. In response to a request of the emperor, Sung Lao reported on the personality of Chang Po-hsing during the latter's fight with Gali over the Examination Hall scandal at Chiang-nan. Sung expressed the opinion that Chang was indeed honest, but not competent in administrative affairs. Since the memorial was sent in the same envelope with a greetings memorial dated KH 51/3/?, it can be assumed that the two were written at the same time.

41. For example, see Chao Hung-hsieh's (governor of Honan) memorial of 1705 (dated KH 44/7/17, Chao Hung-hsieh Archives, no. 592). Lang T'ing-chi's (governor of Kiangsi) memorials of 1706, 1708, and 1710 (dated KH 45/10/6, KH 47/6/15, and KH 49/1/8 respectively, Lang T'ing-chi Archives, nos. 1978, 1982, 2008). Chang Po-hsing's (governor of Kiangning) memorial of 1710 (dated KH 49/6/2, Chang Po-hsing Archives, no. 2191). Wu Chün's (Commander-in-chief of Chekiang) memorial of 1711 (date suggested by context, Wu Chün Archives, no. 1761)

42. Provincial authorities were only allowed to send *ch'ing-an che* starting in 1701 (*CSL*:KH 210.6).

43. This was mentioned in a memorial submitted by Ts'ai Sheng-yüan; see Ts'ai Sheng-yüan Archives, no. 1691, undated. Judging from the post he held as a subchancellor in the *Nei-ko,* the memorial was submitted probably in 1711.

44. For Wang Hung-hsü's short biography by Tu Lien-che, see Hummel, p. 826; for more details concerning the South Library, see my "Nan-shu-fang

chih chien-chih chi ch'i ch'ien-ch'i chih fa-chan" (The founding of the South Library and its early development), in *Ssu yü yen* (Thought and Word), 5, no. 6 (March 1968), 6–12.

45. *WHTP* 78. The instruction was written in the emperor's own hand on very small note paper (8 by 4 cm); a photo of it is in *WHTP* ("*T'u-hsiang*," p. 19).

46. *WHTP* 78.

47. The emperor left the capital every year from the fourth to the ninth month to stay in Jehol.

48. This was a typical greetings palace memorial, of only one sentence: "Your subject Wang Hung-hsü reverently memorializes and inquires of Your Majesay's well-being"; *WHTP* 81

49. *Ibid.*

50. *WHTP* 91. Wang Hung-hsü lost the emperor's favor in 1709 because of his involvement in the heir apparent scandal (*CSL*:KH 236.14). In 1715, he was recalled to Peking to do compilation work in the South Library. As a retired official he was not asked to present any secret palace memorials until 1720. Only three reports submitted by him in 1720 and 1721 have been found in the Palace archives, two of them concerned with the thorny problem of appointing an heir apparent (*WHTP* 94–95).

After Wang Hung-hsü had been dismissed from the presidency of the Board of Revenue and ordered to return to his home province of Kiangsu, Li Hsü, under secret imperial instructions, sent a report on his activities in the South: "I have heard that the former president of the Board of Revenue Wang Hung-hsü, ever since he was dismissed from his office and returned home, has regularly sent his servants to Peking once every month to contact his elder brother Wang Chiu-ling (then censor-general) in order to search out any information about happenings in the palace. He has fabricated things and misled people's hearts"; *WHTP* 866b.

51. *WHTP* 93.

52. *WHTP* 83, 90b.

53. *CSL*:KH 249.5–6b. Although the grand secretaries, the nine ministers and the censors had already begun to use palace memorials by the year 1711, they were apparently not secret ones; *CSL*:KH 246.11b–13b.

54. *WHTP* 90.

55. *WHTP* 866b.

56. *WHTP* 290.

57. *WHTP* 78.

58. *CSL*:KH 249.6; *WHTP* 290 and *passim*.

59. Cf. *WHTP* 90b, where Wang wrote in his palace memorial: "With regard to the affairs which I was instructed secretly to investigate while I was in Soochow, I wrote a *che-tzu* [palace memorial] with my own hand and sealed it very carefully. I presented it through Li Yü [director of eunuchs] for presentation while I was greeting Your Majesty's arrival in Shih-men county . . ."

60. *CSL*:KH 225.17.

61. *CKTP* 201b.

62. Cf. *CKTP* 200.

63. *WHTP* 858b.

64. *CSL*:KH 274.19; for some concrete examples, see *CSL*:KH 280.18; 212.27b.

65. *CKTP* 200.

66. At least as early as the K'ang-hsi period, guards at the Ch'ien-ch'ing Gate were in charge of transmitting imperial instructions orally. The famous Ma-wu, younger brother of the influential grand secretary Maci, was one of these guards; *CSL*:KH 212.15.

67. Literally, the "outer memorial receiving office" or simply Chancery of Memorials (*Tsou-shih ch'u*). Accepting memorials was merely one of the daily routine duties of these guards; a formal chancery never existed in the Ch'ing bureaucracy.

68. *HTK* 8772b.

69. Literally, the "inner memorial receiving office." During the K'ang-hsi reign, Ts'un-chu was the director of this office. His official title was, first, *tsou-shih chu-shih,* and later *tsou-shih chih-i-cheng.* See *CSL*:KH 200.15b; 212.16b.

70. *CSL*:KH 249.6.

71. *CSL*:KH 246.16; 265.14b; 221.19; 249.6.

72. Cf. *WHTP* 293.

73. *WHTP* 93.

74. *WHTP* 308b; 95b.

75. *CKTP* 190–195.

76. See *SH:KH* 9.3 (edict of 1718).

77. Examples are many; see Li Hsü's memorials, Ts'ao Yin's memorials, and Wang Hung-hsü's memorials in *WHTP*

78. When the K'ang-hsi Emperor endorsed Nien Keng-yao's palace memorials, for example, he often endorsed each request with the familiar phrase "you ought to prepare a *t'i-pen* instead"; see *CKTP,* "Nien Keng-yao tsou-che" (Nien Keng-yao's memorials).

79. In 1718 Nien Keng-yao, then governor of Szechwan, presented a palace memorial requesting that he be made governor-general of Szechwan. The K'ang-hsi Emperor granted the appointment by adding the endorsement: "I have already issued an instruction"; *CKTP* 201b–02.

**Chapter VI. Factionalism and the Growth
of the Palace Memorial System**

1. Cf. Hsiao I-shan, I, 795–804; Miyazaki Ichisada, "Shuhi yushi kaidai" (Notes on *The Vermilion Endorsements of the Yung-cheng Emperor*), in *Tōyōshi Kenkyū* (Journal of oriental researches), 15 (March 1957), 7–9.

2. Hsiao I-shan, I, 817–820; Backhouse and Bland, pp. 245–68.

3. For Songgotu's biography, see Hummel, p. 663. When Wang Hung-hsü

secretly reported on how T'o-ho-ch'i blackmailed both officials and common people in the capital city in 1708, the name was actually T'ao ho-ch'i; though the latter is pronounced nearly the same as the one recorded in the *CSL,* the three characters are entirely different (Wang Hung-hsü's memorials, nos. 25, 26, in *WHTP* 92–93).

4. Hummel, p. 268.

5. According to Hsiao I-shan, Asan was an adherent of the Gali faction, though he gives no indication of whether this faction was the same as the Yin-jeng faction (see Hsiao I-shan, I, 804). In view of the fact that Yin-jeng collaborated with Asan and Gali in the Ch'en P'eng-nien and Chang Po-hsing cases respectively, we can at least label them as "collaborators."

6. For details of this incident, see Spence, pp. 240–254. Yin-jeng's role in this incident was essential for an understanding of the true nature of the case: he was the real power behind the associate examiner Chao Chin, as well as the Gali faction as a whole; see *Yung-hsien lu,* p. 306. See Appendix Case B of the present study for more information concerning this case.

7. According to the K'ang-hsi Emperor, the commanders-in-chief and the brigade generals at this time were all on the side of Gali; Li Hsü, among many others, was also partial to Gali. See Appendix, Case A; also, *Chang Ch'ing-ko kung* [Po-hsing] *nien-p'u* (A chronological biography of Chang Po-hsing; 1738), 1.62.

8. *CSL*:KH 250.6.

9. *CSL*:KH 248.15, 250.7b.

10. In the mutual impeachment case of 1712 between Gali and Chang Po-hsing, Ma-san-ch'i submitted a memorial on behalf of Gali requesting that he be retained in office (*WHTP* 292). Ma seems to have been quite influential at court: he constantly received the K'ang-hsi Emperor's favors and was on good terms with the emperor's secret memorialist Li Hsü; see *CSL*:KH 219.22b; 229.14.

11. Cf. *CSL*:KH 235.6.

12. *CSL*:KH 171.20; 171.24b.

13. See Hummel, p. 924.

14. *CSL*:KH 234.19. Actually, Yin-jeng only accompanied the emperor on his last three southern tours (in 1703, 1705, and 1707) excluding the abortive one of 1702. See *CSL*:KH 221.3b; 219.7; 228.4b; and 203.23 on these tours.

15. *CSL*:KH 234.18.

16. *CSL*:KH 251.10b–11.

17. *CSL*:KH 251.10b–11.

18. *Ibid.*

19. *CSL*:KH 212.15b.

20. See *CSL*-KH 212.13b, 17, which lists at least seven Manchu names: A-mi-ta, Ma-erh-t'u, O-k'u-li, Wen-t'e, Shao-kan, T'ung-pao, Weng-o-li. The last two were considered by the emperor to be "absolutely unforgivable."

21. *Ibid.,* 112.16–16b.

22. *Ibid.*, 112.14–14b.

23. *Ibid.*, 234.6–6b.

24. *WHTP* 858.

25. Cf. *WHTP* 858b; *CKTP* 131b. See also *Yung-hsien lu*, pp. 56–57.

26. Hsiao I-shan, I, 804.

27. Ch'en Ju'pi was then a *lang-chung* (department director) in the Board of Personnel. Because he was unwilling to agree to a request by certain supervising censors that their fellow provincials from Chiang-nan be given posts in the Six Sections or in the Censorate at once, the latter falsely charged him with corruption. Apparently as a result of Wang Hung-hsü's secret reports, the K'ang-hsi Emperor flatly rejected the recommendation made by the joint deliberative assembly. He eventually intervened in the case personally, and only then was Ch'en saved from being victimized by his false accusers. Shu-lu and most of the deliberative ministers were properly punished by being lowered two or three ranks. For details of the case, see *WHTP* 79–80: Wang Hung- Hsü's memorials, nos. 4, 5; also *CSL*: KH 220.12b; 221.1b, 3, 6b.

On another occasion, Ch'en Ju-pi was blackmailed for 600 taels by Prince Yin-t'ang through a certain supervising censor named Ch'in Tao-jan (*WHTP* 13b).

28. *WHTP* 80b.

29. For Ch'en P'eng-nien's biography by C. P. Wong, see Hummel, p. 95.

30. *Kuo-ch'ao ch'i-hsien lei-cheng ch'u-pien* (Classified biographies of eminent men of the Ch'ing period; 1884–1890), compiled by Li Huan, 164.18; also see Hummel, p. 96.

31. For his biography by Fang Chao-ying, see Hummel, p. 64.

32. Hummel, p. 96.

33. *CSL*:KH 234.4.

34. This clearly indicates that the emperor had discovered Yin-jeng's evil deeds as early as in the late 1690's. He had nevertheless been made regent twice.

35. *CSL*:KH 234.2–9b.

36. *CSL*:KH 234.7.

37. During his last southern tour of 1707, the K'ang-hsi Emperor received a report that a certain Fan Fu (and many others, as well) was forcing the common people to sell their young daughters, acting "in the name of those who are close to the emperor." The emperor transmitted a secret instruction to Wang Hung-hsü to engage in secret investigations on this matter. According to Wang's three secret reports (see *WHTP* 90–91, Wang Hung-hsü's memorials, nos. 20–22), a certain powerful figure described as the "number one man before the throne" (*yü-ch'ien ti-i jen*) was intimately involved in this scandal; the mysterious personality was neither a eunuch nor an imperial bodyguard. It is unlikely that he referred to Yin-t'ang or Yin-ssu, not only because they had not accompanied the emperor to the South, but also because Wang was affiliated with their fac-

tion. Neither could it have been the K'ang-hsi emperor's most trusted bodyguard Ma-wu; indeed, it was probably Ma-wu who reported Yin-jeng's evil acts in the South to the emperor, thus contributing to the downfall of the crown prince (see *Yung-hsien lu*, p. 324). The figure referred to, therefore, was probably the heir apparent. Only in his name could Fan Fu have dared request local officials to use official warrants and force the common people to sell their young daughters. Only Yin-jeng could be regarded as the "number one man before the throne"; he was the only one who could make Wang Hung-hsü feel "extremely fearful in his heart" and ask the emperor to conceal his name. A year later, when Yin-jeng was deposed in 1708, the emperor made special reference, among other crimes committed by Yin-jeng, to his audacious acts during the imperial southern tours. In condemning Yin-jeng's oppression of the people, the *CSL* only used vague terms, such as that the heir apparent "had acted audaciously and strangely in every possible way." The emperor said it would "make me blush if I opened my mouth [to describe it]." He also described Yin-jeng's acts as "shameful" (*pu-shih lien-ch'ih*) and said it was "not proper to describe them plainly in words" (*yu pu-k'o yen-che*); see *CSL*:KH 234.3, also 253, 9b. According to the depositions of Ch'in Tao-jen, Yin T'ang, ninth son of the emperor, engaged in similar practices; but he had not accompanied the emperor on this tour, so that the above report cannot have alluded to him (see *WHTP* 15b and *CSL*:KH 228.4b).

38. Matteo Ripa, *Memoirs of Father Ripa* (London, 1855), p. 83.

39. *Chosŏn wangjo sillok* (or *Yijo sillok*) (The annals of the Yi dynasty), Sunzong reign (Seoul, 1955–1958), ch. 47.20.

40. For this episode, see *CSL*:KH 234.206; 235.3b, 19b–20; 237.4, 14–14b; 235.23b; 261.8–9b. On the coup, see Wang Chung-han, *"Ch'ing Shih-tsung to-ti k'ao-shih"* (The Yung-cheng Emperor's struggle for the right of succession), *Yen-ching hsüeh-pao* (Yenching journal of Chinese studies), 36, no. 62 (June 1949), 212–214.

41. *CSL*:KH 250.6–6b.

42. *CSL*:KH 249.5b.

43. Cf. also *CSL*:KH 251.9b. Father Ripa, an eyewitness when the heir apparent was handcuffed before the emperor, recorded: "In a public manifesto he [the emperor] subsequently deposed the unfortunate prince [Yin-jeng] on suspicion of treason"; Ripa, p. 83.

44. *CSL*:KH 248.11.

45. For his short biography by Fang Chao-ying, see Hummel, p. 552.

46. The crucial part Lungkodo played in the subsequent succession struggle shows all the more importance of this military post in the capital city. For more details of the struggle, see Chapter VII.

47. *CSL*:KH 248.14.

48. *CSL*:KH 250.6b.

49. *CSL*:KH 248.15.

50. According to the emperor, Keng-o should have been executed during the time of the Songgotu incident in 1703, but the emperor had generously pardoned him; see *CSL*:KH 248.17b.

51. *CSL*:KH 248.15–18b.

52. This sentence was deleted from the *CSL*:KH but is preserved in *SH:KH* 24.3b.

53. *CSL*:KH 249.5–6b.

54. Cf. *CSL*:KH 249.7, 277.10b, 250.6.

55. Cf. *CSL*:KH 250.4b. According to the *Ch'ing-shih* (History of the Ch'ing dynasty; Taipei, 1961), 4006, Wang I's name should be Wang I-te (the *CSL* probably left out the last character by error). The *Ch'ing-shih* also includes part of a memorial submitted by another supervising censor, Kao Hsia-ch'ang, which reveals some of the tyranny of the commandant in detail.

56. *CSL*:KH 250.5b–6; the content of this memorial was not recorded in the *CSL*.

57. *CSL*:KH 250.6b.

58. *CSL*:KH 250.6–7b.

59. *CSL*:KH 250.10.

Chapter VII. Changes in the Palace Memorial
System in the Yung-cheng Reign

1. *CSL*:KH 253.10b.

2. *Yung-hsien lu*, p. 84.

3. *CSL*:KH 266.5–5b; ECCP 925. For Chao Shen-ch'iao's connection with Yin-jeng, see *Yung-hsien lu*, p. 69.

4. *CSL*:KH 266.5–5b; Hummel, p. 925.

5. For details, see *CSL*:KH 277. 6.12b, 30b–31.

6. For details, see *CSL*:KH 291.25b–28b.

7. See edict of the Yung-cheng Emperor dated YC 4/5/9, in *SYNK*.

8. Ho T'u's deposition, in *WHTP* 5.

9. *CSL*:KH 281.16b; Hummel, p. 930.

10. *CSL*:YC 44.30; Jean Mourao's deposition, in *WHTP* 1.

11. Ch'in Tao-jen's deposition, in *WHTP* 4.

12. Chang Hsia-tzu's deposition, in *WHTP* 5b.

13. *Yung-hsien lu*, p. 83.

14. For some of the versions, see references quoted in Hsiao I-shan, I, 856–857.

15. The two most influential studies on the subject are: Meng Sen, "Shih-tsung ju-ch'eng ta-t'ung k'ao-shih" (A study of the Yung-cheng Emperor's succession), in his *Ch'ing-tai shih* (History of the Ch'ing dynasty; Taipei, 1960), ed. Wu Hsiang-hsiang, pp. 477–510, and Wang Chung-han, pp. 205–261. Other studies have amplified their thesis without basic modifications.

16. *CSL*:KH 235.27b.

17. Wu Chen-yü, 3.3b; Yoshimoto Hakusen, Kōki *taitei* (K'ang-hsi the

Great; Tokyo, 1941), which includes a poem scroll (reproduction no. 3) designated as "the calligraphy of K'ang-hsi the Great." It very much resembles that of Yin-chen.

18. Cf. edict of YC 2/8/22, in *SYNK*.

19. *CSL*:YC 4.64b.

20. Huang Ping's memorials, dated YC 1/1/25, 1/5/24, in *CPYC*.

21. *Yung-hsien lu,* p. 70.

22. Vermilion endorsement noted on Sai-leng-o's memorial dated YC 5/2/10, in *CPYC*.

23. *Shih-tsung Hsien huang-ti sheng-hsün* (Sacred instructions of the Yung-cheng Emperor; 1965 Taiwan reprint), 7.5.

24. *Ibid.,* 22.1.

25. *SL* 998.15b. The immediate cause of withdrawal was that the supervising censor, Ts'ui Chih-yüan, had falsely accused his superior in a palace memorial (*SL* 998.11b). As a matter of fact, the censors never functioned properly in serving as the emperor's "ears and eyes" until the very end of the Yung-cheng period (Cf. *SL* 12b–16b, 25–30).

26. *Shih-tsung sheng-hsün,* 7.1.

27. If boxes had not yet been issued, palace memorials were securely sealed in boards (*chia-pan*) for dispatching. See *CPYC,* palace memorials of Chao Hung-en dated YC 12/6/10.

28. Cf. *Man-Han ming-ch'en chuan* (Biographies of eminent Manchu and Chinese officials), 28.23–23b

29. Cf. Wu Chen-yü 23.36–4b; Miyazaki Ichisada, "Kaidai," 12.

30. Cf. *CPYC,* Chu Kang's memorial dated YC 3/1/7.

31. For further discussion on this matter, cf. Wu Chen-yü 23.4; Miyazaki Ichisada, "Kaidai," p. 12; Huang P'ei, pp. 38–40.

32. *CSL*:YC 96.6; *Shih-tsung sheng-hsün,* 7.5–5b.

33. These matters apparently concerned new policy decisions which were beyond the prescribed powers of the Six Boards.

34. Presumably, the informal inner *Nei-ko,* which later became the Grand Council, was the most important one. For discussion of the Grand Council, see Chapter VIII.

35. Although the financial and judicial commissioners were given the privilege of supplying secret information in palace memorials, they were not allowed to present a *t'i-pen* to the emperor, according to administrative regulations.

36. *SYNK* dated KH 61/11/23.

37. *SYNK* dated KH 61/11/27; *CSL*:YC 1.26b; and *WHTP* 290, compiler's note. The *Yung-hsien lu* which is often quoted by historians (e.g., see Spence, p. 224 n. 53) gives a wrong date for this edict (KH 61/12/3–15); thus this source should be used cautiously.

38. *HT* 51.14b.

39. *CSL*:KH 270.5b–6.

40. In view of the fact that palace memorials of the Yung-cheng period are

extant in huge numbers, examples for this part of the study will be drawn from four major memorialists: Nien Keng-yao, T'ien Wen-ching, Li Wei, and O-erh-t'ai. (For their respective short biographies, see Hummel, pp. 587, 714, 720, 601.) Nien lost imperial favor after the end of the second year of Yung-cheng (1724), when he was summoned for a special audience. He was convicted and allowed to commit suicide in the third year. Li, T'ien, and O-ehr-t'ai remained in the Yung-cheng Emperor's favor; they are known by historians as the "three most trusted provincial officials of the Yung-cheng Emperor." See Miyazaki Ichisada, *Yō-sei-tei* (The Yung-cheng Emperor; Tokyo, 1950), p. 98; Hummel, 720.

41. This is not to say that the K'ang-hsi Emperor did not use memorials at all to transmit moral exhortations to the memorialists. In fact, he once clearly stated that he often advised his memorialists how to be good officials and how to love the common people (*CSL*:KH 221.19). But all his vermilion endorsements consisted of only a few sentences, and his exhortations can hardly be compared with the lengthy essay-style endorsements of the Yung-cheng Emperor, which often consisted of hundreds or even more than a thousand characters.

42. The *Chu-p'i yü-chih* is a collection of palace memorials submitted by 235 memorialists, bearing the Yung-cheng Emperor's personal vermilion endorsements. It was first printed in 1732, with additional memorials included in 1738; see Hummel, p. 919. For a brief discussion of the value of the *Chu-p'i yü-chih*, see Miyazaki Ichisada, "Kaidai," pp. 25–28. Mr. Yang Ch'i-chiao, of the Research Institute for Humanistic Studies, Kyoto University, has kindly informed me that, after having compared all the memorials included in the CPYC against the corresponding original memorials (only a few thousand pieces) extant in the National Palace Museum archives in Taipei, he has found that many of the original memorials were edited before publication. In addition to polishing the uncouth wording used in the vermilion endorsements, passages were occasionally deleted; but only in rare cases were endorsements deleted because they were "inconvenient to the Yung-cheng Emperor" (Yang's letter to the author, dated Jan. 6, 1970).

43. This figure is a rough estimate based on two considerations: (1) According to the emperor's own statement, the *CPYC* contains over 10,000 palace memorials, but this figure only constitutes 20–30 percent of the total volume he had received by 1732, when the collection was first published. (2) During the following four years a fair amount should be added to the above figure. Therefore, the grand total should be at least around 50,000. As to the daily inflow of secret palace memorials from the provinces, the emperor testified that he "sometimes received twenty to thirty pieces, or even fifty to sixty memorials" (*CSL*:YC 96.6). Simple arithmetic shows, on the basis of an estimate of 50,000 memorials for the entire reign, that the daily average of palace memorials handled by the Yung-cheng Emperor during his thirteen-year reign would be 10 or so. It must be remembered that the emperor endorsed all palace memo-

rials with his own hand, and that this was extra work in addition to many routine memorials (*t'i-pen*) that had to be acted upon and all major decisions to be made on state affairs.

The National Palace Museum archives contains 6,483 pieces of unpublished palace memorials of the Yung-cheng period. They were not intended for publication and were classified by Ch'ing official archivists as "palace memorials not to be published (*pu-lu che,* or *pu-lu tang-an*). In addition, there are 5,964 pieces under the classification of "palace memorials not yet published" (*wei-lu che,* or *wei-lu tang-an*); letter of Liu chia-chü to author dated June 24, 1968.

No one was charged with caring for the secret palace memorials; they were simply locked up in the Mao-ch'in Hall. *WHTP* 101, 290, compiler's notes.

44. *CSL*:YC 96.6b.

45. *CPYC,* "Preface."

46. Cf. *CPYC,* Yang Lin's memorial dated YC 1/9/15.

47. Cf. *CPYC,* Li Wei's memorial dated YC 2/9/6.

48. *CPYC,* Fan Shih-i's memorial dated YC 4/8/28.

49. Once while still a prince he endorsed in the following manner a *ch'ing-an che* sent by his household servant, a circuit intendant in Fukien province at that time: "How could [we be so stupid that we should] enjoy smelling a fart as if it were fragrant incense?" See *WHTP* 103.

50. *CPYC,* Ma Ti-po's memorial dated YC 3/3/7.

51. *CPYC,* Shen T'ing-cheng's memorial dated YC 8/3/21.

52. *CPYC,* Huang Kuo-ts'ai's memorial dated YC 3/8/12.

53. *CPYC,* I Chao-hsiung's memorial dated YC 6/1/24.

54. *CPYC,* Li Lan's undated memorial.

55. For an example, see *CPYC,* Li Fu's memorial dated YC 4/11/21. Of course, such interlinear endorsements sometimes were compliments rather than harsh words.

56. For an example, see *CPYC,* Yang Ming-shih's memorial dated YC 5/3 intercalary/8; also K'ung Yü-hsün's memorial dated YC 6/10/20.

57. *CPYC,* "Preface," pp. 2, 2b.

58. For some interesting references, see Hsiao I-shan, I, 886–887.

59. Li Wei was only an intendant when Yin-chen was enthroned, but he became the governor-general of Chekiang within five years.

60. *CKTP* 223b.

61. This memorial was submitted on YC 3/7/6; *WHTP* 229. Similar lengthy spy reports may be found in *WHTP* and *CPYC, passim.*

62. *CSL*:YC 51.30–32b; Appendix, Case C.

63. See Appendix, Case C.

64. See Appendix, Case C.

65. Rescript to O-erh-t'ai's memorial dated YC 5/1/25, in *CPYC.* This source also reveals that the Yung-cheng Emperor read and endorsed 90 percent of the palace memorials from the provinces at night.

66. *Ibid.*

67. *CPYC* 30.63b.

68. Literally, "being unstable in anger and joy" (*CSL*:KH 235.26).

**Chapter VIII. The Grand Council and the
New Communication-Decision Structure**

1. *CSL*:YC 1.8b–9.

2. *CSL*:YC 29.10b–13. For rebukes that the Yung-cheng Emperor laid upon Yin-ssu during the mourning period, see edicts in *CSL*:YC dated 2/4/7, 2/5/14, 2/8/22, 2/11/13, and *passim.*

3. Yin-t'ang was also put in prison and died in the same year; see Hummel, p. 927.

4. *SYNK,* edict dated YC 1/11/8.

5. *SYNK,* edict of YC 1/7/11.

6. *Nei-ko hsiao-chih,* pp. 7–8.

7. *SYNK,* edict dated YC 3/3/19.

8. See, e.g., *CPYC,* Fan Shih-i's memorial dated YC 5/1/2, no. 2.

9. *CKTP* 39b.

10. For examples, see *CKTP* pp. 39–45, under "Ch'ing Sheng-tsu yü-chih" (Instructions of Emperor Sheng-tsu). Also see *Jung-tsun yü-lu* (Recorded sayings of Li Kuang-ti, 1829), 31.10, which records that the emperor sent a letter to Li Kuang-ti through a Hanlin official, Wei T'ing-chen, in 1716.

11. *Ibid.*

12. For a photo reproduction of an original letter, dated KH 55/9/17 (Oct. 31, 1716), that the emperor sent to Western missionaries, see Antonio S. Rosso, *Apostolic Legations to China of the Eighteenth Century* (1948), pp. 307–308; also *CKTP* 42 for an example concerning missionaries in Kwangtung. The court letter was transmitted through officials who were taking charge of the imperial manufactury and escorting Westerners (missionaries) from the Yanghsin Hall and the Wu-ying Hall and other inner court offices.

13. *Ch'ing-shih,* p. 4033.

14. Or "his father"; the term *fu-tzu* appears ambiguous in this text.

15. Chao Hung-hsieh Archives, no. 622, dated KH 59/2/2.

16. Edict of YC 7/10/20, Dec. 10, 1729, in *CSL*:YC 87.18b–19.

17. Huang Ping Archives, no. 4694, dated YC 2/1/28.

18. The allegedly earlier court letter referred to in a memorial of Kao Ch'i-cho dated YC 1/12/20, as mentioned in Fu Tsung-mao, seems to be a "vermilion instruction" instead of a court letter. So it is with the "secret vermilion instruction" that Li Wei mentioned in his memorial dated YC 4/10/25, *CPYC.*

19. See more examples in Fu Tsung-mao, pp. 345–349. Even after the Grand Council was established, other agents in the capital were still occasionally asked to transmit court letters; see *CPYC,* memorial of Mai Chu dated YC 12/12/4, no. 3; Fu Tsung-mao, p. 425 n. 32. Throughout his discussions on the subject,

Fu seems to have failed to differentiate between the "vermilion instructions" and the "court letters."

20. See *CPYC*, an undated memorial of Wang Kuo-tung, which he submitted in response to a court letter he received in YC 6/12/?; also see *CPYC*, memorial of I Chao-hsiung dated YC 5/3 intercalary/22. The Yung-cheng Emperor forbade provincial authorities to deal with routine financial problems in palace memorials because, in his own words, "the governors and governors-general may take advantage and encroach upon the powers and duties of the Six Boards" (*CSL*:YC 96.6); thus, the financial problems referred to here are those which could not be dealt with by the Board of Revenue on the basis of precedents and administrative regulations.

21. *CPYC*, Li Wei's memorial dated YC 4/10/9.

22. Cf. *CPYC*, Wang Kuo-tung's undated memorial (pp. 108–09), which he submitted in response to a court letter he received in YC 7/6/17.

23. Cf. I Chao-hsiung's memorial dated YC 5/4/4, in *CPYC*.

24. For instance, on November 12, 1728 (YC 6/10/11), a court letter was sent to Chao Ch'eng, the financial commissioner of Hunan, transmitting the emperor's permission to use palace memorials for secret reports (see *CPYC*, Chao Ch'eng's memorial dated YC 6/10/11). On December 11, 1728 (YC 6/11/11), a court letter was sent to Fan Shih-i, acting governor-general of Chiang-nan and Kiangsi, instructing him to make secret inquiries about the comrades of Tseng Ching, who had attempted to pursuade General Yüeh Chung-ch'i to start a rebellion; this was the famous literary inquisition case involving the scholar Lü Liu-liang (*CPYC*, Fan's memorial; for details of this case, see Tseng Ching's biography by Fang Chao-ying, Hummel, p. 747).

25. See *CPYC*, K'ung Yü-p'u's memorial dated YC 5/11/19. In the earliest stage (roughly from 1725 to 1727), the committee was composed of the three grand secretaries Chang T'ing-yü, Fu-ning-an, and Chu Shih. In the second stage (roughly from 1727 to 1730), it was composed of Prince I and the two grand secretaries Chang T'ing-yü and Chiang T'ing-hsi. (Chiang T'ing-hsi, however, became a grand secretary only in 1728 [YC 6/3/?]; Fu-ning-an died a few months later in the same year. Chu Shih, probably because of his age and ill health, was no longer involved by this time.) It was during the period 1727–1729 that this informal body was entrusted with the secret mission of making military preparations, mainly concerning the transport of military rations to the northeastern region for the projected campaign. Before Prince I's death in 1730 (the eighth year), however, Ma-erh-sai, the new chief grand secretary, had already taken over his role; thus the body again consisted solely of grand secretaries. (See Yen Mao-kung, *Ch'ing-tai cheng-hsien lei-pien* [classified historical records of the Ch'ing dynasty; Taipei, 1961], I, 8, for the appointment dates of the grand secretaries involved.) The fluid role of Prince I will be made clear in subsequent discussion of the origins of the Grand Council.

26. *Ch'ing-shih*, pp. 4033, 4039.

27. *CSL*:YC 82.6–6b.

28. *Nei-ko hsiao-chih,* p. 8. which states: "When the title *Chün-hsü fang* was first used, this office was located in the capital in the Military Manufacturing Office (*tsao-pan ch'u*), a sub-office under the Yang-hsin Hall; but the inner grand secretary Chang Wen-ho [T'ing-yü] alone was on duty in the West Chamber of the South Library."

29. The new office contained three types of officials: the inner grand secretaries, the grand councillors, and the secretaries (*chün-chi chang-ching*). The secretaries dealt only with paper work, not having any deliberative power; the councillors were given deliberative power in matters concerning the military operations; and the grand secretaries were given comprehensive deliberative power on major governmental affairs.

30. *Nei-ko hsiao-chih,* p. 7b.

31. The term *ta-ch'en* is synonymous with *ta-jen;* see *Nei-ko hsiao-chih,* p. 23.

32. The *Ch'ing-shih* also confuses the grand councillors with the inner grand secretaries in the Yung-cheng reign and includes the latter in the "Chün-chi ta-ch'en nien-piao," (Chronological Tables of the Grand Councillors), pp. 2486–2487. A number of ministers who were made grand councillors during the period 1732–1735 are listed in the tables. Ha-yüan-sheng, commander-in-chief of Kweichow, is recorded as the earliest one in the group. He was summoned to Peking in 1732 for a special audience and subsequently was ordered "to be on duty in the *Chün-chi ch'u*" in that year. But grand councillors had already existed in 1731, although the *Ch'ing-shih* fails to mention this fact.

33. See their designations in Wang ta-jen mi-i tsou-p'ien (Short memorials containing secret deliberations of Prince [Yin-hsiang] and other ministers), uncatalogued; National Palace Museum archives, Taiwan.

34. *CSL*:YC 115.7b.

35. *CSL*:YC 112.22.

36. *Shang-yü ch'i-wu i-fu* (Imperial decrees in response to deliberations on banner affairs; Palace ed.) 26.8, which records an imperial instruction that orders some military affairs be deliberated jointly by "Prince Chuang [Yin-lu], Ministers of the Imperial Household, in conjunction with the [inner] grand secretaries including Chiang T'ing-hsi and grand councillors (*Pan-li chün-hsü shih-wu ta-ch'en teng*)."

37. It was not until 1738 that grand secretaries were for the first time made "grand councillors," so that they might continue to handle military affairs in connection with the northwest and "special matters" to be managed promptly nearby (that is, in the palace where the Grand Council was situated); see *CSL*:Ch'ien-lung, 57.6, edict dated 2/11/28.

38. See lengthy discussion in Fu Tsung-mao, pp. 118–125, for the various dates. Also cf. Li Tsung-t'ung, "Pan-li chün-chi ch'u lüeh-k'ao," (A brief study of the founding of the Grand Council) *Yu-shih hsüeh-pao* (The youth journal) 1, no. 2 (1959), 1–19, and Fang Tu Lien-che, "Kuan-yü Chün-chi ch'u ti chien-

chih" (On the establishment of the Grand Council), Occasional Papers, no. 2, Centre of Oriental Studies, Australian National University (Canberra, 1963).

39. The discovery of this date was made by Li Tsung-t'ung: see, Li Tsung-t'ung, p. 6.

40. The authors in note 38 above all agree on this point.

41. Fu Tsung-mao, p. 120.

42. See his "Chün-chi ch'u shu" (An account of the Grand Council) in *HTK*, pp. 8773–8774. It should be noted that, with the exception of this passage, "An account" is essentially concerned with the Grand Council in the Ch'ien-lung period, during which grand secretaries were also made grand councillors.

43. *Nei-ko hsiao-chih*, pp. 7–8.

44. For the date of Shu-ho-te's appointment, see *Shu-yüan chi-lüeh* (A brief account of the Grand Council; 1875), by Liang Chang-chü, 16.1; also see *Nei-ko hsiao-chih*, p. 7.

45. *CSL*:YC 116.2b.

46. Despite the casting of the official seal, the name of this office continued to appear in various forms. One record shows that, as late as 1733, the term *Chün-chi fang*, instead of *Chün-chi ch'u*, was still used by the inner grand secretary Chang T'ing-yü in reference to this office. In his *Ch'eng-huai yüan wen-ts'un* (An anthology of Chang T'ing-yü; 1891), 15.31, Chang records that his son Chang Jo-ai was ordered by the emperor "to be on duty in the *Chün-chi fang*" (*tsai Chün-chi fang hsing-tsou*); also see *Nei-ko chih*, p. 3.

47. Yüeh Chung-ch'i Archives, no. 257, dated YC 8/4/22. The instruction secretly sent to Yüeh was in the form of a court letter; see *ibid.*, no. 493, dated YC 8/5/30.

48. *CSL*:YC 94.6b–7, edict dated YC 8/5/9.

49. *CSL*:YC 99.19b–20, dated YC 8/10/19. The emperor recovered around October; see endorsement to Yüeh Chung-ch'i's memorial dated YC 8/8/8, Yüeh Chung-ch'i Archives, no. 236.

50. *CSL*:YC 101.10–10b.

51. Yüeh Chung-ch'i Archives, no. 67, dated YC 7/12/7, Jan. 25, 1731.

52. Hsü-Jung Archives, no. 11808, Hsü Jung's memorial dated YC 9/5/12. Hsü was then governor of Lan-chou (Shensi). The vermilion endorsement noted on this memorial reads: "Let [this memorial] be filed with the *Pan-li chün-hsü ch'u* and kept on record. As to those items that ought to be deliberated, let them be deliberated [by that office]" (*chiao Pan-li chün-hsü ch'u ts'un-an, ying i-tsou che i-tsou*).

53. Hsien-te Archives, no. 13052: memorial dated YC 9/5/16. Hsien-te was then governor of Szechwan.

54. *SYNK*, edict dated YC 9/3/26, where it is recorded that the emperor's vermilion endorsement noted on a palace memorial concerning "the training of militia" reads: "Let ministers who are managing military supplies [grand coun-

cillors] deliberate on this matter" (*cho pan-li chün-hsü chih ta-ch'en i-tsou*). Also see *CSL*:YC 112.22, edict dated YC 9/11/11, where it is recorded that an imperial rescript ordered that a palace memorial submitted by Fu-erh-tan, the generalissimo of the northern route, be handed down to the *Pan-li chün-chi shih-wu ta-ch'en* (grand councillors) for "deliberation" (*i-tsou*).

55. For instance, in nearly seventy pages of discussion on the various functions of the grand councillors (military and financial matters, public works, civil examinations, judicial and foreign affairs, etc.), Fu Tsung-mao quoted only two memorials of the Yung-cheng period, both of which were submitted by Li Wei, to illustrate the grand councillors' power in deliberating military affairs. See Fu Tsung-mao, pp. 355–423. Fu relied almost solely on documents of the post-Yung-cheng period.

56. According to a letter to the author from Liu Chia-chü, dated Aug. 10, 1968.

57. Wang ta-jen mi-i tsou-p'ien.

58. *Ibid.*

59. *Ibid.* Cf. *CSL*:YC 156.15b; *CSL*:Ch'ien-lung, 5.42b.

60. *CSL*:YC 96.18–19.

61. Wang ta-jen mi-i tsou-p'ien. See Ch'ü T'ung-tsu, p. 74, where the term *ch'ang-sui* is translated as "personal servants." My deviation is based on the context which states that the function of these *ch'ang-sui* was to "protect" the officials.

62. See reports from O-erh-t'ai and the corresponding deliberations in Wang ta-jen mi-i tsou-p'ien.

63. See my "The Memorial Systems of the Ch'ing Dynasty," p. 14, for the uses of the Yellow Book.

64. See Ch'ü T'ung tsu, p. 22, for the origin of this system.

65. Wang ta-jen mi-i tsou-p'ien.

66. *Ibid.*

67. *Ibid.*

68. *Ibid.*

69. Concerning the case of Chang Ching-heng, no references whatever have thus far been found, perhaps because he was found not guilty. In the case of Hsü Chün, the *Ch'ing-shi-lu* contains only a very brief entry (*CSL*:YC 99.2–2b). The important source material entitled *Ch'ing-tai wen-tzu yü tang-an* (Archival collections on literary inquisitions under the Ch'ing) does not contain any documents on Hsü's case. Among contemporary studies on the subject, only Kuei Ching-hsien, in his *Ch'ing-tai wen-yen chi-lüeh* (A brief survey on the literary inquisition under the Ch'ing) (Chungking, 1944), briefly alludes to him. Others, such as L. C. Goodrich in his *Literary Inquisition* (Baltimore, 1935), do not refer to the case.

70. See Chang T'ing-yü and Chiang T'ing-hsi's *tsou-p'ien* (memorials) in Wang ta-jen mi-i tsou-p'ien.

71. *CSL*:YC 99.2–2b.

72. Goodrich, p. 23.

73. Wang ta-jen mi-i tsou-p'ien.

74. *Ibid.*

75. *CSL*:KH 200.8b–9b.

76. For a similar case, see *CPYC,* Hao Yü-lin's memorial dated YC 10/7/26, no. 2.

77. Wang ta-jen mi-i tsou-p'ien.

78. *CSL*:YC 101.15b–16; *CPYC,* Chang Ch'i-yün's memorial dated YC 9/6/8.

79. See *CPYC,* Chang Ch'i-yün's memorials dated YC 8/2/20, 8/6/20, 9/1/22, and 9/6/8.

80. *Fu-chien t'ung-chih* (A general gazetteer of Fukien; 1737) 30.28b; *CPYC,* Chang Ch'i-yün's memorial dated YC 9/10/1.

81. Wang ta-jen mi-i tsou-p'ien.

82. *WHTP* 234–235, dated YC 5/4/28.

83. For the *t'i-pen* bearing the imperial corrections, see *WHTP,* 235–236.

84. For details, see Hao Yü-lin's memorial dated YC 8/3/26 in *CPYC.*

85. *Ming-fa* is actually an adverb-verb compound, meaning that which is publicly issued.

86. *HTK* 8774. Also see *Nei-ko hsiao-chih,* "Preface," p. 1, which states that "when the emperor wanted to issue an edict, he would first instruct the [inner] grand secretary orally. The latter, after having retreated from the imperial presence, would make a draft and present it to the emperor. After the emperor had approved the draft, then it was issued accordingly."

87. *HTK* 8774. From the early Ch'ien-lung period, several grand councillors were summoned to receive oral instructions; this was because Na-ch'in, the chief grand councillor, was afraid that he might not be able to remember all of them.

88. Chao I, *Yen-p'u tsa-chi* (Miscellaneous notes) in *Ou-pei ch'üan-chi* (The complete works of Ou-pei; 1877), 1.4b. For the meaning of *shu-chih,* see *Shu-yüan chih-lüeh,* 22.5b; *SL* 114.21.

89. Wang ta-jen mi-i tsou-p'ien.

90. *Ibid.*

91. *HTK* 8774.

92. Cf. Fairbank and Teng, p. 26: "This office had the special function of receiving documents [palace memorials] sent by express and transmitting them inward and outward from the Court."

93. *HTK* 8774.

94. *HTK* 8774.

95. *HTK* 8774. Of course Chao probably was not aware of the origin of court letters, which, as noted earlier, actually started in the K'ang-hsi era.

96. *CPYC,* "Preface," p. 2.

97. *HTK* 8773b.

98. *Hsiao-t'ing tsa-lu,* 2.13.

99. *HTK* 8773.

100. Chao I, *Yen-p'u tsa-chi*, 1.3.

101. Concrete cases and references can be found in *CSL*:KH 44.2b, 44.4–4b, 135.13b–14b, 164.3–3b, 179.8b–9b, 200.8b–9b, 274.5b–6, 290.14b–15; also *SH:KH* 9.3b–4.

102. See *SYNK*, edicts dated YC 1/3/14 and YC 1/9/22.

103. *SYNK,* edicts dated KH 61/11/29, YC 1/5/6, and YC 2/8/19.

104. *CSL*:YC 83.20.

Chapter IX. Communication, Values, Control

1. These definitions are adapted from two authorities: Lasswell and Kaplan, mentioned above, and Abraham Zaleznik and David Moment, *The Dynamics of Interpersonal Behavior* (New York, 1964), pp. 104–105.

2. See edict of KH 48/10/8 (*SH:KH* 8.1), in which he stressed that "the best policy of ruling the empire is one of harmony [or peace]" (*ho-p'ing*). He exhorted his officials to follow the same principle by using a similar aphorism, "mutual respect and harmony among colleagues" (*t'ung-yin ho-kung*); edict of KH 18/8/12 in *SH:KH* 43.3.

3. See edict of KH 50/9/29 to Governor P'an Tsung-lo (*SH:KH* 46.2), and his vermilion endorsement noted on Ts'ao Yin's memorial dated KH 43/10/13 (*WHTP* 294). In both cases, the emperor used the same popular aphorism to stress his ruling policy: "It is better to keep things as they are rather than create new ones."

4. See edicts of KH 43/1/1 and 50/9/29 in *CSL*:KH 215.2b–4b and *SH:KH* 46.2. This attitude greatly accounts for the factional activities in the first half of the K'ang-hsi reign. See my *"Nan-shu-fang . . ."*

5. *SH:KH* 6.1; *CSL*:KH 266.14–15.

6. For his policy statements in this respect, see *T'ing-hsün ko-yen* (Exhortations of the K'ang-hsi Emperor; Wu-hsing, 1921), p. 51b.

7. Spence, p. 253.

8. Wang Hung-hsü's memorial, no. 24, *WHTP* 92.

9. *Ibid.,* no. 27.

10. See Kent Smith, "O-erh-t'ai and the Yung-cheng Emperor," *Ch'ing-shih wen-t'i*, 1, no. 8 (May 1968), p. 11.

11. Edict of YC 7/6/12, in *SH*:YC 7.1b.

12. Vermilion endorsement noted on Yang Lin's memorial dated YC 1/9/24, in *CPYC*. As Smith also pointed out, "The Yung-cheng Emperor put the officialdom on notice that he would not tolerate the lax administrative practices which had long been accepted procedure"; Smith, p. 11.

13. In his point of view, the moral senses of some officials, especially the Chekiang people in the South, could not be aroused merely by kindness. See vermilion endorsement noted on Ch'en Shih-kuan's memorial dated YC 4/11/16 in *CPYC*, which reads: "I am surprised by the fact that you Chekiangese were unable to be transformed by kindness and grace." Thus, he valued punishment as a necessary means to achieve administrative rehabilitation.

14. P. J. B. Du Halde, *The General History of China* (London, 1736), I, 505.

15. Ch'ien Mu, p. 98.

16. See Karl W. Deutsch, *The Nerves of Government: Models of Political Communication and Control* (London, 1963).

17. James Walker, pp. 211–242.

18. *CSL*:YC 96.6.

19. See Kurt H. Wolff, ed., *The Sociology of George Simmel* (Glencoe, Ill., 1950), pp. 332, 334.

20. There were severe and detailed punitive measures stipulated by the Yung-cheng Emperor to regulate the mutual interpersonal relations among Manchu princes and their bannermen, as well as among Chinese and Manchu ministers.

21. See Chao I's account of Chang T'ing-yü's behavior in *HTK* 8774.

Appendix

Case A

1. See Ts'ao Yin's palace memorial dated KH 48/3/16 in *WHTP* 290b. Also see Governor-general Li Fu's memorial of 1726, in which the Yung-cheng Emperor corrected the memorial because he found that his imperial oral instructions had been misunderstood (*WHTP* 8).

2. A Ch'ing official would often falsify his age, pretending to be younger than he really was in order to stay in office longer.

3. Brunnert and Hagelstrom, 629c.

4. James Legge, *The Chinese Classics* (Hong Kong, 1960), II, 131.

5. William T. de Bary *et. al., Sources of Chinese Tradition* (New York, 1960), pp. 513–514, 524–525.

6. *Ibid.,* p. 525.

7. Because there were no funds allotted to local governments in the Ch'ing financial system they had to find their own means of support.

8. At this time, the privilege of sending the emperor palace memorials was granted on an individual basis. This is why Ch'en Pin thanked the emperor immediately at this juncture for such a privilege.

9. The comment was recorded in *CSL*:KH 266.14b–15b.

10. The poem that appears at this spot is not translated here.

11. The account is taken from the *Ch'en Ch'ing-tuan-kung wen-chi* (Canton, 1868), 1–22. In view of some rather ridiculous repetition in this account, I have edited it in part.

Case B

1. See Spence, pp. 240–254. These documents constituted part of a chapter in the original draft of my study; unknown to each other, Spence and I were

dealing with the same subject, though with separate objectives and from different angles. My chapter (now deleted) was intended to translate all palace memorials submitted by Li and Ts'ao, in extenso, chronologically, in order to show some important aspects of the palace memorial system itself: its effects on factionalism, the comprehensiveness of the contents of the memorials, and the significant role of the heir apparent in these two cases.

2. *CSL*:KH 251.18b.

3. *Li Wen-cheng kung* [*Kuang-ti*] *nien-pu* (A chronological biography of Li Kuang-ti), 2.49–49b.

4. *WHTP* 291.

5. *WHTP* 867. Exact date taken from Ts'ao Yin Archives, No. 2761.

6. *WHTP* 867b.

7. *WHTP* 867b.

8. *WHTP* 291b.

Case C

1. Of course (as has been mentioned), the K'ang-hsi Emperor also sent fans, as well as other gifts, to these memorialists to whom he was closest; but the fundamental difference lies in the nature of the endorsements written by the two emperors. The K'ang-hsi Emperor's emotions were often hidden, whereas those of the Yung-cheng Emperor were rather overt.

2. *WHTP* 134.

3. The Yung-cheng Emperor was very fond of *Ch'an* (*Zen*) Buddhism and styled himself as the "monk of the Yüan-ming Garden."

4. *WHTP* 135b–136.

5. For the relationship between the Yung-cheng Emperor and the Niens, see Hummel, p. 587.

6. *WHTP* 130.

Bibliography

Archives of the National Palace Museum, Taiwan
For catalogued archives, a four-digit number is assigned to a memorial submitted during the K'ang-hsi reign and a five-digit number to a memorial submitted during the Yung-cheng reign.

Chang Po-hsing Archives 張伯行: 2168 to 2198
Chao Hung-hsieh Archives 趙宏燮: 0001 to 1177
Hsien-te Archives 憲德: 04351, 13052 to 13164
Hsü Jung Archives 許容: 04896, 04900, 04901
Huang Ping Archives 黃炳: 04502 to 04609
Lang T'ing-chi Archives 郎廷極: 1926 to 2012, 1942.1
Li Lin-sheng Archives 李林盛: 1817 to 1818
Sung Lao Archives 宋犖: 2400 to 2443
Ts'ai Sheng-yüan Archives 蔡升元: 1691 to 1696
Ts'ao Fu Archives 曹頫: 2845 to 2890
Ts'ao Yin Archives 曹寅: 2709 to 2827
Wang ta-jen mi-i tsou-p'ien 王大人密議奏片 (Short memorials containing secret deliberations of Prince [Yin-hsiang] and other ministers): uncatalogued
Wu Chün Archives 吳郡: 1761
Yüeh Chung-ch'i Archives 岳鍾琪: 00001 to 00728

Published Works
Allport, Gordon W. *Personality and Social Encounter*. Boston: Beacon Press, 1966.
Backhouse, E. T., and J. O. P. Bland. *Annals and Memoirs of the Court of Peking*. [Boston and New York, 1914.]
de Bary, William T., *et al. Sources of Chinese Tradition*. New York: Columbia University Press, 1960.
Bodde, Derk, and Clarence Morris. *Law in Imperial China*. Cambridge: Harvard University Press, 1967.
Brunnert, H. S., and V. V. Halgelstrom. *Present Day Political Organization of China*, trans. A. Belt-Beltchenko and E. E. Moran. Shanghai: Kelly and Walsh, 1912.
Carter, Charles H. *The Secret Diplomacy of the Habsburgs, 1598–1625*. New York: Columbia University Press, 1964.
Chang ch'ing-ko [*Po-hsing*] *kung nien-p'u* 張清恪公年譜 (A chronological biography of Chang Po-hsing). 1738.
Chang-ku ts'ung-pien 掌故叢編 (Collected historical documents). Published by the Department of Historical Records (Wen-hsien-kuan 文獻館), Palace Museum,

Peiping, 1928–1929. Beginning with the eleventh issue the title was changed to *Wen-hsien ts'ung-pien*. The 1964 Taiwan reprint with continuous pagination is used for this study.

Chang T'ing-yü 張廷玉. *Ch'eng-huai yüan wen-ts'un* 澄懷園文存 (An anthology of Chang T'ing-yü), 1891.

Chao I 趙翼. *Yen-p'u tsa-chi* 簷曝雜記 (Miscellaneous notes), in *Ou-pei ch'üan-chi* 甌北全集 (The complete works of Ou-pei [Chao I]), vol. 15. 1877 reprint.

—— *Kai-yü ts'ung-k'ao* 陔餘叢攷 (A collection of miscellaneous notes), in *Ou-pei ch'üan-chi* (see Chao I).

Ch'en Ch'ing-tuan kung wen-chi 陳清端公文集 (The collected essays of Ch'en Pin). Yang-ch'eng 羊城 (Canton), 1868.

Ch'ien Mu 錢穆. *Chung-kuo li-tai cheng-chih te-shih* 中國歷代政治得失 (A critical review of the political institutions in imperial China). Taipei, 1952.

Ch'ing-ch'ao hsü wen-hsien t'ung-k'ao 清朝續文獻通考 (Imperial encyclopedia of the historical records of the Ch'ing dynasty, continued), by Liu Chin-tsao 劉錦藻. 320 chüan. 1904 ed., undated Taiwan reprint used for this study.

Ch'ing-ch'ao wen-hsien t'ung-k'ao 清朝文獻通考 (Imperial encyclopedia of the records of the Ch'ing dynasty). 300 chüan. 1882 ed., undated Taiwan reprint.

Ch'ing-shih 清史 (History of the Ch'ing dynasty). 8 vols. Taipei, 1961; continuous pagination.

Ch'ing-tai wen-tzu-yü tang 清代文字獄檔 (Archival collections on literary inquisition under the Ch'ing). 12 vols. Peiping: National Palace Museum, 1931 et seq.

Chosŏn wangjo sillok 朝鮮王朝實錄 or *Yijo sillok* 李朝實錄 (The annals of the Yi dynasty), Sukchong 肅宗 reign. Compiled by Kuksa P'yŏnch'an Wiwŏnhoe 國史編纂委員會 (The Compilation Committee of the National [Korean] History). Seoul, 1955–1958. A facsimile reproduction of the *T'aebaek-san* 太白山 ed.

Chou Ju-ch'ang 周汝昌. *Hung-lou meng hsin-cheng* 紅樓夢新證 (New studies on the *Dream of the Red Chamber*). Shanghai, 1953.

Chu-p'i yü-chih 硃枇諭旨 (Vermilion endorsements of the Yung-cheng Emperor, including memorials concerned). 112 vols. 1738; preface by the Ch'ien-lung Emperor dated 1738.

Ch'ü T'ung-tsu. *Local Government in China under the Ch'ing*. Cambridge: Harvard University Press, 1962.

Deutsch, Karl W. *The Nerves of Government: Models of Political Communication and Control*. London: Free Press of Glencoe, 1963.

Du Halde, P. J. B. *The General History of China*, trans. R. Brookes. 4 vols. London, 1741. From the French edition: *Description geographique, historique, chronologique, politique, et physique de l'empire de la Chine*, 4 vols. Paris, 1735.

Fairbank, J. K. and S. Y. Teng. *Ch'ing Administration: Three Studies*. Cambridge: Harvard University Press, 1960.

Fairbank, J. K., E. O. Reischauer, and A. M. Craig. *East Asia: Modern Transformation*. Boston: Houghton Mifflin, 1965.

Fang Pao. See *Fang Wang-ch'i ch'üan-chi*.

Fang Tu Lien-che 房杜連喆. "Kuan-yü Chün-chi ch'u ti chien-chih" 關於軍機處的建置 (On the establishment of the Grand Council). Occasional Papers, no. 2,

Centre of Oriental Studies. Australian National University, Canberra, 1963.

Fang Wang-ch'i ch'üan-chi 方望溪全集 (Collected works of Fang Pao), by Fang Pao 方苞. Shanghai, 1936.

Fu-chien t'ung-chih 福建通志 (A general gazetteer of Fukien). 1737.

Fu Tsung-mao 傅宗懋. *Ch'ing-tai Chün-chi ch'u tsu-chih chi chih-chang chih yen-chiu* 清代軍機處組織及職掌之研究 (A study of the organization of the Grand Council and its functions under the Ch'ing). Taipei, 1967.

Goodrich, L. Carrington. *The Literary Inquisition of Ch'ien-lung.* Baltimore: Waverly Press, 1935.

Grant, Hamil. *Spies and Secret Services.* London: Grant Richards, 1915.

Grimm, Tilemann. "Das Neiko der Ming-Zeit von den Anfangen bis 1506," *Oriens Extremus*, 1, no. 2 (1954), 139–177.

Ho Ping-ti. *The Ladder of Success in Imperial China.* New York: Columbia University Press, 1962.

Hsiao I-shan 蕭一山. *Ch'ing-tai t'ung-shih* 清代通史 (A general history of the Ch'ing dynasty), rev. ed. 5 vols. Taipei, 1951–1953.

Hsiao Kung-ch'üan. *Rural China: Imperial Control in Nineteenth Century China.* Seattle: University of Washington Press, 1960.

Hsiao-t'ing tsa-lu 嘯亭雜錄 (Miscellaneous notes on Ch'ing history), by Chao Lien 昭槤. 6 chüan, 1880.

Hsieh, Pao-chao. *Government of China: 1644–1911.* Baltimore: The Johns Hopkins Press, 1925.

Huang P'ei 黃培. "Yung-cheng shih-tai ti mi-tsou chih-tu" 雍正時代的密奏制度 (The secret-report system during the Yung-cheng period), in *Tsing-hua hsüeh-pao* 清華學報 (Tsing Hua journal of Chinese studies), NS 3 (May 1962), 17–52.

Hucker, Charles O. *The Censorial System in Ming China.* Stanford: Stanford University Press, 1966.

Hummel, Arthur W., ed. *Eminent Chinese of the Ch'ing Period.* Washington: U.S. Government Printing Office, 1943–1944.

Inaba Kunzan 稻葉君山. *Ch'ing-ch'ao ch'üan-shih* 清朝全史 (A complete history of the Ch'ing dynasty), trans. Tan T'ao. 2 vols. Shanghai, 1914.

Juan K'uei-sheng 阮葵生. *Ch'a-yü k'o-hua* 茶餘客話 (Random notes on Ch'ing history and institutions). Peking, 1959.

Jung-ts'un yü-lu 榕村語錄 (Recorded sayings of Li Kuang-ti), in *Jung-ts'un ch'uan-shu* 榕村全書 (The collected works of Jung-ts'un [Li Kuang-ti]), ts'e 61–63. 1829.

Kanda Nobuo. 神田信夫. "Shinsho no gisei daijin ni tsuite" 清初の議政大臣について (On the deliberative ministers in the early Ch'ing dynasty), in *Wada hakushi kanreki kinen Tōyōshi ronsō* 和田博士還曆紀念東洋史論叢 (Essays on Asian history in commemoration of Dr. Wada's sixty-first birthday). Tokyo, 1951. Pages 171–185.

—— "Shinsho no bairoku ni tsuite" 清初の貝勒について (On the *pei-le* in the early Ch'ing dynasty), in *Tōyō gakuhō* 東洋學報 (Reports of the Oriental Society), 43, no. 4 (March 1958), 1–23.

Kroeber, A. L. *Anthropology.* New York: Harcourt, Brace, 1958.

Kuei Ching-hsien 歸靜先. *Ch'ing-tai wen-yen chi-lüeh* 清代文讞紀略 (A brief survey on the literary inquisition under the Ch'ing). Chungking, 1944.

Kuo-ch'ao ch'i-hsien lei-cheng ch'u-pien 國朝耆獻類徵初編 (Classified biographies of eminent men of the Ch'ing period), compiled by Li Huan 李桓. 720 chüan with appendixes (12 chüan). 1884–1890.

Lasswell, H. D., and A. Kaplan. *Power and Society*. New Haven: Yale University Press, 1961.

Legge, James. *The Chinese Classics*. 5 vols. Hong Kong: Hong Kong University Press, 1960.

Li Tsung-huang 李宗黃. *Chung-kuo li-tai hsing-cheng t'ung-lun* 中國歷代行政通論 (A historical treatise of the administrative systems in China). Taipei, 1961.

Li Tsung-t'ung 李宗侗. "Pan-li chün-chi ch'u lüeh-k'ao" 辦理軍機處略考 (A brief study of the founding of the Grand Council), in *Yu-shih hsüeh-pao* 幼獅學報 (The youth journal), 1, No. 2 (1959), 1–19.

Li Wen-cheng kung [*Kuang-ti*] *nien-p'u* 李文貞公年譜 (A chronological biography of Li Kuang-ti). N.p.

Man-chou shih-lu 滿洲實錄 (The veritable records of the Manchus). Peking: Kuo-hsüeh wen-k'u 國學文庫 ed., 1927.

Man-Han ming-ch'en chuan 滿漢名臣傳 (Biographies of eminent Chinese and Manchu officials). 90 chüan. Chü-hua shu-shih 菊花書室, n.d.; *Kuo-shih* 國史 ed.

Mayers, W. F. *The Chinese Government*. Shanghai, 1897.

Meng Sen 孟森. "Shih-tsung ju-ch'eng ta-t'ung k'ao-shih" 世宗入承大統考實 (A study of the Yung-cheng Emperor's succession), in *Ch'ing-tai shih* 清代史 (History of the Ch'ing dynasty), ed. Wu Hsiang-hsiang 吳相湘. Taipei, 1960. Pages 477–510.

Michael, Franz. *The Origin of Manchu Rule in China*. Baltimore, The Johns Hopkins Press, 1942.

Miyazaki Ichisada 宮崎市定. *Yō-sei-tei: dokusai no kunshu* 雍正帝—獨裁の君主 (The Yung-cheng Emperor: an imperial dictator). Tokyo, 1950.

——— "Shuhi yushi kaidai" 硃枇諭旨解題 (Notes on *The Vermilion Endorsements of the Yung-cheng Emperor*), in *Tōyōshi kenkyū* 東洋史研究 (Journal of Oriental researches), 15 (March 1957), 1–32.

——— "Shinchō ni okeru kokugo mondai no ichimen" 清朝に於ける國語問題の一面 (One aspect of the Manchu language problem in the early Ch'ing period), in his *Ajiashi kenkyū* アジア史研究 (Studies in Oriental history), 3 (Kyoto, 1963), 336–393.

Mo Tung-yin 莫東寅. *Man-tsu shih lun-ts'ung* 滿族史論叢 (Essays on the history of the Manchus). Peking, 1958.

Mote, F. W. "The Growth of Chinese Despotism: A Critique of Wittfogel Theory of Oriental Despotism as Applied to China," *Oriens Extremus*, 8, no. 1 (August, 1961), 1–41.

Nei-ko chih 內閣志 (An account of the Grand Secretariat), by Hsi Wu-ao 席吳鏊 Shanghai, 1937. *Ts'ung-shu chi-ch'eng* 叢書集成 ed.

Nei-ko hsiao-chih 內閣小志 (A brief sketch of the Grand Secretariat), by Yeh Feng-mao 葉鳳毛. Shanghai, 1940. *Ts'ung-shu chi-ch'eng* ed.

Nishimoto Hakusen 西本白川. *Kōki Taitei* 康熙大帝 (K'ang-hsi the Great). Tokyo, 1941.

Ripa, Matteo. *Memoirs of Father Ripa*. London, 1855.

Rosso, Antonio Sisto. *Apostolic Legations to China of the Eighteenth Century* (South Pasadena, 1948).

Sakata, Yoshio, and John W. Hall, "Motivation of Political Leadership in the Meiji Restoration," *Journal of Asian Studies*, 15, no. 1 (November 1956), 31–50.

Schurmann, Franz. *Ideology and Organization in Communist China*. Berkeley: University of California Press, 1966.

Shang-yü ch'i-wu i-fu 上諭旗務議覆 (Imperial decrees in response to deliberations on banner affairs; Palace ed.)

Shang-yü Nei-ko 上諭內閣 (Imperial edicts of the Yung-cheng Emperor to the *Nei-ko*), that is, *Yung-cheng shang-yü* 雍正上諭. 34 ts'e. 1741. Footnote citation according to date of edict.

Sheng-tsu Jen huang-ti sheng-hsün 聖祖仁皇帝聖訓 (Sacred instructions of the K'ang-hsi Emperor), in *Ta-ch'ing shih-ch'ao sheng-hsün* 大清十朝聖訓 (Sacred instructions of the ten reigns of the Ch'ing dynasty). 60 chüan. 1965 Taiwan reprint.

Shih-tsung Hsien huang-ti sheng-hsün 世宗憲皇帝聖訓 (Sacred instructions of the Yung-cheng Emperor), in *Ta-Ch'ing shih-ch'ao sheng-hsün*. 36 chüan. 1965 Taiwan reprint.

Shu-yüan chi-lüeh 樞垣記略 (A brief account of the Grand Council), by Liang Chang-chü 梁章鉅 and supplemented by Chu Chih 朱智. 1875.

Skinner, C. William. "What the Study of China Can Do for Social Science," *Journal of Asian Studies*, 23, no. 4 (August 1964), 517–522.

Smith, Kent C. "O-erh-t'ai and the Yung-cheng Emperor," *Ch'ing-shih wen-t'i* (Bulletin of the Society for Ch'ing Studies), 1, no. 8 (May 1968), 10–15.

Snyder, Richard C. "A Decision-Making Approach to the Study of Political Phenomena," in Roland Young, ed., *Approaches to the Study of Politics*. Evanston, Ill.: Northwestern University Press, 1958.

Spence, Jonathan D. *Ts'ao Yin and the K'ang-hsi Emperor*. New Haven: Yale University Press, 1966.

Sprenkel, S. van der. *Legal Institutions in Manchu China*. London: Athlone Press of the University of London, 1962.

Sun Ch'eng-tse 孫承澤. *Ch'un-ming meng-yü lu* 春明夢餘錄 (Miscellaneous accounts of the capital city and the central administration in the Ming dynasty). 70 chüan. *Ku-hsiang-chai* 古香齋 1883.

Sun Zen, E-tu. *Ch'ing Administrative Terms*. Cambridge: Harvard University Press, 1961.

Ta-Ch'ing hui-tien 大清會典 (Collected statutes of the Ch'ing dynasty). Shanghai. Kuan-hsü ed., 100 chüan (Taiwan reprint in 1 vol., abbreviated *HT*, used in this study); K'ang-hsi ed., 162 chüan (abbreviated *HT*: KH); Yung-cheng ed.,

100 chüan (*HT*: YC).

Ta-Ch'ing hui-tien shih-li 大清會典事例 (Precedents and edicts pertaining to the collected statutes of the Ch'ing dynasty). 1220 chüan. Shanghai, 1899. 1963 Taiwan reprint with continuous pagination, in 19 vols., used in this study.

Ta-Ch'ing li-ch'ao shih-lu 大清歷朝實錄 (The veritable records of the Ch'ing reigns). Tokyo, 1937. Shun-chih reign, 144 chüan; K'ang-hsi reign, 300 chüan; Yung-cheng reign, 159 chüan; Ch'ien-lung reign, 1500 chüan.

Ta-Ming hui-tien 大明會典 (Collected statutes of the Ming dynasty). 1585 ed.; 1963 Taiwan reprint used in this study.

T'ai-tsung shih-lu 太宗實錄 (Veritable records of T'ai-tsung) or *Ta-Ch'ing T'ai-tsung Wen Huang-ti shih-lu* 大清太宗文皇帝實錄, in *Ta-Ch'ing li-chao shih-lu*. Tokyo, 1937.

T'ang Chi-ho 湯吉禾. "Ch'ing-tai k'o-tao chih kung-wu kuan-hsi" 清代科道之公務關係 (The censorial functions in the Ch'ing administration), in *Hsin she-hui k'o-hsüeh chi-k'an* 新社會科學季刊 (The new social sciences quarterly) 1, no. 2 (1934), 209–211.

Teng Wen-ju 鄧文如 (Teng Chih-ch'eng 鄧之誠). "T'an Chün-chi ch'u" 談軍機處 (On the Grand Council), in *Shih-hsüeh nien-pao* 史學年報 (Historical annual) 2, no. 4 (1937), 193–198.

T'ing-hsün ko-yen 庭訓格言 (Exhortations of the K'ang-hsi Emperor). Wu-hsing 吳興, 1921.

Tung-hua lu 東華錄 (Tung-hua records), by Wang Hsien-ch'ien 王先謙, Ch'ung-te 崇德 reign, 8 chüan; Shun-chih 順治 reign, 36 chüan; T'ien-ming 天命 reign, 4 chüan; T'ien-ts'ung 天聰 reign, 11 chüan. 1911.

Walker, James. "The Secret Service under Charles II and James II," *Royal Historical Society Transactions*, 4th ser., 15 (1932), 211–242.

Wang Ching-ch'i 王景祺. *Tu-shu-t'ang hsi-cheng sui-pi* 讀書堂西征隨筆 (Jottings of a western journey), in *Chang-ku ts'ung-pien*.

Wang Chung-han 王鍾翰. "Ch'ing Shih-tsung to-ti k'ao-shih" 清世宗奪嫡考實 (The Yung-cheng Emperor's struggle for the right of succession), in *Yen-ching hsüeh-pao* 燕京學報 (Yenching journal of Chinese studies), 36, no. 62 (June 1949), 205–261. This article is also reprinted in his *Ch'ing-shih tsa-k'ao* 清史雜考 (Miscellaneous studies on Ch'ing history). Peking, 1957. Pages 147–193.

Wang Shih-chen 王士禎. *Ch'ih-pei ou-t'an* 池北偶談 (Miscellaneous notes and comments). 36 chüan. Preface written in the K'ang-hsi reign. 1950 Taiwan reprint.

Wen-hsien ts'ung-pien 文獻叢編 (Collectanea of historical documents of the Ch'ing dynasty). Peking: Palace Museum, 1930——. 1964 Taiwan reprint, with continuous pagination in 2 vols., used.

Wittfogel, Karl A. *Oriental Despotism: A Comparative Study of Total Power*. New Haven: Yale University Press, 1957.

Wolff, Kurt H., ed. *The Sociology of George Simmel*. Glencoe, Ill.: Free Press, 1950.

Wu, Silas H. L. (Wu Hsiu-liang 吳秀良). "The Memorial Systems of the Ch'ing Dynasty, 1644–1911," *Harvard Journal of Asiatic Studies*, 27 (1967), 7–75.

—— "Nan-shu-fang chih chien-chih chi ch'i ch'ien-ch'i chih fa-chan" 南書房之

建置及其前期之發展 (The founding of the South Library and its early development), in *Ssu yü yen* 思與言 (Thought and word), 5, no. 6 (March 1968), 6–12.

———— "Transmission of Ming Memorials, 1368–1627," *T'oung Pao*, 54, nos. 4–5 (1968), 275–287.

Wu Chen-yü 吳振棫. *Yang-chi-chai ts'ung-lu* 養吉齋叢錄 (Miscellaneous notes from the Yang-chi Study). 35 chüan (including *Yü-lu* 餘錄, 10 chüan); 1896 preface; n.p.

Yen Mao-kung 嚴懋功. *Ch'ing-tai cheng-hsien lei-pien* 清代徵獻類編 (Classified historical records of the Ch'ing Dynasty), vol. I. Taipei, 1961.

Yung-hsien lu 永憲錄 (Historical records of the Yung-cheng period), compiled by Hsiao Shih 蕭奭. Shanghai, 1959.

Zaleznik, Abraham, and David Moment. *The Dynamics of Interpersonal Behavior*. New York: Wiley, 1964.

A-erh-sung-a 阿爾松阿
A-lin 阿琳
an-ch'a-shih 按察使
An-p'ing 安平

cha-erh-ku-ch'i 扎爾固齊
ch'a-i 查議
ch'a-li 察吏
Ch'a Shen-hsing 查慎行
chan-chieh-hou 斬監候
Chan-shih fu 詹事府
Chang Ch'i-yün 張起雲
Chang Ching-heng 張景恒
Chang-chou 漳州
Chang Jo-ai 張若靄
Chang Kuo 張國
Chang Ming-te 張明德
Chang P'eng-ko 張鵬翮
Chang T'ing-yü 張廷玉
Ch'ang-ch'un yüan 暢春園
ch'ang-shih 長史
ch'ang-sui 長隨
Chao Ch'eng 趙成
Chao Chin 趙晉
chao kai-tu so-ch'ing hsing 照該督所請行
Chao Shen-ch'iao 趙申喬
che 摺
che-hsia 摺匣
che-pen 折本
che-tzu 摺子
Ch'e-chia ch'ing-li ssu 車駕清吏司
chen-an 朕安
Chen-chiang 鎮江
chen-kuo chiang-chün 鎮國將軍
chen-kuo kung 鎮國公
Ch'en Ju-pi 陳汝弼
Ch'en Lun-chiung 陳倫炯

Ch'en P'eng-nien 陳鵬年
Ch'en Pin 陳瓆
ch'en-pu 臣部
Ch'en Shih-kuan 陳世倌
ch'en teng tsun-chih kung-ni shang-yü ch'eng-lan 臣等遵旨恭擬上諭呈覽
Ch'en Wang-chang 陳王章
cheng-ch'ao 正鈔
cheng-ch'ien 正籤
ch'eng-chih 承旨
Ch'eng Kuang-k'uei 程光奎
chi-shih-chung 給事中
chi-tzu 寄字
chi-wu 機務
ch'i 氣
ch'i-che 啓摺
ch'i-chien 啓柬
Ch'i-shih-wu 齊世武
chia-pan 夾板
chia-ssu 甲巳
Chiang-ning 江寧
Chiang T'ing-hsi 蔣廷錫
ch'iang-chi 強記
chiao-hui 教誨
chiao pan-li chün-chi ch'u ts'un-an 交辦理軍機處存案
chiao-pu ch'ao-lu ts'un-an 交部抄錄存案
chiao-pu i-fu 交部議覆
Chieh-pao ch'u 捷報處
chieh-t'ieh 揭帖
chien-ch'a yü-shih 監察御史
Chien-chiao shih-kao 堅蕉詩稿
Chien-ning 建寧
ch'ien 錢
Ch'ien-ch'ing men 乾淸門
Ch'ien-ch'ing men shih-wei 乾淸門侍衞
chih 旨，制

chih-tao-le 知道了
chih-tsao 織造
chin-shen 縉紳
chin-shih 進士
chin-tsou ch'ing-chih 謹奏請旨
chin tz'u tsun-chih chi-hsin ch'ien-lai 謹此遵旨寄信前來
chin-yao shih-chien 緊要事件
ch'in-wang 親王
Ching-pao 京報
ch'ing-an che 請安摺
Ch'ing-ho 清河
ch'ing-pao ling-t'ung 情報靈通
"Ch'ing Sheng-tsu yü-chih" 清聖祖諭旨
Ch'ing-tzu 清字
ch'ing-yü lu 晴雨錄
chiu-ch'ing i-tsou 九卿議奏
chiu-ch'ing k'o-tao hui-i 九卿科道會議
cho pan-li chün-hsü chih ta-ch'en i-tsou 著辦理軍需之大臣議奏
Chou-i che-chung 周易折中
chu-ching t'i-t'ang 駐京提塘
Chu-pi yü-chih 硃筆諭旨
Chu-p'i yü-chih 硃批諭旨
Chu Shih 朱軾
Chu T'ien-pao 朱天保
Chu-tzu ch'üan-shu 朱子全書
Chu Wei-chün 朱維鈞
Chu Yün 朱雲
ch'u k'ou 出口
Chü-i lu 居易錄
chü-jen 舉人
chü-pen chin-t'i 具本謹題
chü-t'i 具題
chuan-chih 專制
ch'uan chih 傳旨
ch'uan-feng chih-i 傳奉旨意
Ch'üan-chou 泉州
Chuang-lang 莊浪
chuang-yüan 狀元
chün-chi chang-ching 軍機章京
Chün-chi ch'u 軍機處
Chün-chi fang 軍機房
"Chün-chi ta-ch'en nien-piao" 軍機大臣年表
chün-hsü 軍需
Chün-hsü fang 軍需房
chün-kuo chung-wu 軍國重務
chung-shu (i.e. chung-shu she-jen, or she-jen) 中書 (i.e. 中書舍人, or 舍人)
Chung-shu k'o 中書科

erh-mu chih-kuan 耳目之官

fa-ch'ao 發鈔
Fan Shih-i 范時繹
Fang Ming 方名
fang-ts'un i-luan 方寸已亂
Feng Hsieh-i 馮協一
feng-kuo chiang-chün 奉國將軍
feng shang-yü 奉上諭
fu 福
fu-chien 副件
fu-chun 覆准
fu-kuo chiang-chün 輔國將軍
fu-kuo kung 輔國公
Fu-ning-an 富寧安
fu-pen 副本
Fu-t'ai 傅泰
fu-tzu 父子

Ha Yüan-sheng 哈元生
Hai-t'an chen 海壇鎮
Han chiu-ch'ing 漢九卿
Han p'iao-ch'ien ch'u 漢票籤處
Hao Yü-lin 郝玉麟
ho 和
Ho-nan tao chien-ch'a yü-shih 河南道監察御史
ho-p'ing 和平
Ho-shou 赫壽
ho-shuo ch'ing-wang 和碩親王
ho-shuo pei-le 和碩貝勒
ho-tao tsung-tu 河道總督
Hsi-erh-ta 席爾達
Hsi-ming 西銘
Hsieh Chi-shih 謝濟世
hsien 縣

Hsien san 軒三
hsien-san i-cheng ta-ch'en 閒散議政大臣
hsing 刑
hsing-wen 行文
hsiu-ts'ai 秀才
Hsü Ch'ien-hsüeh 徐乾學
Hsü-chou 徐州
Hsü Chün 徐駿
hsüeh-cheng 學政
hsüeh-shih 學士
hsün 汛
hsün-fu 巡撫
hsün-hsing 巡幸
hsün-yü 訓諭
Hu Jen-yü 胡任輿
Hu-k'o 戶科
Hua-niao 花鳥
hua-t'i 劃題
Huai-an 淮安
Huang Kuo-ts'ai 黃國材
hui-t'ui 會推
Hui-t'ung kuan 會同舘
Hung-pen-shang 紅本上
huo-p'ai 火牌

i 驛
I Chao-hsiung 宜兆熊
I-cheng ch'u 議政處
i-cheng pei-le 議政貝勒
i-cheng ta-ch'en 議政大臣
i-cheng wang 議政王
i-cheng wang ta-ch'en 議政王大臣
i-cheng wang ta-ch'en hui-i 議政王大臣
　會議
i-cheng wang ta-ch'en i-tsou 議政王大臣
　議奏
i-chun 議准
i-i 依議
i-ting 議定
i-tsou 議奏
i-yu 乙酉
i yu chih le 已有旨了

ju-ch'en 儒臣

ju-chin (i.e. pi-chien) 入覲 (i.e. 陛見)

kai chü-t'i 該具題
kai-pu i-tsou 該部議奏
K'ai-feng 開封
Kao Ch'i-cho 高其倬
Kao Shih-ch'i 高士奇
Keng-o 耿額
ko-chih 革職
k'o 尅
k'o-hsiao 可笑
k'o-tao 科道
k'ou-ch'uan yü-chih 口傳諭旨
Ku-pei (-k'ou) 古北 (口)
ku-shan o-chen 固山額眞
ku-shan pei-le 固山貝勒
ku-shan pei-tzu 固山貝子
Ku-t'ien 古田
Ku-t'u-ho 顧圖河
Ku Yüeh-li (lü) 顧悅履
kuan-feng cheng-su shih 觀風整俗使
kuan-li Hu-pu shih-wu 管理戶部事務
k'uan 寬
k'uan-jen 寬仁
k'uan yen hsiang-chi 寬嚴相濟
Kuang-p'ing (fu) 廣平 (府)
kung-hou ch'ing-ting 恭侯欽定
kung-nü 宮女
K'ung-ming-tzu chi 空明子集
K'ung Yü-hsün 孔毓珣
K'ung Yü-p'u 孔毓璞

lai ching yin-chien 來京引見
Lan-chou 蘭州
Lei-chou 雷州
li 例，里
li-fa 立法
Li-fan yüan 理藩院
Li-k'o 吏科
Li Ch'i 李奇
Li Fu 李紱
Li Hsi 李錫
Li Hsü 李煦
Li Kuang-ti 李光地

Li Lan 李蘭
Li Lin-sheng 李林盛
Li-pu 吏部
Li Wei 李衛
liang-i i-wen 兩議以聞
Liang Shih-hsün 梁世勳
Liang Wen-k'o 梁文科
Lin-ming kuan 臨洺關
ling shih-wei nei ta-ch'en 領侍衛內大臣
Liu Chia-chü 劉家駒
liu-chung pen 留中本
Liu-k'o 六科
Liu-pu 六部
Lo Cheng-nien 羅正年
Lu-erh men 鹿耳門
Lü Liu-liang 呂留良
lü-t'ou-p'ai 綠頭牌
Lü-ying 綠營
luan-ch'en tse-tzu 亂臣賊子
Lung-t'an 龍潭
Lung-tsung (men) 隆宗 (門)

Ma-erh-sai 馬爾賽
Ma I-tzu 馬逸姿
Ma-san-ch'i 馬三奇
ma-shang fei-ti 馬上飛遞
Ma Ti-po 馬覿伯
Mai-chu 邁柱
Man chiu-ch'ing 滿九卿
Man Han chiu-ch'ing 滿漢九卿
Man-pao 滿保
Man-p'ei 滿丕
Man p'iao-ch'ien ch'u 滿票籤處
mao 卯
Mao-ch'in (tien) 懋勤 (殿)
mi-che 密摺
mi chi-hsin 密寄信
mi-chih 密旨
mi-hsing shih-chien 密行事件
mi-pao 密保
mi-pen 密本
mi-yü 密諭
miao-chiang shih-i 苗疆事宜
miao-wu 苗務

mien-ch'eng 面承
ming-fa (shang-yü) 明發 (上諭)
ming-pai-le 明白了
Mu-ho-lun 穆和倫

Nan-ao chen 南澳鎮
Nan-ch'ang 南昌
nan-fang 南方
Nan-ho tsung-tu 南河總督
Nan-shu-fang 南書房
Nan-shu-fang chin-feng 南書房謹封
nei chung-t'ang 內中堂
Nei hung-wen yüan 內宏文院
Nei-ko 內閣
Nei-ko chung-shu 內閣中書
Nei-ko hsing-wen 內閣行文
Nei kuo-shih kuan 內國史館
Nei pi-shu yüan 內祕書院
Nei san-yüan 內三院
nei tsou-shih t'ai-chien 內奏事太監
Nei-yüan 內院
ni-kao 擬稿
Nien Hsi 年熙
"Nien Keng-yao tsou-che" 年羹堯奏摺
nu-ts'ai 奴才

O-erh-t'ai 鄂爾泰
O-lun-t'e 額倫特
O-shan 鄂善

Pa-hsi 巴錫
pa-shih 罷士
pa ta-ch'en 八大臣
Pai Huang 白潢
Pai-ting 擺頂
pan-li chün-hsü shih-wu ta-ch'en 辦理軍
    需事務大臣
pan-tu 伴讀
P'an Tsung-lo 潘宗洛
pang-yen 榜眼
pao-mu 媬母
Pao-ting 保定
Pei-ho-no 貝和諾
pei-le 貝勒

P'ei-wen yün-fu 佩文韻府
pen-chang 本章
pi-chien 陛見
pi-t'ieh-shih 筆帖式
pi-tz'u 陛辭
p'i-pen ch'u (i.e. hung-pen-shang) 批本處
piao 標
p'iao-ni 票擬
Ping-pu huo-p'ai 兵部火牌
ping-shen 丙申
Po Ch'i 白琦
pu-cheng shih 布政使
pu-chung chih shih, pu-k'o k'o-chiu 部中之事，不可苛求
pu-lu che 不錄摺
pu-lu tang-an 不錄檔案
pu-pen 部本
pu-shih lien-ch'ih 不識廉恥
pu-yüan 部院
P'u-ch'eng 浦城
P'u-ch'i 普奇
p'u-ping 舖兵

san-fa-ssu 三法司
sha-i ching-pai 殺一儆百
Sha-mu-ha 沙木哈
Shan-yang (hsien) 山陽（縣）
shang-yü 上諭
she-jen (i.e. chung-shu) 舍人
shen-shang hao-mo 身上好麼
Shen T'ing-cheng 沈廷正
sheng-hsün 聖訓
sheng-yüan 生員
shih 是
shih-tu 侍讀
shih-tu hsüeh-shih 侍讀學士
shu-chi yün-ch'ou chih chu 樞機運籌之助
shu-chih 述旨
Shu-lu 舒輅
shu-ming 署名
shui-i 水驛
ssu-kuan 司官

ssu-lun pu 絲綸簿
Su-chou 肅州
Su Hsün 蘇壎
sui 歲

ta-ch'en 大臣
ta-chi 大計
ta chiu-ch'ing 大九卿
ta-hsüh-shih 大學士
ta-jen 大人
Ta-li ssu 大理寺
t'ai-chi 太極，台吉
T'ai-chi [t'u shuo] 太極（圖說）
T'ai-ho (men) 太和（門）
T'ai-tsu 太祖
T'ai-tsung 太宗
T'ang-shan 湯山
tao 道
t'e-wu jen-yüan 特務人員
t'e-wu tsu-chih 特務組織
ti-fang shih-i 地方事宜
t'i-chun 題准
t'i-pen 題本
t'i-t'ang 提塘
t'i-t'ang ch'eng-ch'ai 提塘承差
t'iao-ch'en 條陳
tieh-huang 貼黃
t'ien-ming 天命
T'ien Wen-ching 田文鏡
ting 定
t'ing-chi (shang-yü) 廷寄（上諭）
T'ing-hai 定海
to-lo chün-wang 多羅郡王
to-lo pei-le 多羅貝勒
T'o-ho-ch'i (T'ao ho-ch'i) 託和齊（陶和氣）
tou 斗
Tsa-lu 雜錄
tsai Chün-chi ch'u hsing-tsou 在軍機處行走
tsai mi-fang 再密訪
Ts'ai T'ien-lüeh 蔡添略
Ts'ai T'ing 蔡珽
Tsao-pan ch'u 造辦處

ts'ao-ch'ien 草籤
ts'ao-yün tsung-tu 漕運總督
Ts'ao Yung 曹頫
Tseng Ching 曾靜
Tso Pi-fan 左必蕃
tsou-che 奏摺
tsou-hsiao 奏銷
tsou-pen 奏本
tsou-p'ien 奏片
tsou-shih chih-i-cheng 奏事治儀正
shou-shih chih-jen 奏事之人
tsou-shih chu-shih 奏事主事
Tsou-shih ch'u 奏事處
tsou-shih t'ai-chien 奏事太監
tsou-t'ieh (i.e. tsou-che) 奏帖
tsuan-ni (i.e. ni-chih) 撰擬 (i.e. 擬旨)
Tsung-jen fu 宗人府
tsung-li shih-wu wang ta-ch'en 總理事
　務王大臣
Tsung-ti 宗地
tsung-tu 總督
Tu-ch'a yüan 都察院
tu-ts'ai 獨裁
tu-t'ung 都統
Tung-ch'ao-fang 東朝房
Tung Yung-chi 董永芰
T'ung-cheng ssu 通政司
t'ung-pen 通本
t'ung-yin ho-kung 同寅和恭
tzu 咨, 字
tzu-chi 字寄
tz'u-chien tang-ts'an 此件當參
tz'u-p'u (kuan) 詞譜 （館）
tz'u pu-kuo hsiao-shih, chin ta-shih i-
　ch'eng 此不過小事，今大事已成

wai-ch'ao 外鈔
wai chung-t'ang 外中堂
Wai taou-shih ch'u 外奏事處
wang 王
Wang Ch'ao-en 王朝恩
Wang Hung-hsü 王鴻緒
Wang I (te) 王懿 （德）
Wang Kuo-tung 王國棟

Wang Shan 王掞
Wang Shao-hsü 王紹緒
Wang ta-jen mi-i tsou-p'ien tsai-nei 王
　大人密議奏片在內
Wang Tung 王棟
Wang Tzu-chung 汪自重
Wei-lu che 未錄摺
wei-lu tang-an 未錄檔案
Wen-kuan 文舘
Wu-ch'ang 武昌
Wu-hsü wen-kao 戊戌文稿
Wu Pi 吳泌
Wu Sheng 吳陞
Wu Ta-ch'an 吳達禪
wu ta-ch'en 五大臣
Wu Ying 吳英

yang 陽
Yang Ch'i-chiao 楊啓樵
Yang-hsin tien 養心殿
yang-lien yin 養廉銀
Yang Lin 楊琳
Yang Ming-shih 楊名時
Yang Wen-ch'ien 楊文乾
Yao Chen-tsung 姚振宗
Yao T'ang 姚堂
Yeh Chiu-ssu 葉九思
Yeh Erh 葉二
yen-ch'a i-tsou 嚴察議奏
yen-kuan 言官
yin 陰
Yin-chen 胤禎
Yin-chi-san 尹繼善
Yin-chih 胤祉
Yin-ch'ing piao 陰晴表
Yin-hsiang 胤祥
Yin-jeng 胤礽
Yin-lu 胤祿
Yin-ssu 胤禩
Yin-t'ang 胤禟
Yin-t'i 胤禵 (or 禵)
yin-wen 印文
Ying-chih 胤祉
Ying i-tsou che i-tsou 應議奏者議奏

ying pu-chun k'ai-hsiao 應不准開銷
yu pu-k'o yen-che 有不可言者
yü 諭
Yü Cheng-chien 余正健
yü ch'ien ti-i jen 御前第一人
Yü-chih wen-chi 御制文集
yü-men t'ing-cheng 御門聽政

yü-shih 御史
Yü Shih-ch'eng (ch'en) 俞世承（臣）
yü-shui ch'ing-hsing 雨水情形
Yüan-chien lei-han 淵鑒類函
Yüan Hsing-jo 員星若
yüan-wai-lang 員外郎
yung-wei ting-li 永爲定例

A-erh-sung-a, 83
A-lin, 133, 140
Allport, Gordon, 5
A-mi-ta, 165n20
An-ch'a-shih, 22
Asan, 53, 56–57, 165n5
Assassination, 58, 68
Assembly of Deliberative Princes and Ministers, 10–13, 17–18, 33; functions, 12–13, 56; abolition, 105–106
Assembly of Nine Ministers and Censors, 10, 13, 14, 33, 64, 106; functions, 13; ineffectiveness, 18–19
Audiences, 20–23; morning, 20–21, 48; farewell, 22; special, 22–23; personal, 69

Bandits, 137
Banners, 38; origin, 10; commanders of, 12; organization of, 12; in South, 25, 53; five inferior, 60
Beile, see Pei-le
Board of Personnel (or Civil Appointment), 79, 93, 128
Board of Punishments, 9, 19
Board of Revenue, 31, 40, 91
Board of Rites (or Ceremonials), 14, 99
Board of War, 94, 96
Board of Works, 97
Bondservants, 36, 38–42, 109
Book of Changes, 130
Book of History, 75, 131
Bribery, 64, 144

Censorate, 13, 23, 32, 155n1, 156n18
Censors, 19, 24, 62, 70, 108, 115; general, 12, 23; supervising, 23; function, 23–24
Cha-erh ku-ch'i, 155n5
Ch'a-i, 71
Ch'a-pi-na, 93
Ch'a Shen-hsing, 46
Chan chien-hou, 66
Chancery of Memorials, 49, 70, 71, 164nn67,69. *See also* Eunuchs; Palace guards
Chang Ch'i-yün, 100

Chang Ching-heng, 98, 99, 176n69
Chang Hsia-tzu, 168n12
Chang Jo-ai, 175n46
Chang K'ai, 75
Chang Kuang-ssu, 97
Chang Kuo, 133
Chang Ming-te, 59–60
Chang P'eng-ko, 24, 142, 143–148
Chang Po-hsing, 26, 53, 113, 139, 142–148
Chang T'ing-yü, 98, 101, 173n25; and Grand Council, 84–86, 90; and Inner Grand Secretaries, 92–94, 96; and court letter format, 104
Chang Ying, 57
Chang Yüan-tso, 103
Ch'ang-ch'un yüan, 128, 138, 141
Ch'ang-ning, 18
Ch'ang-shih, 17
Ch'ang-sui, 95, 176n61
Chao Ch'eng, 173n24
Chao Chin, 143, 146, 165n6
Chao Hung-hsieh, 41, 82
Chao I, 87, 88, 104, 106
Chao-lien, 105
Chao Shen-ch'iao, 66, 131, 168n3
Che, 43, 161n8. *See also* Memorials, palace
Che-pen, 30
Che-p'ien, 103
Che-tzu, 161n8, 163n59. *See also* Memorials, palace
Ch'e-chia ch'ing-li ssu, 28
Chen-kuo chiang-chün, 156n9
Chen-kuo kung, 156n9
Ch'en Ju-pi, 56, 113, 166n27
Ch'en Lung-chiung, 99, 100
Ch'en P'eng-nien, 57, 113
Ch'en Pin, 20, 22, 127, 132–133, 179n8
Ch'en Wang-chang, 96
Cheng-ch'ao, 31
Cheng-ch'ien, 30
Ch'eng-chih, 102
Ch'eng Kuang-k'uei, 143, 146, 147
Chi-shih-chung, 23
Ch'i-chien, 94

Ch'i-shih-wu, 61, 64; death of, 66
Chia-pan, 169n27
Chiang Huang, 55
Chiang Ping, 88
Chiang T'ing-hsi, 84–86, 90, 92, 94, 96, 98, 173n25; in South Library, 82
Chiao-pu i-fu, 32
Chieh-pao ch'u, 103
Chieh-t'ieh, 29
Chien-ch'a yü-shih, 23
Ch'ien-ch'ing Gate, 21, 49, 128, 161n8
Ch'ien-lung Emperor, 87, 105
Ch'ien Mu, 6
Chih, 32, 130
Chih-tao-le, 50, 114
Chih-tsao, 36
Chin-shih, 97, 129, 138, 160n4
Chin-tsou ch'ing-chih, 93
Ch'in Tao-jen, 166n27, 166n37, 168n11
Ch'in-wang, 79
Chinese Registry, 29, 30, 31
Ching-pao, 31
Ch'ing-an che, 36, 37, 40, 41, 44, 45, 109, 110, 113, 143, 161n9
"Ch'ing Sheng-tsu yü-chih," 172n10
Ch'ing-shih-lu, 13, 24, 127; reliability of, 59; on T'o-ho-ch'i, 60, 61; on Grand Council, 89
Ch'ing-yü lu, 37
Chiu-ch'ing i-tsou, 32
Chiu-ch'ing k'o-tao hui-i, 10
Chu-ching t'i-t'ang, 28
Chu Hsi, 98
Chu-p'i, 81
Chu-p'i yü-chih, 73, 76, 81, 118, 170n42
Chu Shih, 101, 173n25
Chu T'ien-pao, 66–67
Chu Wei-chün, 82
Chü-i-lu, 20
Chü-jen, 14, 131, 138, 143, 145
Chü-pen chin-t'i, 43
Chü-t'i, 50, 119
Chuan-chih, 6
Ch'uan-chih, 82
Chün-chi chang-ching, 91, 174n29
Chün-chi ch'u, 6, 85–92, 106, 116, 120, 122, 127, 175n46; translation, 84; functions, 92; and court letter, 103; and palace memorial system, 104; and communication-decision structure, 105; as symbol of power, 122. *See also* Grand Council
"Chün-chi ch'u shu," 175n42

Chün-chi fang, 88, 90–91, 175n46
Chün-chi ta-ch'en, 85, 86
"Chün-chi ta-ch'en nien-piao," 174n32
Chün-hsü fang, 87, 89, 174n28
Chung-shu, 29, 88
Chung-shu k'o, 17
Chung-shu she-jen, 88
Collected Statutes, Ch'ing, 17, 29, 72
Commissioner: financial, 22; judicial, 22; educational, 128
Communication, 1–4, 20, 31, 62, 104, 117; network, 1; in contemporary China, 3, 154n10; typology of, 4; between South and Peking, 35; predecisional, 99–102; channels, 104–105. *See also* Communication-decision structure; Decisions
Communication-decision structure, 1–4, 104–106, 118–120; importance of term, 1; discussed, 2–4; of Yung-cheng bureaucracy, 102; components, 107; flaws, 108; role change, 118–119; pioneering studies in, 153n7. *See also* Communication; Decisions
Concurrent titles, 41, 84, 105, 110
Couriers Office, 103
Courier posts, superintendents, 28, 31
Court of Colonial Affairs (Mongolian Superintendency), 12, 32
Court of Historiography, Inner, 15
Court of Judicature and Revision, 13
Court letters, 70, 80–84, 88, 102–103, 122–123, 172n19; origins, 80–84, 177n95; earliest, 83–84; example, 101; transmission, 103; and palace memorial system, 104
Court of Literature, Inner, 15
Court of Secretariat, Inner, 15

Decisions: system, 1; private, 6; routine, 9; imperial, 9, 99–100; "high policy," 10; types, 33; procedure of, under Ming, 155n20. *See also* Communication; Communication-decision structure
Deliberative bodies, 9, 32, 107–108, 155n1; structure, 10–14; evolution, 10–17; joint sessions, 10, 13–14, 19, 46; procedures and problems, 15, 17–19, 108; types of decisions, 32–33; and military affairs, 86, 92. *See also* Assembly of Deliberative Princes and Ministers
Department director, 128
Deutsch, Karl, 117
Director-general of grain transport, 35

Dorgon, Regency of, 12, 15
Draft rescript system, 28, 29, 32, 80, 160nn18,31; origin, 16; institutionalized, 17; procedure, 29–33, 99–100

Eleuths, 67, 89
Emperor: power and position, 9; in communication-decision network, 118–119; relationship with officials, 121
Erh-mu chih kuan, 23
Espionage, *see* Spies
Eunuchs, 48, 49, 70, 81
Examination Hall scandal, 142

Factionalism, 7, 18, 101, 107, 115, 165n5; defined, 52; and palace memorials, 61; under Yin-ssu, 67
Fan Fu, 166n37
Fan Shih-i, 74, 173n24
Fang Ming, 143
Feng Hsieh-i, 136
Feng-kuo chiang-chün, 156n9
Feng shang-yü, 94
Fortune-teller, 148–149
Fu-chien, 92
Fu-ch'üan, 18
Fu-chun, 32
Fu-erh-tan, 89
Fu-kuo chiang-chün, 156n9
Fu-kuo kung, 156n9
Fu-ning-an, 101, 173n25
Fu-pen, 28
Fu-t'ai, 102

Galdan, 42, 162n24
Gali, 53, 142, 144–147
Gifts, imperial, 78, 141, 149, 150, 180n1
Grand Canal, 35, 36
Grand Council: and South Library, 82; origins, 84–92; secretaries, 91, 174n37; types of officials, 174n29. *See also* *Chün-chi ch'u*
Grand councillors, 85, 91, 174n37, 175n54
Grand Secretariat, *see Nei-ko*
Grand secretaries, 12, 15, 84–92, 116; functions, 92–102; role in deliberative bodies, 156n21; appointed grand councillors, 174n37
Great Accounting, 22
Green-head tablet, 20, 158n4
Green Standards, 12

Ha-yüan-sheng, 174n32
Han p'iao-ch'ien ch'u, 29
Hanlin Academy, 16
Hao Yü-lin, 101, 102
Ho-nan tao chien-ch'a yü-shih, 23
Ho-shou, 144, 146, 147
Ho-shuo ch'in-wang, 156n9
Ho-tao tsung-tu, 97
Hsi-erh-ta, 24
Hsi-ming, 130
Hsi Wu-ao, 29, 33
Hsiao I-shan, 25, 165n5
Hsieh Chi-shih, 101
Hsieh-en che, 127
Hsieh Pao-chao, 2
Hsien-san i-cheng ta-ch'en, 18
Hsing-wen, 103
Hsiu-ts'ai, 143, 147
Hsiung Tz'u-li, 113
Hsü Ch'ien-hsüeh, 39, 45, 98
Hsü Chün, 98
Hsü Jung, 93, 94
Hsüeh-cheng, 128
Hsüeh-shih, 15
Hsün, 94
Hsün-yü, 81
Hu Jen-yu, 129
Hu-k'o, 31
Hua-t'i, 19
Huang Kuo-ts'ai, 171n52
Huang Ping, 84
Hui-t'ui, 18
Hui-t'ung kuan, 28
Hung-pen fang, 30
Hung-pen-shang, 30
Huo-p'ai, 28

I, 28
I Chao-hsiung, 97, 171n53
I-cheng ch'u, 105
I-cheng pei-le, 155n2
I-cheng ta-ch'en, 10
I-cheng wang, 10
I-cheng wang ta-ch'en hui-i, 10
I-chun, 33
I-i, 32
I-ting, 33
I-tsou, 175n54
Ideology: defined, 34, 108–109; Neo-Confucian, 109, 111
Imperial: decisions, 9, 38, 99–102; commissioners, 24–26, 142; advisors, 35, 155n5; gifts, 78, 141, 149, 150, 180n1;

assistants plenipotentiary, 79; instructions, 81–82, 93, 102–103, 172nn18,19, 179n1
Imperial Clan Court, 9
Imperial Dispatch Office, 28
Imperial Household, 25, 38
Imperial Instruction Book, 31
Imperial Manufactory, superintendents, 37
Imperial Patent Office, 17
Imperial Printing Establishment, 81

Jehol, summer palace at, 46, 81
Jesuits: on espionage, 6; and K'ang-hsi Emperor, 34; and Yung-cheng Emperor, 116
Ju-chin, 21

Kai chü-t'i, 119
Kai-pu i-tsou, 32
K'ang-hsi Emperor, 17, 19, 25, 33, 44–45, 59, 63, 73, 135–139, 168n17; and Yung-cheng Emperor compared, 1, 5–7, 68, 72–73, 76, 111, 115, 170n41; and palace memorials, 4, 34, 49; and Ming rulers compared, 6, 21, 34–35; audiences, 20–22, 141; policy toward censors, 23–24; and imperial commissioners, 24, 145; tours, 24–26, 159n22; and Ts'ao Yin, 38; intention to abdicate, 53; assassination attempt on, 58; values, 111, 138–139; and Wang Hung-hsü, 114; on honest officials, 135, 139
Kao Ch'i-cho, 74, 99, 100
Kao Hsia-ch'ang, 168n55
Kao Shih-ch'i, 44, 45, 56
Keng-o, 61, 168n50
K'o-tao, 13
Kroeber, A. L., 36
Ku-shan o-chen, 11
Ku-shan pei-le, 11
Ku-shan pei-tzu, 156n9
Ku T'u-ho, 129
Ku Yüeh-li, 129
K'ua-se, 69
Kuan-feng cheng-su shih, 99
Kuan-li Hu-pu shih-wu, 80
Kung-hou ch'in-ting, 100
K'ung-ming-tzu chi, 98
K'ung Yü-hsün, 97, 101, 102, 171n56

Lai-ching yin-chien, 100
Lamas, 60

Lan-chou, 93, 94
Land-poll tax, 26, 135
Lang-chung, 19, 128, 166n27
Lasswell, H. D., 2
Lei-chou, 128, 129
Li Ch'i, 144, 146, 147
Li-fan yüan, 12
Li Fu, 171n55
Li Hsi, 131
Li Hsü, 43, 56, 58, 109, 110, 113, 144, 165n7; palace memorials, 36–38, 47, 48, 142; and K'ang-hsi Emperor, 38; and Ts'ao Yin, 39; character, 39–40; as salt censor, 41; and Wang Hung-hsü, 45, 163n50
Li-k'o, 158n14
Li Kuang-ti, 142, 172n10
Li Lan, 171n54
Li Lin-sheng, 42–43, 47
Li Wei, 74–76, 100, 121, 169n40, 171n59, 172n18
Li Yü, 163n59
Liang-i i-wen, 18
Liang Shih-hsün, 144, 146
Liang Wen-k'o, 136
Ling shih-wei nei-ta-ch'en, 47
Literary inquisition, 97–99
Liu chia-chü, 170n43
Liu-chung pen, 30
Liu-k'o, 15
Liu-pu, 9
Liu Shih-shu, 97
Lo Cheng-nien, 84
Lu-erh-men, 132
Lü Liu-liang, 173n24
Lü-t'ou-p'ai, 20
Lü-ying, 95
Lung-tsung Gate, 85, 87
Lungkodo, 61, 68, 79–80, 148, 149

Ma-erh-sai, 90, 92, 173n25
Ma-erh-t'u, 165n20
Ma I-tzu, 144, 147
Ma-san-ch'i, 53, 165n10
Ma-shang fei-ti, 103
Ma Ti-po, 171n50
Ma-wu, 164n66, 166n37
Maci, 59, 60, 79, 80
Man-pao, 133, 137
Man-p'ei, 69
Man p'iao-ch'ien ch'u, 30
Manchu: policy, 3; acculturation, 8; script, 14

Manchu Registry, 30
Mao-ch'in Hall, 170n43
Memorials, palace, 1, 4, 5, 7–8, 27, 69–70, 92, 104, 109–111, 117–119, 170n43; earliest, 41–43; transmission, 46, 118; and Li Hsü, 36–38, 47, 48, 142; size, 48; endorsements, 49–50; contents, 50–51
Memorials, red, 30–32, 158n14
Memorials, traditional, 4, 27; draft, 19; retained, 30; confidential, 31; board, 32; provincial, 32; transmission, 159nn3,14
Messengers, 29, 48–49, 70, 143
Mi-che, 44
Mi-chi-hsin, 101
Mi-chih, 72
Mi-pao, 106
Mi-pen, 31
Mi-yü, 45
Miao affairs, 94
Miao-chiang shih-wu, 94
Miao-wu, 94
Michael, Franz, 11
Mien-ch'eng, 102
Military affairs, 85, 86, 91
Military Manufacturing Office, 85, 174n28
Ming emperors, 41
Ming-fa shang-yü, 102
Ming-pai-le, 50, 114
Mingju, 18, 39
Missionaries, 67, 81, 172n12
Motives, 4–5, 40, 68, 108
Mourao, Jean, 168n10
Mu-ho-lun, 23, 61

Nan-ao, 100
Nan-ho tsung-tu, 97
Nan-shu fang chin-feng, 47
National Palace Museum, 41, 42, 91, 92, 113
Nei chung-t'ang, 80
Nei hung-wen yüan, 15
Nei-ko (Grand Secretariat), 3, 4, 12, 20, 21, 23, 27, 71, 72, 82, 83, 87, 92, 94, 107, 120; establishment, 14–17; and draft rescripts, 28; composition, 29–30; secretaries, 88; as open channel, 104; organizational breakup, 106; procedure in, 159n17
Nei kuo-shih kuan, 15
Nei pi-shu yüan, 15
Nei san-yüan, 15
Nei-yüan, 156n21

Ni-chih, 103
Ni-kao, 19
Nien Hsi, 83, 148–149
Nien Keng-yao, 51, 76, 83, 169n40; and Yung-cheng Emperor, 77, 180n5 (Case C); as faction leader, 80; family, 148–149; palace memorials, 148–150, 164nn78,79
Nine ministers, 13
Niru, 14
Nurhaci, 10–11, 14

Oboi, 7, 17
O-erh-t'ai, 78, 94, 95, 100, 121, 169n40
O-k'u-li, 165n20
O-lun-t'e, 133
O-shan, 53, 61

Pa-hsi, 24
Pa ta-ch'en, 11
Pai Huang, 139
Palace guards, 49, 70, 164n66
Palace report, 48
Pan-li chün-chi ch'u, 85, 89
Pan-li chün-chi shih-wu ta-ch'en, 91, 175n54
Pan-li chün-chi yin-hsin, 89
Pan-li chün-hsü ch'u, 91, 175n52
Pan-li chün-hsü ta-ch'en, 91
P'an Tsung-lo, 131, 178n3
Pei-ho-no, 24
Pei-le, 2, 7, 10–12, 15, 155n2
Peking Gazette, 4, 31, 40, 134
Pen-chang, 27, 71, 104–106. *See also* Memorials, traditional
Pi-chien, 21, 127
Pi-t'ieh-shih, 14, 71
Pi-tz'u, 22
P'i-peng ch'u, 30
P'iao-ni, 16, 29–33
Ping-pu huo-p'ai, 94
Pirates, 59, 136–137
Poems, imperial, 141
Postal system: Ch'ing, 27–28; soldiers in, 28; stations, 28; death toll of horses, 159n14
Prices: in Taiwan, 131, 136; in South, 143
Provincial officials, 35, 134, 162n42, 179n2; weather reports of, 41; and palace memorials, 42, 44, 137; role in decisions, 99–102; character, 101, 135, 138, 140; qualifications, 138
Pu-cheng-shih, 22

Pu-lu che, 170n43
Pu-lu tang-an, 170n43
Pu-pen, 32
P'u, 28
P'u-ch'i, 66
Public opinion, 145–148

Remount Department, 28
Rescript, 32, 130
Ripa, Father M., 59, 167n43
Rumors, 41, 50, 143

Sai-leng-o, 169n22
Salt censor, 41, 109
San-fa-ssu, 9
Sha-mu-ha, 133
Shang-yü, 102
She-jen, 88
Shen T'ing-cheng, 171n51
Sheng-hsün, 81
Sheng-yüan, 131, 143
Shu-chih, 103, 127, 153n11, 177n86
Shu-ho-te, 88, 91, 175n44
Shu-lu, 56, 166n27
Shu-ming, 19
Shui-i, 159n6
Shun-chih Emperor, 7, 16
Simmel, George, 121
Singde, 39
Six Boards, 9, 12, 18, 32, 72, 105, 107, 156n18; early status, 15; powers, 169n33
Six Sections, 15, 16, 23, 31, 32, 158n14; organization, 160n21
Smith, Kent, 115
Songgotu, 18, 53, 55–56, 61, 111, 168n50
South: cultural significance, 35; economic significance, 35–36; effects of court politics on, 40
South Library, 35, 48, 113, 162n44, 163n50, 174n28; origins, 44–45; and court letter system, 81; and Grand Council, 82, 85
Special messengers, 28
Speech officials, 23
Spies, 6, 41, 76, 118
Ssu-kuan, 19
Ssu-lun pu, 31
Su-chou, 93, 94
Su Hsün, 144
Succession struggle, 59–60, 66–67
Sun Ch'eng-tse, 15
Sung Ho, 57
Sung Lao, 43–44, 56, 58, 162nn38,40

Sunu, 18
Surgaci, 10
Surtax, 131, 135

Ta-ch'en, 12, 83, 85, 155n5, 174n31
Ta-chi, 22
Ta chiu-ch'ing, 13
Ta hsüeh-shih, 15, 86
Ta-jen, 92, 174n31
Ta-li ssu, 13, 155n1
Taiwan, 128, 129, 135; population, 128, 136; prices, 131, 136
T'ai-chi t'u shuo, 130
T'ai-ho Gate, 16, 87
T'ai-tsung (Abahai), 7, 11, 12, 14
T'ang-shan, 141
Textile commissioner (superintendent of Imperial Manufactory), 36, 109
Three Feudatories, 21
Three Inner Courts, 15
Three Judiciary, 9
T'i-chun, 32
T'i-pen, 27, 32, 41, 43, 50, 51, 72, 94, 101, 119, 134, 145, 169n35. *See also* Memorials, traditional
T'i-t'ang ch'eng-ch'ai, 28
T'iao-ch'en, 158n15
T'ieh-huang, 17, 28–29
T'ien Wen-ching, 75–78, 101, 121, 169n40
Ting, 32
T'ing-chi yü-chi, 88, 102
To-lo chün-wang, 156n9
To-lo pei-le, 156n9
T'o-ho-ch'i, 54, 60, 62, 64, 112, 164n3–165; death, 66
Tours, by K'ang-hsi Emperor, 24–26, 46, 110, 159n22, 165n14
Transmission Office, 13, 28, 29, 31, 107
Tribute-rice, 35–36
Tsai Chün-chi ch'u hsing-tsou, 85
Tsai Chün-chi fang hsing-tsou, 175n46
Ts'ai T'ien-lüeh, 100
Ts'ai T'ing, 46
Tsao-pan ch'u, 174n28
Ts'ao-ch'ien, 30
Ts'ao Fu, 37–39
Ts'ao Yin, 47–48, 58, 109, 110, 113, 143; and palace memorials, 37, 40–41, 142; family, 38, 39; and Li Hsü, 39; as textile commissioner, 39; as salt censor, 41
Ts'ao-yün tsung-tu, 35
Ts'ao Yung, 37
Ts'e-wang, 89

Tseng Ching, 173n24
Tso Pi-fan, 142, 143, 146
Tsou-che, 1, 4, 27, 34, 43. *See also* Memorials, palace
Tsou-hsiao, 96
Tsou-pen, 27, 34. *See also* Memorials, traditional
Tsou-p'ien, 92, 93, 95–103. *See also* Memorials, palace
Tsou-shih chih-i-cheng, 164n69
Tsou-shih chih-jen, 49
Tsou-shih chu-shih, 164n69
Tsou-shih ch'u, 49, 164n67
Tsou-shih t'ai-chien, 49
Tsou-t'ieh, 37. *See also* Memorials, palace
Tsuan-ni, 103
Ts'ui Chih-yüan, 169n25
Ts'un-chu, 164n69
Tsung-jen fu, 9
Tsung-li shih-wu wang ta-ch'en, 79
Tu-ch'a yüan, 13
Tu-t'ung, 156n7
Tung Fu, 15
Tung Yung-chi, 133
T'ung-cheng ssu, 13, 161n8
T'ung Kuo-wei, 18
T'ung-pao, 165n20
T'ung-pen, 32
Tzu, 31, 102, 104, 128
Tzu-chi, 102

Upper White Banner, 38

Values, 5, 112; of K'ang-hsi Emperor, 5, 111, 113–114; of Yung-cheng Emperor, 5, 115, 117, 120; defined, 108–109
Vermilion endorsements, 75, 81, 114, 148, 171n49
Vermilion instructions, 81

Wai-ch'ao, 31
Wang, 12, 92
Wang Ch'ao-en, 133
Wang Chiu-ling, 163n50
Wang Hung-hsü, 45, 56, 110, 111, 118, 166n37; and palace memorials, 44–48, 114; in succession struggle, 60; lost imperial favor, 163n50
Wang I(-te), 63–64, 168n55
Wang Shan, 56, 67

Wang Shao-hsü, 101, 102
Wang Tung, 77
Wang Tzu-chung, 93
Water post, 159n6
Weather reports, 34, 37–38, 41
Weber, Max, 1
Wei-lu che, 170n43
Wei-lu tang-an, 170n43
Wei T'ing-chen, 172n10
Wen-kuan, 14
Wen-ta, 61
Wen-t'e, 165n20
Weng-o-li, 165n20
Wittfogel, Karl, 1–2
Wu-hsü wen-kao, 98
Wu Pi, 143, 144, 146, 147
Wu Sheng, 133–134
Wu Ta-ch'an, 42
Wu ta-ch'en, 11
Wu Ying, 140
Wu-ying Hall, 81, 172n12
Wu Yüan-an, 88

Ya-erh-ha-shan, 88
Yang Ch'i-chiao, 170n42
Yang-hsin Hall, 172n12, 174n28
Yang K'un, 96
Yang-lien yin-liang, 97
Yang Lin, 74, 139
Yang Ming-shih, 74, 171n56
Yang Wen-ch'ien, 75
Yangchow massacre, 35
Yao Chen-tsung, 144
Yao T'ang, 136
Yeh Chiu-ssu, 144, 147
Yeh Feng-mao, 29, 85, 88, 89
Yellow Book, 96–97
Yen-ch'a i-tsou, 93
Yen-kuan, 23
Yin and *yang*, 130
Yin-chen, 65, 68–69. *See also* Yung-cheng Emperor
Yin-chi-shan, 98
Yin-chih (Prince Ch'eng), 67–68, 82
Yin-ch'ing piao, 37
Yin-hsiang (Prince I), 69, 71, 79, 80, 83, 84, 92, 96, 97, 102, 149, 173n25; death, 90
Yin-jeng, 25, 52–61, 63–68, 81, 142, 166n37; faction of, 53, 165n5; sexual aberrations, 54, 58–59, 112; deposition, 58–60, 64–65, 112, 167n43; in Korean records, 59; values, 111

Yin-lu, 82

Yin-ssu, 52, 53, 68, 79, 112, 166n37; in succession struggle, 59–60, 67; and Yung-cheng Emperor, 79

Yin-t'ang, 67, 69, 76, 166nn27,37; death, 172n3

Yin-t'i (eldest brother), 59, 60, 67–69, 112

Yin-t'i (fourteenth brother), 67–68

Yin-wen, 29

Ying i-tsou che i-tsou, 175n52

Ying pu-chun k'ai-hsiao, 97

Yü, 32

Yü Cheng-chien, 130, 139

Yü-chih wen-chi, 140

Yü-men, 21

Yü-men t'ing-cheng, 20

Yü-shih, 23

Yü Shih-ch'en(g), 144

Yüan-chien lei-han, 138

Yüan-wai-lang, 36

Yüeh Chung-ch'i, 85, 89–91, 173n24

Yung-cheng Emperor, 52, 65, 92, 100, 116, 122, 148, 171n49, 179nn20,1; and K'ang-hsi Emperor compared, 1, 5–7, 68, 72–73, 76, 111, 115, 170n41; despotism, 5–6, 117; and Ming rulers compared, 6; and palace memorials, 71–72, 119, 171n65; and Yin-ssu, 79; values, 115; and trusted officials, 121; religious concepts, 149–150; and Nien Keng-yao, 180n5(Case C)

Yung-hsien lu, 169n37

Yung-wei ting-li, 99

1. *China's Early Industrialization: Sheng Hsuan-huai (1844–1916) and Mandarin Enterprise.* By Albert Feuerwerker.
2. *Intellectual Trends in the Ch'ing Period.* By Liang Ch'i-ch'ao. Translated by Immanuel C. Y. Hsü.
3. *Reform in Sung China: Wang An-shih (1021–1086) and His New Policies.* By James T. C. Liu.
4. *Studies on the Population of China, 1368–1953.* By Ping-ti Ho.
5. *China's Entrance into the Family of Nations: The Diplomatic Phase, 1858–1880. By Immanuel C. Y. Hsü.*
6. *The May Fourth Movement: Intellectual Revolution in Modern China.* By Chow Tse-tsung.
7. *Ch'ing Administrative Terms: A Translation of the Terminology of the Six Boards with Explanatory Notes.* Translated and edited by E-tu Zen Sun.
8. *Anglo-American Steamship Rivalry in China, 1862–1874.* By Kwang-Ching Liu.
9. *Local Government in China under the Ch'ing.* By T'ung-tsu Ch'ü.
10. *Communist China, 1955–1959: Policy Documents with Analysis.* With a foreword by Robert R. Bowie and John K. Fairbank. (Prepared at Harvard University under the joint auspices of the Center for International Affairs and the East Asian Research Center.)
11. *China and Christianity: The Missionary Movement and the Growth of Chinese Antiforeignism, 1860–1870.* By Paul A. Cohen.
12. *China and the Helping Hand, 1937–1945.* By Arthur N. Young.
13. *Research Guide to the May Fourth Movement: Intellectual Revolution in Modern China, 1915–1924.* By Chow Tse-tsung.
14. *The United States and the Far Eastern Crises of 1933–1938: From the Manchurian Incident through the Initial Stage of the Undeclared Sino-Japanese War.* By Dorothy Borg.
15. *China and the West, 1858–1861: The Origins of the Tsungli Yamen.* By Masataka Banno.
16. *In Search of Wealth and Power: Yen Fu and the West.* By Benjamin Schwartz.
17. *The Origins of Entrepreneurship in Meiji Japan.* By Johannes Hirschmeier, S.V.D.
18. *Commissioner Lin and the Opium War.* By Hsin-pao Chang.
19. *Money and Monetary Policy in China, 1845–1895.* By Frank H. H. King.
20. *China's Wartime Finance and Inflation, 1937–1945.* By Arthur N. Young.
21. *Foreign Investment and Economic Development in China, 1840–1937.* By Chi-ming Hou.

22. *After Imperialism: The Search for a New Order in the Far East, 1921–1931.* By Akira Iriye.
23. *Foundations of Constitutional Government in Modern Japan, 1868–1900.* By George Akita.
24. *Political Thought in Early Meiji Japan, 1868–1889.* By Joseph Pittau, S.J.
25. *China's Struggle for Naval Development, 1839–1895.* By John L. Rawlinson.
26. *The Practice of Buddhism in China, 1900–1950.* By Holmes Welch.
27. *Li Ta-chao and the Origins of Chinese Marxism.* By Maurice Meisner.
28. *Pa Chin and His Writings: Chinese Youth between the Two Revolutions.* By Olga Lang.
29. *Literary Dissent in Communist China.* By Merle Goldman.
30. *Politics in the Tokugawa Bakufu, 1600–1843.* By Conrad Totman.
31. *Hara Kei in the Politics of Compromise, 1905–1915.* By Tetsuo Najita.
32. *The Chinese World Order: Traditional China's Foreign Relations.* Edited by John K. Fairbank.
33. *The Buddhist Revival in China.* By Holmes Welch.
34. *Traditional Medicine in Modern China: Science, Nationalism, and the Tensions of Cultural Change.* By Ralph C. Croizier.
35. *Party Rivalry and Political Change in Taishō Japan.* By Peter Duus.
36. *The Rhetoric of Empire: American China Policy, 1895–1901.* By Marilyn B. Young.
37. *Radical Nationalist in Japan: Kita Ikki, 1883–1937.* By George M. Wilson.
38. *While China Faced West: American Reformers in Nationalist China, 1928–1937.* By James C. Thomson Jr.
39. *The Failure of Freedom: A Portrait of Modern Japanese Intellectuals.* By Tatsuo Arima.
40. *Asian Ideas of East and West: Tagore and His Critics in Japan, China, and India.* By Stephen N. Hay.
41. *Canton under Communism: Programs and Politics in a Provincial Capital, 1949–1968.* By Ezra F. Vogel.
42. *Ting Wen-chiang: Science and China's New Culture.* By Charlotte Furth.
43. *The Manchurian Frontier in Ch'ing History.* By Robert H. G. Lee.
44. *Motoori Norinaga, 1730–1801.* By Shigeru Matsumoto.
45. *The Comprador in Nineteenth Century China: Bridge between East and West.* By Yen-p'ing Hao.
46. *Hu Shih and the Chinese Renaissance: Liberalism in the Chinese Revolution, 1917–1937.* By Jerome B. Grieder.
47. *The Chinese Peasant Economy: Agricultural Development in Hopei and Shantung, 1890–1949.* By Ramon H. Myers.
48. *Japanese Tradition and Western Law: Emperor, State, and Law in the Thought of Hozumi Yatsuka.* By Richard H. Minear.
49. *Rebellion and Its Enemies in Late Imperial China: Militarization and Social Structure, 1796–1864.* By Philip A. Kuhn.
50. *Early Chinese Revolutionaries: Radical Intellectuals in Shanghai and Chekiang, 1902–1911.* By Mary Backus Rankin.